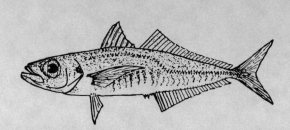
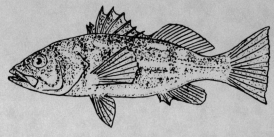

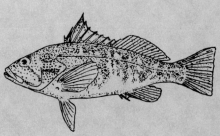

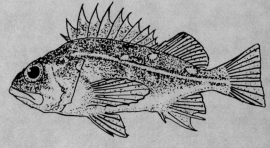

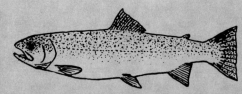

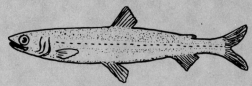

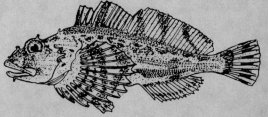

Pacific North!

Pacific North!

Sea Trails for the Sportsman on the North Pacific Rim

By

DON HOLM

ILLUSTRATED WITH PHOTOGRAPHS AND CHARTS

The CAXTON PRINTERS, Ltd.
CALDWELL, IDAHO
1969

Standard Book Number 87004-134-7

Library of Congress Catalog Card No. 72-84780

Lithographed and bound in the United States of America by
The CAXTON PRINTERS, Ltd.
Caldwell, Idaho   83605
112254

Mon Dieu, votre mer est si grand,
et mon bateau est si petit!

FISHERMAN'S PRAYER

Table of Contents

Chapter   Page

PART ONE
OFFSHORE

1. Making the Run for Blue Water Tuna - - - - - - - - - - - - - -   1

2. Legends of the North Pacific - - - - - - - - - - - - - - - -   8

3. Moving in on the Rim - - - - - - - - - - - - - - - - - - - 13

4. The Offshore Trollery - - - - - - - - - - - - - - - - - - 18

5. Pioneering the Sport Fishery - - - - - - - - - - - - - - - 23

6. Offshore Banks, Pelagic Predictions, and Intruders - - - - - - - 26

7. Three Thousand Nights - - - - - - - - - - - - - - - - - - 30

PART TWO
ALONGSHORE

1. Chinook! - 45

2. The Mightiest Bar of All - - - - - - - - - - - - - - - - - 54

3. The Cruise of the "Question Mark?" - - - - - - - - - - - - - 62

4. Action at Kiwanda - - - - - - - - - - - - - - - - - - - 68

5. I Like Humpback Salmon - - - - - - - - - - - - - - - - - 73

6. Those Amazing Dorymen of Cape Kiwanda! - - - - - - - - - - 79

7. Port Alberni in the Dark - - - - - - - - - - - - - - - - - 84

Chapter   *Page*

   8. JUNEAU STRIPTEASE - - - - - - - - - - - - - - - - - - - 87

   9. A SEAGOIN' CHEECHAKO - - - - - - - - - - - - - - - - - 90

PART THREE
THE TIDAL SHELF

   1. SALMON IN THE SURF - - - - - - - - - - - - - - - - - - 95

   2. COHO GO FOR FLIES - - - - - - - - - - - - - - - - - - - 100

   3. ADMIRALTY ISLAND CLAMBAKE - - - - - - - - - - - - - - 108

   4. DOZIN' FOR STRIPERS - - - - - - - - - - - - - - - - - - 115

   5. AQUAVIT ON THE MILLICOMA - - - - - - - - - - - - - - - 118

   6. HARVEST'S THE TIME FOR CUTS - - - - - - - - - - - - - 120

   7. NUGGET GOES FOR SEA-RUNS - - - - - - - - - - - - - - 123

   8. WINTER STEELHEADERS ARE A BREED APART - - - - - - - 125

   9. THOSE "OTHER" FISHES - - - - - - - - - - - - - - - - - 128

 10. WINTER BLACKMOUTHING - - - - - - - - - - - - - - - - 133

 11. DIGGING FOR TROUT - - - - - - - - - - - - - - - - - - 135

 12. LET'S GO CLAMMING! - - - - - - - - - - - - - - - - - - 137

 13. NORTH PACIFIC SHELL GAME - - - - - - - - - - - - - - 142

 14. FISH POISONING - 147

PART FOUR
PLACES TO GO

   1. NORTHERN CALIFORNIA - - - - - - - - - - - - - - - - 151

   2. OREGON - 164

   3. WASHINGTON COAST - - - - - - - - - - - - - - - - - - 179

Chapter   *Page*

4. STRAIT OF JUAN DE FUCA - - - - - - - - - - - - - - - - 186

5. PUGET SOUND - 191

6. VANCOUVER ISLAND - - - - - - - - - - - - - - - - - - 196

7. BRITISH COLUMBIA MARINE PARKS - - - - - - - - - - - - 199

8. FISHING BRITISH COLUMBIA WATERS - - - - - - - - - - - 200

9. QUEEN CHARLOTTE ISLANDS - - - - - - - - - - - - - - - 202

10. SOUTH COAST BRITISH COLUMBIA - - - - - - - - - - - - 203

11. UPPER COAST BRITISH COLUMBIA - - - - - - - - - - - - 205

12. ALASKA WATERS - - - - - - - - - - - - - - - - - - - 207

13. SOUTHEAST ALASKA (THE PANHANDLE) - - - - - - - - - - 217

14. ALASKA WESTWARD - - - - - - - - - - - - - - - - - - 227

PART FIVE
THE NORTH PACIFIC FISHES

1. DEMERSALS, PELAGICS, ANADROMOUS - - - - - - - - - - - - 233

2. DEMERSALS - 235

3. STURGEON - 237

4. SHAD - 239

5. SMELT - 240

6. SEA-RUN TROUTS - - - - - - - - - - - - - - - - - - 241

7. SPECIES ONCORHYNCHUS - - - - - - - - - - - - - - - - 243

8. SALMON NOMENCLATURE - - - - - - - - - - - - - - - - 246

9. PACIFIC SALMON HISTORY - - - - - - - - - - - - - - - 248

10. RANGE OF PACIFIC SALMON - - - - - - - - - - - - - - 250

11. SALMON AT THE MARKETPLACE - - - - - - - - - - - - - 252

12. SUPER SALMON COMING - - - - - - - - - - - - - - - - 254

13. CONSERVATION AND OUTLOOK - - - - - - - - - - - - - - 258

Chapter   *Page*

PART SIX
NORTH PACIFIC GRAB BAG

1. THERE'S ALWAYS BEEN A DORY - - - - - - - - - - - - - - - - 265

2. WEATHER, SAFETY AND BOAT HANDLING - - - - - - - - - - - 270

3. BAIT, TACKLE AND GEAR - - - - - - - - - - - - - - - - 276

4. MARINE GAME SPECIES OF NORTH PACIFIC - - - - - - - - - - 280

List of Illustrations

	Page
Dory fishermen greet the morning sun off the coast of Oregon	3
The *Della*, steam schooner on the Nestucca River	4
The author with an albacore caught offshore	5
Wayne Harding, pastor of the Cloverdale Baptist Church	6
Salmon fishing offshore	7
New boat harbor at Depoe Bay	15
Salmon troller working offshore	21
Fish on! Salmon anglers offshore	24
Sea lions on the Pacific coastline	29
Hoyt Barnett	31
A troller off Cape Disappointment	46
Chinook caught off the Columbia Bar	47
Part of the charter fleet heading into Ilwaco, Washington	48
Typical trailer park during the salmon season	49
Fish cleaning station at a Columbia River port	51
Boat harbor at Ilwaco, Washington	52
Coast Guard vessel patroling the Columbia	55
The Coast Guard tows in a distressed boat	58
Offshore fishing in the 1940's was uncrowded	60
Patrol boat on the Columbia Bar	63
Joe Munson, skipper of the *Question Mark*?	64
Jack Moys landing a salmon	65
Sport fishing in the old days	66
Rigging up gear for salmon offshore	67
This type of dory is no longer in general use at Cape Kiwanda	69
Paul Hanneman retrieving his dory from the surf	70
The view from a dory as you launch into the surf	71
A bright humpbacked or pink salmon caught off Lummi	74
Reef netters fishing the straits of Lummi Island	75

Page

Close-up of a reef netter - 77

A dory fisherman unloading his catch - - - - - - - - - - - - - - - - - 80

A successful dory trip ends. The Rock is in the background - - - - - - - - 82

The author and a companion with a limit of salmon - - - - - - - - - - - 83

A surf and rock angler on the Northwest Coast - - - - - - - - - - - - - 96

Salmon can be caught in the surf - - - - - - - - - - - - - - - - - - - 97

For surf fisherman it's the lonely sea and sky - - - - - - - - - - - - - - 98

Surf casting for salmon in the Georgia Strait near the Canadian border - - - - 98

The author spinning for salmon in the surf - - - - - - - - - - - - - - - 99

Coho flies tied with polar bear hair - - - - - - - - - - - - - - - - - 101

The author landing a 15-pound coho - - - - - - - - - - - - - - - - - 103

The Siletz River "Jaws" near Taft, Oregon - - - - - - - - - - - - - - - 104

Landing a large salmon requires lots of room - - - - - - - - - - - - - - 106

Bank plunking for striped bass on the Coos River - - - - - - - - - - - - 114

Tidal waters are for shad and striped bass - - - - - - - - - - - - - - - 115

Part of Seattle's salmon fleet - 116

Bill Roberts, Coos Bay, playing a fighting shad - - - - - - - - - - - - - 117

Fishing the Millicoma for shad in the evening - - - - - - - - - - - - - - 119

Floating for sea-run cutthroat - 121

Fishing writer Francis Ames and Bill Osborne with a catch of harvest trout - - - - 122

Motor-driven canoes skim the water - - - - - - - - - - - - - - - - - 124

The author and an 11-pound winter steelhead - - - - - - - - - - - - - 126

Young Puget Sound angler with a catch of assorted "bottom" fishes - - - - - - 129

Typical catch of Pacific marine game species - - - - - - - - - - - - - - 130

Jetty fishermen with a catch of rockfish - - - - - - - - - - - - - - - - 131

A mixed catch of rockfish - 132

To hunt clams, you need a "clam gun" and sharp eyes - - - - - - - - - - - 138

Shellfish hunters in the Puget Sound islands - - - - - - - - - - - - - - 140

"Gunning" a clam - 141

Crab fisherman beaching his craft after a trip - - - - - - - - - - - - - - 143

Surf dories used by crabbers - 145

Chinook salmon and striped bass - - - - - - - - - - - - - - - - - - 153

Angler measures abalone for size - - - - - - - - - - - - - - - - - - 154

Double catch of chinook salmon and striped bass - - - - - - - - - - - - 156

Clamming at Pismo Beach - 157

Party boat off Santa Cruz - 158

An abalone catch from the San Mateo beaches - - - - - - - - - - - - - 159

A hefty catch of chinook and stripers - - - - - - - - - - - - - - - - - 161

Spawning salmon fighting their way up the Trinity River - - - - - - - - - - 162

Typical unused surf and rock fishing stretch of Oregon coast - - - - - - - - - 166

Page

Coquille River mouth and jetties at Bandon-by-the-Sea - - - - - - - - - - - - - - 167

Oregon coast near Florence - 168

Fog and windblown day along the south coast of Oregon - - - - - - - - - - - - - 169

Yaquina Bay and Newport, Oregon - - - - - - - - - - - - - - - - - - - 170

Salmon Harbor at Winchester Bay - - - - - - - - - - - - - - - - - - - 171

The little "dog hole" at Depoe Bay - - - - - - - - - - - - - - - - - - 173

The excellent small boat harbor at the mouth of the Chetco River - - - - - - - - - - 174

Nehalem Bay - 175

Quinault Indian dugout canoes are used with modern outboard motors - - - - - - - - - 180

An Indian practices his drum beating - - - - - - - - - - - - - - - - - - 180

A section of the raw Olympic Peninsula coastline - - - - - - - - - - - - - - - 180

The small boat harbor at Westport, Washington - - - - - - - - - - - - - - - 181

Grays Harbor, looking west - 182

Willapa Bay - 182

Bellingham Bay and breakwater - 183

Port Angeles on the Strait of Juan de Fuca - - - - - - - - - - - - - - - - 183

Quinault River below the lake - 184

U.S. Indian Service at Lake Quinault Station - - - - - - - - - - - - - - - - 185

A 15-pound "blackmouth" caught off Sekiu - - - - - - - - - - - - - - - - 188

The harbor at old Port Townsend - - - - - - - - - - - - - - - - - - - 189

A dangerous tidal channel along Whidbey Island - - - - - - - - - - - - - - - 193

Deception Pass, a picturesque waterway - - - - - - - - - - - - - - - - - 194

A snug harbor in the San Juans - - - - - - - - - - - - - - - - - - - 195

Dr. Dean Watt gathering clams - 208

Steelhead of Kispiox River, British Columbia - - - - - - - - - - - - - - - - 209

A record halibut caught near Ketchikan - - - - - - - - - - - - - - - - - 212

Pre-World War II adventurer in Alaskan waters - - - - - - - - - - - - - - - 215

A nice chinook caught on sport tackle near Juneau - - - - - - - - - - - - - - 215

Juneau harbor and the "AJ" mine - - - - - - - - - - - - - - - - - - - 219

Juneau harbor with Coast Guard cutter Haida, and the Douglas Bridge - - - - - - - - 220

Salmon being brailed into a cannery tender - - - - - - - - - - - - - - - - 224

Salmon drying on the rack along lower Yukon River - - - - - - - - - - - - - - 229

The author visiting a village on the Yukon River near Circle - - - - - - - - - - - 230

Frank Haw with a rockfish caught under the Tacoma Narrows Bridge - - - - - - - - - 236

A "red" or sockeye salmon - 244

Comparison of "natural" salmon fingerlings with "super salmon" - - - - - - - - - - 255

Coho salmon with a marked left maxillary - - - - - - - - - - - - - - - - 256

Range of chinook salmon from Sacramento system - - - - - - - - - - - - - - 260

Modern square-stern dory under construction - - - - - - - - - - - - - - - 266

Frame and method of construction of a dory - - - - - - - - - - - - - - - - 267

Page

Sketch of the classic square-stern dory - 268
North Pacific salmon trolling dory - 269
Wave forms on North Pacific coastline - 271
Sport fisherman returning to harbor in a sheltered "dog hole" - - - - - - - - - - - - - 272
A nearby deserted beach along the North Pacific - - - - - - - - - - - - - - - - - - - 273
Seas crashing against the buttress of the North American coastline draw spectators - - - - - - 274

LIST OF MAPS

The Columbia River meeting the Pacific Ocean - 56
The best razor clam areas in the Northwest are along the Washington coast - - - - - - - 139
Principal salmon rivers and coastal ports in California - - - - - - - - - - - - - - - - 152
The ports of the Oregon coast - 165
Fishing areas of the Washington coast - 180
Waters of the Strait of Juan de Fuca - 187
Key saltwater fishing areas of Washington state - - - - - - - - - - - - - - - - - - - 192
Victoria to Nanaimo - 197
Nanaimo to Kelsey Bay - 197
Queen Charlotte Islands - 202
Sunshine coast-Horseshoe Bay-Powell River-Stuart Island - - - - - - - - - - - - - - - 204
Kelsey Bay-Prince Rupert Ferry - 205
Alaska state ferries - 206
The Seward Highways - 210
The Cordova area - 210
Anchorage, Alaska, a "jumping-off" point for anglers and hunters - - - - - - - - - - - - 211
The Palmer-Matanuska District - 211
The Nome area, first class fishing and surprisingly accessible - - - - - - - - - - - - - - 213
The Kotzebue area, gateway to the Brooks Range - - - - - - - - - - - - - - - - - - - 213
The Kodiak area, one of the leading commercial fishing ports of the world - - - - - - - - 214
Bristol Bay has some top sport fishing - 214
Fishing spots of the Seward-Homer area - 218
Ketchikan anglers must go by boat or float plane - - - - - - - - - - - - - - - - - - - 218
The Petersburg area has many fine sport fishing spots - - - - - - - - - - - - - - - - - 221
Wrangell offers good sport - 221
Admiralty Island can be reached from Juneau - 222
Baranof Island and the Sitka area - 222
The Haines Highway, access to the Skagway area, and Juneau's road system - - - - - - - - 223
Juneau-Douglas area - 223
The remote Yakutat offers superb fishing - 223
Map tracing routes of Washougal River Hatchery coho salmon during 1964 - - - - - - - - 259
Range of chinook salmon from Sacramento system - - - - - - - - - - - - - - - - - - 260

Acknowledgments

The assistance and cooperation of a large number of individuals and organizations made possible the preparation of this volume.

Among these were an old college chum, free-lance author, and sailing school master, Hoyt Barnett, of Sausalito, California; and a fishing and hunting companion on many a trip, Jim Conway, who is also television's "Outdoor Sportsman."

Permission to quote from Zack Taylor's boating column in *Sports Afield* is gratefully noted. Portions of the contents also have appeared previously in one form or another in the *Oregonian, Outdoor Life* magazine, *Northwest Magazine, Alaska Magazine,* and several unpublished manuscripts.

Recognition is also given to such sources of materials as the Alaska Department of Fish and Game; the California Department of Fish and Game; Oregon State University Marine Science Center; Oregon State University "Albacore Central," Corvallis; University of California, Scripps Institution of Oceanography; U.S. Fish and Wildlife Service, Department of Sport Fisheries and Wildlife; U.S. Bureau of Commercial Fisheries; Smithsonian Institution Press; U.S. Corps of Engineers; Oregon State Game Commission; Washington State Department of Fisheries.

I am also indebted to Dr. Carl L. Hubbs, Scripps Institution of Oceanography; Col. Robert L. Bangert, Corps of Engineers, Portland District; Anders Richter, director, Smithsonian Institution Press; James L. Squire, Jr., assistant director, Tiburon Marine Laboratory, Fish and Wildlife Service, Belvedere-Tiburon, California; Jerry Harrell, information officer, California Department of Fish and Game; Bob Baade, Alaska Department of Fish and Game; Don Reed, Washington State Department of Fisheries.

In addition to the author's photographs and sketches, some valuable contributions were made by James Vincent, staff photographer, the *Oregonian;* Leonard Bacon, staff writer and photographer, the *Oregonian;* U. S. Corps of Engineers; California Department of Fish and Game; the Washington State Department of Fisheries; Smithsonian Institution; Jim Conway; U.S. Coast and Geodetic Survey.

Although the subject of the North Pacific is relatively "new," a number of excellent reference works are available. These include: *A Field Guide to Some Common Ocean Sport Fishes of California,* California Fish and Game, Marine Resources Operation; *Field Identification of Northeastern Pacific Rockfish,* by Charles R. Hitz, U.S. Bureau of Commercial Fisheries, Circular

203; *Fishes of North and Middle America* (four volumes), by David Starr Jordan and Barton Warren Everman (Smithsonian Institution); *McClane's Standard Fishing Encyclopedia,* ed. by A. J. McClane (Holt, Rinehart & Winston, Inc.); *Fishes of the Pacific Northwest,* by W. A. Clemens and G. V. Wilby; *A History of the Pacific Northwest,* by George W. Fuller (Alfred A. Knopf); *Seashore Animals of the Pacific Coast,* by Myrtle Elizabeth Johnson and Harry James Snook (Dover Publications, Inc.); *This Great and Wide Sea, an Introduction to Oceanography and Marine Biology,* by R. E. Coker (Harper & Row, Publishers); *The Marine Mammals of the Northwestern Coast of North America,* by Charles M. Scammon (Dover Publications, Inc.); *New Worlds of Oceanography,* by Capt. E. John Long, U.S.N.R. (Ret.) (Grosset & Dunlap); *The Sea Around Us,* by Rachel L. Carson (Oxford University Press); *How To Fish the Pacific Coast,* by Ray Cannon (Lane Magazine and Book Company); *Fishing the Oregon Country,* by Francis H. Ames (The Caxton Printers, Ltd.); *Captain Joshua Slocum,* by Victor Slocum (Sheridan House); *The Voyages of Captain Cook Around the World* (Creset Press, London, 1949); *Atlas of Eastern Pacific Marine Game Fishing,* by James L. Squire, Jr., U.S. Bureau of Sport Fisheries and Wildlife, Circular 164; *Fish and Ships,* by Ralph W. Andrews (Superior Publishing Company); *Inshore Fishes of California,* by John L. Baxter and *Offshore Fishes of California,* by John E. Fitch, both of the California Department of Fish and Game; *United States Coast Pilot,* Vols. 7, 8, and 9; *British Columbia Pilot,* Vols. 1 and 2; *A Guide to Fishing Boats and their Gear,* by Carvel Hall Blair and Dyer Ansel Willits (Cornell Maritime Press); *Northwest Angling,* by Enos Bradner (A. S. Barnes & Co.); *Marine Game Fishes of the Pacific Coast from Alaska to Equator,* by Lionel A. Walford (University of California Press).

In addition the following periodicals and monographs have proven fascinating reading: Various reports and bulletins from the Pacific Marine Fisheries Commission, Portland, Oregon; *Sea and Pacific Motor Boat* magazine; the *American West Magazine,* Wallace Stegner, editor in chief; Washington Historical Society; *Rudder* magazine; the *Alaska Sportsman* magazine; Bureau of Commercial Fisheries research vessel cruise reports; various issues of the *National Geographic Magazine;* and the *Fishermen's News* (Seattle).

PHOTO CREDITS

The following, in addition to the author, contributed photos and artwork: Leonard Bacon—pages 15, 29, 96, 143, 145, 271, 272, 273, 274; James Vincent—pages 24, 48, 51, 52, 55, 58; Clyde Hudson—page 4; U.S. Corps of Engineers—pages 167, 170, 171, 173, 174, 175, 181, 182, 183; California Department of Fish and Game—pages 152, 153, 154, 156, 157, 158, 159, 161, 162; Washington Department of Fisheries—pages 129, 130, 131, 132, 138, 139, 140, 141, 188, 236; Oregon Game Commission (Milt Guymon)—pages 255, 256; U.S. Bureau of Commercial Fisheries—page 244; Alaska Department of Fish and Game (Lou Bandirola)—page 215 bottom, 224; Dr. Dean Watt, Midwest Research Institute—page 208; British Columbia Department of Recreation and Conservation, Fish and Wildlife Branch—page 209.

Introduction

The explorer, Alvar Núñez Cabeza de Vaca, during the golden era of Spanish conquest in North America, wrote of the vast unknown that tantalized him:

"We ever held it certain that going toward the sunset, we would find what we desired."

No one recorded exactly what red-bristled Balboa uttered when he crossed the summit of the Isthmus and beheld at last the great South Sea, which he called "Pacific."

We do have Captain William Clark's charming syntax, scribbled in his rain-soaked notebook, as the wet, hungry, miserable Corps of Discovery paddled down the Columbia and reached the brackish water of the estuary in the vicinity of Pillar Rock:

"Ocian in view! O! the joy . . . !"

Professor Frederick Jackson Turner was to write much later, from the more advantageous perch of scholarly hindsight, that this was the "age of the Pacific Ocean—mysterious and unfathomable in its meaning to our future."

An otherwise obscure Secretary of State, John Hay, once wrote:

"The Mediterranean is the ocean of the past; the Atlantic is the ocean of the present; and the Pacific is the ocean of the future."

Indeed, the North Pacific now remains all that is left of America's westering dream. It is the last frontier, in free man's imagination, and in geographic fact.

It covers about one-sixth of the surface of the earth, washes against the rim of three continents, stretches across a region measuring about 3,500 by 5,000 miles, covers a submerged landscape broken by immense canyons, soaring seamounts, unknown abyssal plains. Around the eastern rim the continental shelf drops away abruptly into deep fractures and abysses having an average depth of fourteen thousand feet.

A youthful region, geologically speaking, the North Pacific is yet rimmed with the fires of subterranean cauldrons—more than half of all Earth's volcanoes are found here—and rumbling earthquakes periodically shake and resettle the cooling crust, sometimes sending *tsunamis*—seismic sea waves popularly known as "tidal waves"—hurtling over distances of several thousand miles at speeds up to five hundred knots.

It lies mostly in the horse latitudes and its prevailing winds are westerly. The northern limit of the northeast trade wind skirts its southernmost boundary. Its climate is controlled by the warm North Pacific Drift, the North Equatorial Current, and the cool California Current, the warm Kuroshio (or Japan) Current, and the Alaska Current.

The waters of the North Pacific contain twenty-six known elements ranging from oxygen to radon, support thousands of known forms of marine life, and no doubt more thousands not yet catalogued. Of these more than two hundred species are regarded by sportsmen as game fish and by commercial enterprises as food to be harvested.

That, probably, is the theme of this book.

Most fishermen, however, be they sports or be they motivated by profit (or both) are singularly curious, inquiring, individualistic, and sensitive persons constantly seeking attunement to their environment; and therefore they are not content with mere manuals of technique, catalogues of equipment, and essays by Old Local Experts on the finer points of baiting a hook.

They respond deeply to total involvement of ecology and esthetics and abstractions of their world, if the writers of "fishing books" would only know.

Oddly, the relatively new and unknown North Pacific was one of the earliest objects of interest to the explorers and discoverers who emerged from the Dark Ages to take a look around the world outside.

There exist ancient records of Afghanistani monks who explored the coast of North America. For at least two centuries, the Pacific was a Spanish lake from which other colonial aspirants were discouraged. When the Pilgrims landed at Plymouth Rock, a regularly scheduled galleon service had already been in operation between Manila and Acapulco for nearly a century.

Men seeking the fabulous cities of Quivira and the mythical Strait of Anián, and later the Northwest Passage, haunted the North Pacific. It is even said that Gulliver's Brobdingnag was located somewhere along the North Pacific coast.

The names of Balboa, Pizarro, Magellan, Cabrillo, Sir Francis Drake, Sebastián Vizcaíno, Juan de Fuca, Vitus Bering, Chirikov, Juan Pérez, Bruno Heceta, Bodega y Quadra, Captain Cook, Jean François de la Pérouse, Captain Robert Gray, George Vancouver, and John Jacob Astor are part of its historical fabric.

Today the maps and charts ring with the sound of place names like Humboldt, Chuginadak, Akutan, Baranof, Augustine, Argonne, Applegate, Beaver, Carlisle, Bainbridge, Bertocini, Juneau, York, Wrangell, Dutch Harbor, Eureka, Tillamook, Hole-in-the-Wall, Ozette.

Long before the United States was a free nation, the remote Nootka Sound, on the west coast of Vancouver Island, was a busy harbor, crowded with ships of a half-dozen far-off nations. Today it is a remote and forgotten place.

For a period equal to that of United States history beginning with the Civil War and stretching to present times, the vast region rimmed by the Gulf of Alaska was a Russian imperial colonial empire.

When Lewis and Clark reached the Pacific by land in November, 1805, they were latecomers who found adult natives in whom coursed the blood of earlier white sailors and aborigine maidens.

Even the dour Yankee, Captain Robert Gray, who sailed across the Columbia bar in May, 1792, was a newcomer, having been anticipated by other traders and explorers a century past.

Therefore it seems incredible today that in the North Pacific there are still bays, inlets, and offshore banks that have never been charted, that the science of oceanography is only now inquiring into these waters seriously, and into what lies under the surface, and perhaps even under the floor of the ocean.

For almost four hundred years now the swirling fogs and weather fronts have shrouded much of this region in foreboding and mystery, legend, and even intrigue. Now it is being discovered again; and again it is a new and fascinating frontier for the curious, the adventurer, the outdoor sports-man, the seeker of freedom and elbowroom in a world now too crowded, for the escapist from the nagging madness of a pressurized, transistorized society.

If you will first glance at a map of the North Pacific for orientation, you will be struck by a number of anomalies—and perhaps even some surprises.

The Hawaiian Islands, rather than being in the tropics, instead straddle the Tropic of Cancer and extend well into the North Pacific, surprisingly close to the extreme tip of the Aleutian Islands, which incidentally lie west instead of north of Seattle.

The International Date Line runs along the 180th degree of longitude on a line that bisects the Bering Strait, lies considerably east of Attu, and just west of Midway.

The Great Circle route between Panama and Yokohama, 7,682 nautical miles, almost touches the Aleutian Islands, as does the Los Angeles to Manila track of 6,530 nautical miles.

Straight south from Dutch Harbor to Honolulu it is 2,040 nautical miles. From San Francisco to Dutch Harbor on the Great Circle it is 2,051 nautical miles.

If you wanted to sail a boat from Mexico to Manila, you would take a track just south of the Hawaiian Islands where you would be helped by the Northeast Trades and the North Equatorial Current. Coming back, however, you would want to steer considerably north of the islands, picking up the Northeast Drift and the prevailing westerlies which would bring you on a wide circle down along the west coast of North America.

Which is as true today as it was in the sixteenth century when the clumsy Spanish galleons began making the round trip.

It is also true today that once you have put out from the Northwest coast and dropped the continent behind you, you are back again in a world as big and wide and free and unknown as it was to the earliest adventurers.

This book deals not in great detail about the specifics of angling. There is no lack of chamber-of-commerce types and of fish and game publicists who, with the slightest encouragement, will inundate a prospective visitor with brochures and guides and directories in living color.

The main purpose of this book is to build the profile of a frontier, through the experience, reactions, and motivations of a fisherman who has lived around it for quite a few years, for the possible enjoyment of those who haven't.

Perhaps even, to paraphrase old Izaak himself:

"Doubt not but it will prove to be so pleasant that it will, like virtue, be a reward unto itself."

PART ONE

Offshore

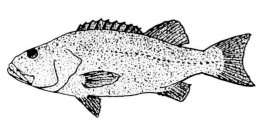

Black Sea Bass

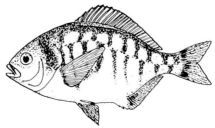

Redtail Surfperch

Bonito

I.

Making the Run for Blue Water Tuna

It is 5:30 A.M. and I have been awake most of the night, thinking of the next day's fishing and wondering if it will be just a routine dory trip along shore for salmon, or if it will be a wild offshore run for albacore tuna which are found only in the blue water, far out in the Pacific.

I hear Paul Hanneman start the engine on his beach buggy with which he pulls the trailer from which he launches his *Kiwanda Klipper 5*—a twenty-three-foot square stern of local design. Paul is a veteran ocean guide, a local civic leader in Tillamook County, and a state representative. I have known and fished with him for more than fifteen years.

In a few minutes he will pound on the cabin door, and we will throw our gear aboard along with an extra fifty gallons of gas—just in case this is to be a run for tuna —and drive the three miles or so from his re-sort on the Nestucca River to the launching site under the lee of Cape Kiwanda.

It is late August and the eastern sky is rosy as we pull up on the wet sand. There is a damp chill in the air and heavy dew on the motor, gas cans, and the dory's seats are cold and clammy and beaded with moisture. Other dorymen are there, waiting to decide about the day's fishing, and the ocean is fairly flat with a fogbank hanging offshore

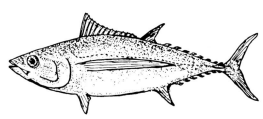

Albacore Tuna (Longfin)

Striped Bass

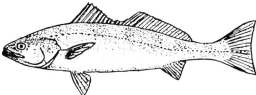

White Seabass

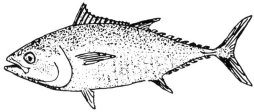

Bluefin Tuna

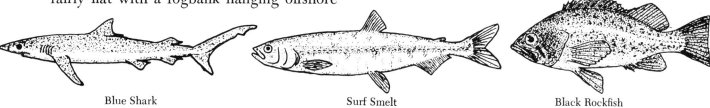

Blue Shark   Surf Smelt   Black Rockfish

about fifteen miles. To the east Oregon's Coast Range is now tinged with copperish pink, and there is a mackerel sky overhead. The surf is light. You cannot see whitecaps through the Jughandle on the Rock, which is one of the signs.

Paul confers with Ted (Shorty) Howe, who's there with his *Dink Howe* to accompany us as a "buddy boat"—just in case it's tuna. Shorty has been out in the blue water every day for two weeks looking for the albacore schools.

"I've been driving in so much fog my eyeballs are blistered," he jokes.

If Shorty and Paul decide we go for albacore, I have a whole bag of worries to take along; if it's for salmon alongshore, just outside the surf, it'll be more certain, but I'll be a little disappointed, too.

So will Paul, who hasn't made the run for albacore for eleven years. Sport fishing for tuna has been done on and off by a few adventurous anglers in the Pacific Northwest since the early 1930's, but only in large ocean-type cruisers with plenty of range, fuel, and sea-kindliness.

Tuna fishing in one of these incredible Kiwanda dories is yet a new sport for North Pacific anglers—but one that will someday become this region's most exciting fishing adventure. I have long hoped I'd be the first to bring back a story and pictures—not for any particular glory attached but because, as they say, *it's there.*

I look at Paul and Shorty conferring, standing head to head in their fishermen's hip boots which hang folded down from the knees. The gentle surf swirls up and around their legs, and recedes. I look at the beautiful sunrise, at the battered sandstone cape, at the monolith called "the Rock," standing darkly offshore half a nautical mile from the tip of Kiwanda—and at the distant horizon

where some unknown happening awaits. Perhaps.

Shorty is telling about the last two weeks and his daily run out trying to find the tuna, and running always into fog or weather; and sometimes even squalls and, on one occasion, having finally to run into Depoe Bay because he can't get back through the surf.

"It's going to be a fast-running sea," Paul says.

Paul and Shorty now go among the dorymen standing around, and come back with two recruits: Wayne Harding, pastor of the Cloverdale Baptist Church and a first-year doryman; and Bob Speldbrink, of Pacific City.

With decision Paul brings Wayne over and introduces him. "I guess it's going to be a run for blue water," he says.

I jump into the *Kiwanda Klipper* 5 and Wayne and Paul shove us off. This amazing boat floats on two inches of water. They hold her for the first good wash coming up on the sand and then launch and jump in.

I think of that old sailor's ditty: "Evening red and morning gray, you're sure to have a fishing day!"

It had started out just the other way around, and moreover the Coast Guard had hoisted small craft warnings the night before, expecting trouble today. But these dorymen I would trust before all else on this ocean. They have been going to sea through the surf under the lee of Cape Kiwanda for nearly a hundred years and so far have not had a fatality or even a serious accident. I can live with these odds.

In another moment we are leaping a little over the gentle breakers and into the mild swell of the open sea with the gulls swooping low over us quizzically, and then we are planing. The surf had indeed been tame

Dory fishermen greet the morning sun on the albacore grounds off the coast of Oregon

and the offshore swell mild and barely noticeable until you pick up speed. Paul twists full throttles on his two thirty-five-horsepower outboards to keep up with Shorty who carries one sixty-five-horsepower in his well.

At thirty knots the gentle swells become launching pads. Our dory, even loaded with three people and fifty gallons of extra gas, takes off from each crest and crashes down with such force I am sure the bottom will collapse. Standing in the bow, Wayne and I try to hang on, but it is almost impossible. It is something like being churned in a cement mixer at the business end of a pile driver.

We pass between the Rock and the Cape running abreast, and then Shorty pulls ahead. We leap from crest to crest, straight for Japan, crashing down and leaping up again, the bonebreaking force a thing of immediacy that one cannot escape and one cannot live with. I do not think I can take even five minutes of this, but indeed I am to take more than an hour of it before relief comes with cut throttles.

As we put the coastline behind us, the copper sun blazing over Cape Lookout to the north and Cascade Head to the south is a rare and beautiful sight—and one I'd wanted to photograph in color for many years. But right now I am trying to hang on with both hands. I yell at Paul to slow down so I can shoot a couple of pictures, but he can't hear me above the roar and merely smiles back.

We run westward for an hour, finally slowing down to a more endurable speed in the longer offshore swells. By now I feel like a bundle of parts rather than a whole person, but it has the effect of keeping my mind off my bag of worries. Once the North American continent drops behind the fog-bank, I then ponder why Paul has chosen a man of God to help crew the boat. Do you suppose he knows something I don't?

A large steamship, hull down to the northwest, disappears from our view. But the fog has dissipated. The greenish water of the continental shelf turns to a dazzling blue as the copper sun now breaks through the haze to the south and east. It turns out to be a breathtaking, magnificent day on a sparkling blue Pacific, and one that is frequent in late summer—even on the North Pacific.

We start looking for "tunny birds," as the offshore fishermen call them, which turn out to be what seem like frigate birds.

Shorty cuts his engine and reaches over the side to test the water. For tuna you look

for temperatures ranging from sixty to sixty-eight degrees. I look around. We are absolutely alone on this big ocean. We are now about an hour and a half's run off the beach.

I see Shorty's poles go overboard. "Time to rig up," Paul says. We set four sport rods out, including my salmon spinning gear with the big saltwater reel loaded with sixteen-pound line. We tie on weighted feather jigs, ones Paul has left over from his last trip eleven years before. By the time we're rigged up, we see Shorty and Bob now a mile or so off, reeling in madly.

"They must be on the school!" Paul shouts.

Albacore fishing is like nothing else. Since these fish feed on the run, you have to keep up with the school, and this means trolling at speeds up to eight knots or more which makes it a rough business when there is a southwest swell running, as there is now.

Tuna are still a mysterious and exotic pelagic fish. They spawn somewhere in the South Pacific, on the run, and move northward thousands of miles at a rate of eight to ten knots, feeding as they go in periods of frenzy, their torpedo-shaped bodies constantly on the move. Off the Oregon and Washington shore they sometimes swing in as close as ten miles, but usually they are from 25 to 150 miles off, depending on the winds and currents.

Along here the tuna are still immature, weighing little more than twenty or thirty pounds, but by the time they get to the Japanese waters they may run as big as a hundred pounds; then they swing back

The *Della*, a locally built steam schooner, on the Nestucca River.

The author with an albacore caught from a dory about 35 miles offshore.

down into the South Pacific again to start the cycle over.

The principal species are bluefin, yellowfin, and albacore or longfin. The albacore is truly the chicken of the sea, with its prized white flesh, almost all solid meat; but in fighting qualities it is more like the tiger of the sea. A twenty-pound albacore will make a forty-pound salmon look like a sissy.

They appear off the Northwest coast in spring and the commercial season runs through October. Sport fishing for tuna in this area is not only an undeveloped potential but an almost unknown one—and until recent years not really possible before modern boats and gear became available. But this is the exotic and adventurous sport fishing of the future in this region, without doubt.

No sooner has Shorty got his lines over than he has fish coming across the gunwales. We are still rigging up. We head for the *Dink Howe*. By the time we get there, they have landed two more. Then Wayne's rod bends double. We are trolling close to eight knots. Paul slows down, which is a mistake. When trolling for albacore you must keep going when you get a strike. A tuna closes his mouth on the bait and will not let go as long as there is tension on the line. Paul has forgotten this in eleven years, but it comes back quickly when the albacore takes the line and circles the boat. We lose this one and another. I lose one, too, that hits and runs before I am ready.

The southwest wind now kicks up stronger, and after playing our tuna and losing them and getting lines tangled up and losing one of Paul's precious jigs, we settle down to business. By now Shorty and Bob have nine tuna in the boat, and are almost hull down out of sight to the southwest. When they come up into sight again we see they have four tuna on at once and have thrown over their marker buoy with the red flag.

Then we hit a school. We have fish on all the lines, even my light spinning tackle. I play this one for fifteen minutes, pumping it up and working the line in with much effort and uninhibited excitement. Wayne lands the first one, a beautiful creature of twenty pounds, dark steel blue on the back with an iridescent yellowish sheen on the undersides, and a tail that buzzes with such power and speed it takes both of them to subdue him in the boat. That's the secret of their tremendous speed—that powerful tail. The Navy ought to look into the design of a tuna.

I pump my fish up until we can see him slashing through the water. Paul yells, "Hurry up, there's a shark after him!" I pump harder hoping to beat the shark. Paul pokes at the shark with a long oar, trying to keep it away. The shark veers off and circles the boat. Just as I bring my tuna to the net the shark cuts in suddenly and grabs it and everything goes limp.

But we are still on the school, and rods go down violently again. Line screeches out against drags. A school of dolphins is now playing tag with us, leaping across our bow and blowing startlingly close. Tuna are often found underneath dolphin, so we know we must be right on top of them.

Paul maneuvers the boat while playing his own fish. By the time we lose the school again we have eight twenty-pound albacore aboard. And they are trying to kick the slats out of this tiny boat of ours.

The sea is building up, too. For a while we lose Shorty and Bob in the *Dink Howe,* but pick them up on the little portable CB radio we have and we try to rendezvous. Shorty has a miss in his motor. We all feel a little tired and let down after the fast action. We are surprised to note that it is already 2:00 P.M.

For some reason we all confer on the proper course to get back ashore, although we have a perfectly good compass there, right under our noses. But there is some doubt about where we are in respect to land. One thinks we're off Cape Lookout, another says we're off Cascade Head. Somebody wants to run southeast for another hour before heading in.

In the end we take up a course of sixty degrees and in a half hour's run pick up the prominence of Mount Hebo above the haze lying against the North American continent.

The sea, which has been building up in the southwest breeze, now flattens out except for long swells that alternately cause the motors to labor and race. We pass a floating log with a lone sea gull standing on

Wayne Harding, pastor of the Cloverdale Baptist Church

it. Everywhere the sea is alive with birds, especially what sailors call "steamboat ducks," because of the way they look like tiny paddle-wheel steamers as they beat the water with their wings trying to escape. Some of them barely make it under our bows as we overtake and scatter them.

The breeze now dies to gentle gusts and cat's paws which sweep hither and thither over the surface. We pass frequent slicks and as we pick up the Rock ahead of us, the surface of the ocean turns to a glassy millpond. A few salmon dories are off the Nestucca trolling around the Rock. I can see on the beach many boats, people, and pickup campers—come to enjoy the gentle surf and sun.

To me salmon fishing alongshore just out-

Offshore salmon fishing. At left is Don Rickles, a Network TV announcer

side the breakers now seems tame. It will never be the same again.

We close the distance and enter the passage between the Rock and the Cape, heading for the landing beach through a mild surf. This is the first time I have seen the Cape and Rock from seaward. There are caves on the north side of the Cape, and horn spouts on the west side of the Rock.

In another moment we are surfing. Paul cuts the engines and we slither up on the wet sand and come to an abrupt stop. A small wave comes after us and breaks alongside, just to remind us that this is an ocean.

I do not feel exactly the way Balboa must have felt, but there is an overpowering elation. We have made the run for albacore tuna and have been successful beyond our hopes. We have spent a day upon a rare and beautiful Pacific engaged in a most unusual and exclusive and adventurous sport.

And I have brought back the very first story and photos of it—no one can ever again claim that.

2.

Legends of the North Pacific

The North Pacific legend really begins about A.D. 458 with the wanderings of a buddhist monk named Hwui Shan who made a voyage around the Great Circle and down along the Alaska, British Columbia, Washington, Oregon, and California coastline, putting in frequently to observe the natives and their customs; and thence to Mexico where much time was spent—perhaps even to start a colony—and from there to a place he called the "Country of the Women." Returning to the mainland of China, Hwui Shan reported his findings to the official historian, and the voyage was considered important enough to become part of the state records of the Sung Dynasty.

Seem incredible that America should be discovered ten centuries before Columbus by an Oriental?

Consider then the case of the *Ryo Yei Maru*, a one-hundred-ton Japanese fishing schooner from Misaki, which left its home port December 5, 1926, and a year later was sighted off Cape Flattery by the S.S. *Margaret Dollar* and towed to Port Townsend. Only two bodies of the original crew were still on board. No one knows what happened, but obviously the vessel was carried by wind alone to the North Pacific coast.

Hwui Shan in his detailed log called Japan the "Island of Jesso"; the Aleutians the

"Country of Marked Bodies"; Alaska, "Great Han Country"; California, "Fu-Sang."

Next, and perhaps more credible to European descendants, and certainly of more substantial record, comes Vasco Nuñez de Balboa, a mercurial, red-haired, adventurous Spaniard, to that cockpit of intrigue, piracy, conquest, convicts, and militant monks —the Caribbean.

On September 1, 1513, with two hundred men and a pack of bloodhounds trained to hunt Indians, Balboa set out across the jungles of the Isthmus with the smell of gold in his nostrils. Three weeks after leaving Santa Maria on the Atlantic, he crossed the summit between the two oceans and reached the Gulf of San Miguel on the South Sea, which he called "Pacific."

In 1519 the governor of Cuba sent Hernando Cortez to Mexico to explore and plunder. Two years later he pushed across the mainland to the Pacific coast. In 1522 he founded San Blas as a base for exploration of the Pacific. In 1532 he sent Diego Hurtado de Mendoza north to look for the mythical Strait of Anián that tantalized the imaginations of Europeans for three hundred years. Mendoza got as far as what is now San Diego.

Pearls were found in the Bay of La Paz,

but no gold. A few years later he founded Santa Cruz. Other expeditions were outfitted and sent north, usually to meet with disaster.

Meanwhile Ferdinand Magellan had sailed the long way around, and across the Pacific in 1521. In 1542 Juan Cabrillo reached the Santa Barbara Islands off California, dying on the voyage. Bartolomé Ferrelo, the pilot, took command and sailed farther north. Spain officially occupied the Philippines in 1565 and began a regularly scheduled galleon service between Acapulco and Manila. The galleons on the westward passage picked up prevailing winds and currents, but on the return trip tended to the more northern latitudes to get help from easterly winds. This made knowledge of the Northwest coast imperative, for these clumsy vessels were often carried helplessly onto unknown coasts by storms.

Sir Francis Drake considered preying upon rich Spanish galleons not only ripping good sport but highly profitable. Sailing through the Strait of Magellan in 1578, he worked along the west coast of South America, Mexico, Lower California, and into the unknown and uncharted waters off northern California and Oregon. During this trip, with unbounded ebullience, he put into a small bay near the entrance to San Francisco Bay for repairs and refitting, and claimed the entire country, which he called New Albion, for England.

After leaving the coast he made off westward and eventually circumnavigated the world on the track of Magellan's epic voyage.

In 1602, Sebasián Vizcaíno pushed farther north along the eastern rim of the Pacific, was turned back by a storm. The second attempt brought him to Monterey Bay and northward to Cape Blanco.

Back in the merchant capital of Venice, a Greek mariner from the island of Cephalonia, with the soul of a con man, looked up a British diplomat and financier named Michael Lok and sang him a song of riches beyond all dreams, discovered by him on one of his voyages to the Northwest Coast of America.

After mutiny by the crew the expedition turned back. He said he sailed with a pinnance and caravel to 47 degrees north where he discovered a broad entrance leading to inland waters where the natives were clad in animal skins and where the country was rich in gold, silver, and pearls. This time he was driven off by the natives.

Now an old man, he sought nothing but a modest pension for his long service to mankind and science. In return, he told Lok, he would pilot a British vessel through the Northwest Passage he had discovered.

The Greek, whose name was Juan de Fuca, died before an expedition could be organized and financed.

Juan de Fuca achieved immortality when J. N. Bellin, a prominent cartographer of his day, placed on the map of 1755 the Strait of Juan de Fuca in latitude 47 degrees north.

Later explorers discovered such a strait at 47 degrees 30 minutes north.

The next wave of exploration came from the north, from Russia, led by a Danish navigator named Vitus Bering in the service of Peter the Great's navy. A Cossack named Popoff had done some exploring around Kamchatka about 1711, but little of record was noted. With the passing of Peter and the ascension of Catherine, Bering was appointed to a command to explore the North Pacific. On July 9, 1728, the *Gabriel* was launched on the Pacific coast of Kamchatka and the famed voyage began. On the second expedition, Bering had along the German naturalist, George William Steller, who left an incredible catalog of flora and fauna unknown to science.

From Bering's voyages until the American Revolution, the North Pacific was virtually a Russian lake, as completely as had been Spain's domination of the Pacific for two hundred years previous. Russia did not grasp the importance, however. Spain began extending her possessions northward from Mexico, still seeking the Strait of Anián, but probably prodded more by Russia's presence.

In 1769 the San Diego mission was founded and the Spaniards pushed up the coast by land. On January 24, 1774, the *Santiago* with a crew of eighty-eight under Juan Pérez sailed north from San Blas, and after many stops along the way to establish claims, refit and reprovision, reached 42 degrees north on July 4. Exploring farther north, looking for suitable harbors, he eventually reached 54 degrees 40 minutes.

Next on the scene were Bruno Heceta and Juan Francisco de la Bodega y Cuadra, joint leaders of a new expedition to map the Northwest coast. They very nearly discovered the Columbia River—which would have been disastrous for the claims of the weak young nation known as the United States of America—and in August and September 1775 reached as far north as Mount Jacinto, now Mount Edgecumbe.

Captain James Cook, perhaps one of history's greatest geographer-explorers, turned his attentions to the North Pacific on his third voyage, leaving England in 1776 in the *Resolution* and *Discovery*. This voyage was considered of such importance to humanity that Benjamin Franklin, then minister to France, gave Cook official protection from armed ships of the United States, then at war with Great Britain.

Cook arrived in the Sandwich (Hawaiian) Islands in early February, 1778, and on March 7, 1778, reached the Oregon coast at 44 degrees north. The expedition thoroughly explored the coast, stopping at Nootka Sound on the west coast of Vancouver Island, trading with the Indians, going northward to map Edgecumbe, Fairweather, and St. Elias. He discovered what is now Cook Inlet and Dutch Harbor, moved into the Bering Sea and turned around at about 70 degrees 44 minutes north. Sea otter pelts picked up in trade were later to start a stampede.

Back in the Islands, trouble with the natives led to Cook's murder while leading a detachment of marines ashore to punish minor theft.

Six years later another Englishman, James Hanna, flying a Portuguese flag, sailed from Macao to Nootka and picked up 560 sea otter pelts. The next year he returned with a larger vessel.

After Hanna came a parade of trader-adventurers, and a long list of official and quasi-official voyages spurred on by the imaginative writings and lectures of an American named John Ledyard, who had been with Cook. Louis XVI sent Comte de la Pérouse on a scientific mission. Captain James Strange, for the East India Company, showed up at Nootka with two ships, the *Captain Cook* and the *Experiment*. John Meares, another English trader-freebooter, also appeared on the scene. From 1785 to 1795, in fact, Nootka Sound, on remote Vancouver Island, was a major port to which came vessels from Kamchatka, from the Sandwich Islands, from the Orient and Mexico, and from Boston.

Meares built the first ship on this coast, the *Northwest America*, launched September 19, 1788. Other free-lancers arrived smelling fabulous riches from trade with the Indians—a sea otter pelt purchased for a copper nail at Nootka on the Northwest coast, was worth up to five hundred dollars in Canton.

Spain again became alarmed and sent an expedition north to take possession of Nootka. In April, 1789, two American ships, the *Columbia* and the *Washington* under Captain Robert Gray and John Kendrick were in Nootka, prowling for profit. Gray returned to Boston with a cargo of spices and baubles from China, purchased with skins from the Northwest, to become the first American ship to sail around the world. On his next voyage, Gray beat out the British, the Spaniards, the Russians, and the Portuguese to the discovery of the great River of the West, which he named after his ship on May 11, 1792.

With a chart supplied by Gray, George Vancouver later entered the river and subsequently tried to claim discovery, to Vancouver's everlasting discredit.

Others, known and unknown, came and went, such as Portlock, Dixon, and a hundred others. In 1791 more than twenty-eight ships anchored in Nootka. From 1799 to 1802, about 50,000 sea otter pelts were shipped to Canton for fabulous profits. One Russian was said to have made $500,000 on one voyage.

By Lewis and Clark's time, the peak had already passed for the freebooting seafarers, and places like Nootka and Clayoquot faded away into obscurity. Today they are as isolated and nondescript as they were before the Spaniards arrived, havens only for salmon trollers and an occasional visiting yacht or mail boat.

3.

Moving In on the Rim

The settlers on the Northwest coast, who followed the trail of Lewis and Clark westward to the Pacific, found an ancient Indian fishery all along the coast from California to Alaska, and most having come from the Eastern seaboard, they were immediately impressed by the fecundity of marine life and particularly the incredible runs of anadromous fishes such as the Pacific salmon —a close relative of the Atlantic salmon which had been fished commercially and for sport in Europe since early times—and the sea-run rainbow trout, now called the steelhead.

Most of the Northwest coast—which was fairly well populated by permanent Indian towns every few miles—came to be settled by whites in the middle 1800's, by land by the covered-wagon emigrants and by sea by sailors who jumped ship to head inland to the new gold fields of California and Oregon. The same pattern generally settled the Washington coast, and from there the northward movement to British Columbia and Alaska was all by boat along the coastline, but for the same reasons.

Fishing and lumbering became the two principal ingredients of the coastal strip, with recreation starting early along the Oregon and California coast, and becoming number one in importance.

The early Indian fishery on the Columbia alone, mentioned in the journals of Lewis and Clark and others, has been estimated at eighteen million pounds of salmon annually. The first commercial exploitation of Columbia salmon began in 1830 as a part of a grandiose scheme of Nathaniel Wyeth to establish a commercial empire on Sauvie Island to rival the Hudson's Bay Company operation. In the period of the early settlers, vessels sailed upriver as far as what is now Portland, taking on cargoes of salted salmon bound for the United States, England, South America, China, and Europe. Columbia River salmon became so famous in Europe that it was known as the "Royal Chinook" salmon—a commercial label that still marks the top-grade salmon pack today.

Modern salmon canning, however, was begun on the Sacramento River during the days of the Forty-niners by William Hume and two other men from New England, Perry Woodson and James Booker, who founded a crude cannery in a cabin on the river to preserve salmon for sale in the booming mining camps. They were joined by Andrew S. Hapgood, from Augusta, Maine, in 1864, a man who had experience as a canner of lobster and who even had some machinery with him. They canned two thousand cases of salmon the first year of this partnership. The cans were painted a bright red and sold as "red salmon."

A couple of years later they discovered the fabulous runs of the Columbia River and moved operations north where a fifty-year boom was ignited. The salmon packing industry spread from there to Grays Harbor, to Puget Sound, British Columbia, and finally to Alaska—the greatest salmon producer of them all, where for years the annual salmon pack far exceeded the value of all the Territory's other wealth combined, including gold production.

Like the North Atlantic, the North Pacific was the hunting ground of the New England whalers, who began rounding the Horn in the early 1820's. In the 1830's and 1840's the whalers pushed into northern waters, working the bowhead and the right whale, into the Gulf of Alaska, through the Bering Strait into the Bering Sea and even the Arctic Ocean. Returning, they sailed home by way of the Hawaiian Islands or along the west coast of North and South America.

Along the coast they found the gray whale in great numbers and easy to kill. The gray migrated south along the coast in great numbers from the Arctic waters to give birth to calves in the warm waters of Lower California. There were plentiful humpback whales along the coast, too, and from ports in Monterey Bay and San Diego fleets of whaleboats used to put out after the huge mammals, and, towing home their kills, to try them out in huge pots on the beach.

The gray whale was hunted to near extinction—down to an estimated one hundred survivors before the species was protected. Today there are about five thousand of these mammals, which are often seen as they migrate north and south.

By 1880 San Francisco was the largest whaling center in the world, and with the coming of transcontinental railroads, the oil could be shipped overland to the East instead of by the long Cape Horn passage. About this time the steam whaling ship was developed, designed for Arctic waters, and trips of two and even three years were made through the Bering Sea and around the bulge of the continent to Herschel Island where the fleet usually wintered. Often as many as two dozen ships would be wintering at Herschel, locked in the ice pack until spring. The decks would be roofed over with lumber and made snug. Some captains brought their wives along, and the long months were spent with dances, card parties, concerts, and winter sports. There is even record of a baseball game held on the ice to celebrate July 4.

The oil fields of Pennsylvania, Texas, and California put an end to the whaling business in the North Pacific after the turn of the century. Moreover, whalebone corsets went out of style.

Some minor whaling is still done, however, out of Astoria and a couple of other places, for the whale is still valuable for fine oil used in industrial instruments, for dog and cat food to humor the personal pets of an affluent society, and for shoe polish, margarine, and cosmetics.

The modern whaling fleets of the world, however, now operate mostly in the southern hemisphere, in Antarctic waters where these magnificent mammals are being relentlessly exterminated.

Most lovers of sea stories and many armchair adventurers have heard of Captain Joshua Slocum and his classic voyage around the world alone in the sloop *Spray*. Few are aware that as a young, adventurous seaman, he found himself on the West Coast, first in San Francisco where he

New boat harbor at Depoe Bay

learned about salmon fishing, and later in the 1860's on the Columbia River where he claimed to have originated the design of the traditional twenty-five-foot double-ended gill-netter with its leg-o'-mutton sail.

Later getting a command, Captain Slocum made many voyages up and down the coast, into Puget Sound, and north to Alaska. On his honeymoon he took his bride, whom he met and married in Australia, on a lengthy voyage to Cook Inlet in Alaska for a cargo of salt salmon shortly after the United States purchased Alaska from the Russians for $7,200,000. He was shipwrecked there, made his way to Kodiak and eventually back to San Francisco, where he was given another command.

But probably the most incredible voyage Captain Slocum ever made, not excepting that of the *Spray*, was the one with his wife and young family, ages three to five, in the forty-five-ton schooner *Pato* (Spanish for duck) through the South China Sea to Hong Kong, and from there to Yokohoma, thence to Kamchatka and Petropavlovsk-Kamchatski, where his wife gave birth to twins, and on to the Sea of Okhotsk to fish the newly discovered North Pacific cod-banks.

Meeting up with an old friend, master of the *Constitution*, which was full of fish and about to jettison its excess salt, Captain Slocum filled his hold and with the whole family manning handlines, soon loaded the *Pato* to her marks. Slocum sailed with his cargo for the States, brought it into the harbor of Portland, Oregon—the first cargo of salt cod to enter that state—sold it for a profit, then sailed to San Francisco and Honolulu where he sold the schooner for $5,000 in gold, ending an odyssey of eight thousand miles.

Later, in one of literature's great understatements, the Captain remarked, "The whole voyage was a great success."

The Siberia codbanks, later the Bering Sea banks, and the halibut fishery of the Gulf of Alaska, Bristol Bay sockeye (to say nothing of pelagic sealing) created great fleets of North Pacific ships, usually based in San Francisco or Seattle, with a romance all their own. Most famous, probably, were the "Stars"—*Star of Alaska, Star of India, Star of England,* and some sixteen others in this famous fleet of the Alaska Packers Association.

Lesser known, perhaps, but more colorful were the Bristol Bay gillnetters. Into this shallow estuary flowed the rich salmon rivers with names like Nushagak, Kvichak, Naknek, Egegik, Ugaskik, and Togiak—all producers of immense numbers of sockeye (commercially called "red") salmon.

A closely regulated fishery, the salmon were (and still are) taken by gillnets manned by one or two men from the double-ended sailboats first used on the Columbia River. For seventy-five years this commercial fishery yielded as much as thirty million dollars annually. In modern times, however, unregulated fishing by huge Japanese fleets just outside the bay, as well as other factors, may well have pushed this fishery past the point of no return.

The "Star" fleet usually tied up in the Oakland estuary during the winter, heading north in the spring for the canneries and fishing grounds in Alaska. The ships would be jammed with workers, usually Italians and Scandinavians who did the actual fishing, Germans as cannery technicians and mechanics, Chinese, Mexicans, or Filipinos

to clean and can the catch. They returned in the late fall loaded with the season's pack.

The Pacific salmon and the can, incidentally, came together as naturally as the sardine and the tuna did. All five species of Pacific salmon (plus a sixth species native to the Asiatic rivers), and steelhead trout to a lesser degree, proved ideal for preserving in this way. The early fishermen started by salting the salmon down in barrels, like cod and herring had been done for centuries. But many people did not like the taste of salted salmon, and, salted, it lost its rich oily taste and appearance (smoked and kippered salmon, however, have always been popular). The development of the vacuum "tin" can in the middle 1800's, and refinement of canning machinery, including the invention of the famous "Iron Chink," probably had more impact on the region than any other single thing since Captain Cook's third voyage to the North Pacific discovered the sea otter's value in the markets of China.

Along with commercial fishing, there was lumbering in the heavily forested coastal areas from San Francisco to southeastern Alaska (redwood in California, Port Orford cedar in Oregon, Douglas fir, spruce, and hemlock in Oregon, Washington, British Columbia, and Alaska). The immense growth inspired the two-masted and three-masted bald-headed lumber schooners, and later the steam schooners which sailed up and down the coast, to put into what the sailors called "Dog Holes"—small coves, bays, and shallow estuaries—to pick up lumber. Often this lumber was loaded by means of chutes from cliffs or by means of highlines. In early days few could provide the luxury of a dock or wharf.

Today, these dog holes are more important as sport fishing and recreational centers, and they include Drake's Bay, Bodega Head, Fort Ross, Gualala, Greenwood, Albion, Noyo, Mendocino, Fort Bragg, Eureka, Crescent City, Chetco, Gold Beach, Port Orford, Bandon, Coos Bay, Winchester Bay, and dozens of others from San Francisco to Puget Sound.

The early halibut fisheries on the high seas of the North Pacific at one time were so extensive that halibut nearly became extinct. Only last-ditch cooperation between the United States and Canada, limiting the fishery by treaty and setting up a regulatory commission east of an arbitrary demarcation line, helped the situation. (In recent years, continued predations of Russian and Japanese factory fleets operating along the Alaska, British Columbia, Washington, and Oregon coasts, on the king crab and alongshore salmon runs, led to a joint U.S.-Canada arbitrary twelve-mile zone—which, incidentally, is frequently violated with contempt.)

Out of the high seas halibut fishery evolved the classic halibut "schooner" of modern design, salty and seaworthy, with a high bow and fantail stern, equipped for working the handlines and cleaning fish on the afterdeck and hatch. Many of these were also equipped with purse seines, and were adapted to king crab fishing in Alaska in the post World War II period. King crabbing today has become such an important industry that boats are specially designed for this work.

But probably the most unique boat to evolve from the North Pacific fisheries was the oceangoing troller. The troller took on many designs and variations, because often they were home-built, but the classic one was on the order of thirty feet over all, with a ten-foot beam and a draft of three to four feet. It had a small pilothouse forward over a combination engine room, galley, and cabin. The afterdeck was taken up by a hatch to a fishhold, a smaller steering hatch on the fantail for use when fishing, a pipe framework overhead for the gurdies and rigging, and usually bins on deck for holding fish while cleaning is under way. The troller usually carried four outrigger poles, each handling a heavy wire line to which were attached individual leaders and lures at intervals of a couple of fathoms.

On one such craft, named the *Helen M.*, I spent an entire winter in southeastern Alaska with two buddies in the halcyon pre World War II days just after graduation from high school. It was a long, crowded, often cold and miserable and completely unprofitable winter aboard the *Helen M*, but one of unbridled personal freedom and high adventure—unequalled by anything before or since.

The modern offshore troller today is generally a seagoing craft of thirty-six to fifty feet in length, often equipped with refrigeration, with radios, depth sounders and radar, fuel capacity for a week or two at sea, and relatively luxurious accommodations for two or three men, and frequently for a married couple. Hundreds of these range up and down the coast from San Francisco to Alaska, working the salmon runs, and going far offshore for tuna in season.

None of them puts the owner-operators into the high-income brackets, but they are the last stronghold of the free and independent fisherman who, like the free trappers of the mountain-man era in Western lore and legend, have found the last frontier of individual freedom on the raw and rugged North Pacific.

4.

The Offshore Trollery

A season trolling off the Alaska coast, plus a few trips off California, British Columbia, and Washington, and about sixty-five crossings of the Columbia River bar, still leaves me in the amateur class—but then the number of sport anglers who have had offshore experience along the Northwest coast at this writing could form a very exclusive club indeed.

The smallest craft I ever attempted to go offshore in was a Cape Ann dory I owned in Alaska, which had been imported from New England and was an authentic craft. While the Coast Guard frowns on amateurs going out on the broad Pacific in such craft, I'm reminded that these have been used in the North Atlantic for a couple of hundred years by fishermen in all manner of weather —and, presumably, a fisherman who makes his living in a small boat would get into some other line of work if he thought he was risking his life to get his daily bread. Moreover, several of said dories have been sailed —even *rowed*—across the Atlantic, which seems to speak for their seaworthiness.

Nevertheless, I don't recommend offshore trips in such small open boats. And I am forced by conscience to admit that my buddy, Tony Kuhn, and I did get into trouble once with our Cape Ann, spending a night upon a black angry sea with a broken out-board motor before being rescued by a tug and towed into port. But then, I did a lot of things in my misspent youth, some of which are best not repeated.

I can only add to all this that the biggest boat I ever went offshore fishing in was the sixty-five-foot *Marigold* (and I had felt infinitely safer in the Cape Ann, as I recall). The most comfortable boat I ever went offshore in was a twenty-four-foot home-built keel sloop which was surprisingly well designed and built, for a backyard job, and with its ballast it rode the waves like a sea gull with a gentle motion that inspired confidence even in six-foot swells. The skipper-owner, whose name I don't recall, was picking up a few bucks running charters on weekends during the fishing season. He told me, however, that he was an accountant or something who was deskbound all week, and each weekend all year around— barring typhoon-type weather—he went aboard his little sloop and headed out to sea.

At this writing, offshore sport fishing in the North Pacific is a "new" and completely unexploited and unspoiled outdoor recreation (although party boats and a charter fleet have been operating off the central and southern California coast for a long time).

Ironically, it was the albacore tuna migration offshore, discovered in the early

1930's, that sparked the first sport fishing off the beach. Here in Pacific salmon country, ocean fishing for these species was almost unknown until after World War II.

While the first settlers and traders found the coastal Indians carrying on an extensive fishery in the ocean, few of these tribes actually bothered to go beyond the surf. For one thing, they didn't have to—the fecundity of fish and game within easier reach made it unnecessary. An exception to this was the Makkah and other tribes of the Cape Flattery and Olympic Peninsula coasts. There the Indians regularly launched their cedar dugouts through the surf and went out to fish the halibut banks with bone hooks and sinew lines.

These Indians had discovered what most commercial fishermen along the north coast later found out—the tender, white, and succulent flesh of the halibut is unsurpassed, even by chinook salmon. When I fished in Alaska, in fact, the rarest delicacy a man could enjoy was halibut cheek.

Because ocean trollers have been the closest thing to an offshore sport fishery the North Pacific had known until recent years (commercial trollers are not far removed from sport fishermen anyway, otherwise they would certainly find an easier way to make a living), a word about these is in order.

Ocean trolling for salmon probably began first off the California coast. In the early 1880's there was a fleet operating out of Monterey. Although salmon canning started on the Sacramento River in the 1860's it was a mild curing process developed at Monterey which supported its offshore fleet. These early trollers were all propelled by leg-o'-mutton sails, and later power boats were used. By 1914 the troll fishery extended from Monterey to Point Reyes,

and even north to Fort Bragg, Shelter Cove, off Humboldt Bay, and as far north as Crescent City.

The early trollers were in the twenty- to thirty-foot class, and were all hand operations using two or four poles, fishing as many as nine lines, with four or more hooks on each line. By the end of World War II, more than 1,100 trollers were landing ocean-caught fish off northern California.

The presence of salmon along the shore in Oregon was discovered and the troll fishery spread north. The first trolling off the Columbia began about 1912 by former gillnetters. Sometimes they would gillnet in the river at night and go trolling offshore in the daytime. After 1915 the troll fishery developed rapidly and by 1919 more than two thousand boats operated off the mouth of the Columbia.

In the early 1920's fishermen discovered that they could catch more salmon on the feeding banks than they could if they waited around the mouths of rivers for the spawning runs to start. Then the fishery went in for larger boats that could stay outside several days and carry ice.

These large trollers were also ideal for offshore tuna when the schools were discovered out in blue water. Thereafter the larger boats trolled for salmon on the banks in April, May, and June, and went out after tuna in July, August, and September.

These trollers were by nature restless, independent, and free souls at heart, and thus while one could say that five hundred boats were based in Oregon ports, for example, they actually operated from California to Alaska, following the action wherever it was. Prior to World War II, a troller regarded the location of productive banks as a secret to be guarded at any cost, in about the same manner that a prospector who came to town to file a claim on a new gold strike would go to extreme ends to foil any would-be followers when he left. I can recall, fishing in southeast Alaska, when the location of "highlines" was a troller's most prized possession, even before his boat or his squaw.

After World War II, when small, compact, and efficient two-way radios became available at relatively modest cost and lonely fishermen discovered their utility, the air began to crackle with boats gossiping back and forth, trading information, even broadcasting the location of a school for all the world to hear—anything for an excuse to get on the mike and yak. Today, offshore, the marine high frequency spectrum is a mass of heterodynes, and the trend now is to FM-VHF gear for short range, and to Single Sideband Suppressed Carrier for long-distance communications. Although not approved necessarily by the Coast Guard, the Citizen Band channels are also used extensively now by both commercial fishing boats and sport craft.

The mild curing process for chinook salmon also was originally a factor in the offshore troll fishery along the Washington coast, Strait of Juan de Fuca, Puget Sound, and Vancouver Island. It should be added that troll-caught fish, and particularly chinook salmon, are of better quality and more highly prized market fish.

The Indians along this coast, who were among the most accomplished watermen in the world, had trolled for fish long before the white man arrived. Some of the adventurous settlers also took it up, adapting the Indian ways to their use. The first modern troll fleet appeared in the early 1900's. By 1918 about five hundred trollers operated off Neah Bay, more off Grays Harbor, and about two thousand off the Columbia.

Also included in the troll fleet were many converted gillnetters and small boats called "kelpers" that fished the rocky shoreline around Flattery. The small boats that operate off the Washington coasts today are usually referred to as "kickers."

The nature of the waters north of the Columbia is such that the trollers tended to develop larger types. The main fishing banks were off Grays Harbor, off the Quillayute River near La Push, fifty miles north, the Destruction Island area; then around Tatoosh and the cape to Neah Bay, the reefs and banks from Umatilla Reef northward. Because of the long runs, it was usually necessary to stay out several days.

Swiftsure Bank is about two hours' run from Neah Bay. Forty Mile or La Pérouse is about five hours. Northward, around Vancouver Island, there were a number of other popular banks such as Amphitrite Point, Leonard Island, Sidney Inlet, Rafael Point, Esperanza Inlet, and Quatsino Sound.

There is a bank in Heceta Strait known to trollers as the Horseshoe, which attracted Canadian as well as United States fishermen.

Although trolling can hardly be called a "sport" in the usual sense of the word, nevertheless it is the sporting element of this method of taking salmon particularly which is a principal factor in the development of this fishery. Because it is "hook and line" fishing, a brief description might be in order.

The modern troller carries four poles and fishes six lines. The bow poles are from twelve to twenty feet long, with one line fished from each pole. The main poles are longer and usually carry two lines, one on the tip and the other from the center, or from a sucker pole attached to it.

Each line (stainless steel usually) is

spooled on "gurdies" now operated by power, although a few still use hand gurdies. Each line runs through a "safety pin" clip attached to a "tag line" at the end of the pole, then down into the water with a heavy lead "cannon ball" on the end. Leaders with hooks and lures on the end are attached to the line at intervals, usually about four to a line, so that fully rigged the six-line troller might have twenty-four lures or baits out at the same time, as he trolls along about three miles an hour.

The fisherman operates the boat and handles the lines from a small hatch on the stern with remote controls for the engine and steering apparatus. Also within reach are the controls for the gurdies. It is not unknown for a troller to hit a school and get fish on all hooks at once, which can make things busy as well as interesting for a time, especially if the sea is a little rough and there are many other boats in the vicinity.

When a fish is hooked the line is reeled in with the gurdy, and each leader in turn is unsnapped from the line and put aside until the one with the fish on is reached. The fish is then clubbed on the head, gaffed, and brought aboard. Immediately the line is let out again as the leaders are snapped on as it goes down.

On deck the salmon is held in bins until the fisherman gets a free moment, then it is cleaned and dropped in the main hold which usually is full of cracked ice, although modern boats used artificial refrigeration.

When a load is aboard, or the run is lost, the fisherman heads for the nearest buyer or the nearest port to sell his catch.

In Alaska before the war, when the state was still a territory and ruled by the fish-packing monopolies, the best fishing grounds in among the islands were blocked by huge floating fish traps that took not just a few fish but entire runs at a time. The canneries hired watchmen to ride shotgun

A lonely, but independent, salmon troller working offshore

on these traps. Often elderly or retired fishermen themselves, they lived in shacks on top of the traps. At regular intervals the tender from the cannery would show up to brail the salmon out of the holding pens and haul them to the cannery.

Many a hardscrabble troller, trying to make a living with his boat in the face of this competition, became a troller by day and a "fish pirate" at night, usually with the tacit approval if not downright collusion of the watchman. Of course, the watchman usually was keenly aware that the fish pirate was going to brail out a load with or without his consent, if necessary at the point of a .30-30 rifle. So the smart watchman who wanted to retire someday to a skidroad hotel in Seattle or Los Angeles, simply made sure the troller wasn't a spy and then helped him brail out a load for a split of the profits.

It probably was some sort of moral retribution that the pirated salmon were usually sold to the same cannery that owned the fish trap in the first place.

As mentioned before, offshore sport fishing first began in California and spread northward, first on albacore (and even sailfish in the early days), and then for salmon. After World War II the sport fishing along the coast developed steadily, if not rapidly, as port and harbor facilities improved and as better boats, motors, and gear were available. The postwar prosperity plus the installment plan and the shorter work week, also were factors in this sport as in most other recreational pursuits.

With the beginning of the 1960's sport fishing along the Oregon and Washington coasts in particular, and to a lesser degree only because of fewer people and distances involved, off British Columbia and Alaska, has begun a fantastic boom. Such popular sport fishing centers as Westport, Neah Bay, Coos Bay, Winchester Bay, Chetco, and a dozen minor "Dog Holes," are jammed with people and boats all summer long. The number of charter boats runs into the hundreds and the investment into millions of dollars.

For a story published in 1968, I did some extensive research which indicated the indirect and direct value of sport salmon fishing to the state of Oregon alone at between $100 million and $200 million! Approximately the same ratios existed in Washington and northern California. Obviously, this salmon fishing is a multi-million-dollar sport and a major "new industry" to the Pacific Northwest—a fact which the business community in general and a lot of chamber of commerce gents still don't fully comprehend.

5.

Pioneering the Sport Fishery

One of the pioneers in the Northwest's present extensive charter fleet (as distinguished from "party boat" fleet) is Jim Conway, of Portland, Oregon. Now producer of the "Outdoor Sportsman," a half-hour hunting and fishing program that is shown on television in thirty or forty Western cities, Jim spent about eight years after World War II in commercial fishing and in taking out charter parties. He was one of the first to operate out of Depoe Bay, and for a long time if you wanted to charter a boat out of Ilwaco (which now has a fleet of several hundred), you went with Jim Conway. His *Jimco*, in fact, is at this writing still in use as a charter boat, and there is now a *Jimco II*, built to specifications especially for the offshore charter business, and run by the present owners.

Jim operated offshore from Depoe Bay for several years when few boats would even attempt it. Day after day, for weeks on end, he and his crew would get up and take out a scheduled party, regardless of weather, when other boats were cancelling or turning down business. On occasion other skippers would tag along, following his example at times in seas that opened up the planking and forced them to turn back.

"It was rough on passengers in those days," he told me, "but we never cancelled a charter because of weather. We just got up and went. Our sports sometimes took a beating, but we almost never came back without fish."

Conway began taking sportsmen out after tuna long before most people knew the schools were there. In fact, when the albacore showed up, he usually quit salmon fishing and went offshore. When he did not have any sports to take out, he would go out fifty miles or so and stay a week or so on a commercial run.

When the other charter boats began taking parties out for tuna, often Conway would come back with seventy or eighty fish aboard, while others who fished right alongside would bring back two or three. Back in port the other skippers would come over, examine his gear and lures, measure his rods, test the line, trying to discover the secret.

They never did find out that the "secret" was simply rubber couplings on the drive shaft. Albacore are spooky and can't stand the noise. It's the quiet boat that gets 'em.

From his experience, Conway passed on some of his tips. The albacore, by far the most desirable of the tuna species, arrive off Oregon and Washington about mid-July, with the peak period in August and early September. They are always found in the warmer "blue water" offshore about twenty-five to thirty miles during the summer months. Sometimes, due to weather and wind, this current may swing in to as close as ten miles.

"Regardless of current," Conway said, "a good skipper will carry a thermometer and when sixty-eight-degree water is reached, you're in business."

The fishing is by trolling with whalebone jigs, plastic squid, weighted-head feather jigs, and similar lures. Almost anything trolled through the water fast enough will induce a tuna to strike. Trolling should be done at about eight knots. When a fish is hooked, the boat should double back and cover the same area unless the school is moving in the same direction. If no strikes are experienced, troll a square pattern, run-

ning five minutes to each four points of the compass. If still no strikes search for bottom schools. Watch the birds, as this is a sure sign of feeding fish. If you sight birds, run wide open until you reach them.

"The boat isn't built that can outrun a tuna, so *move* if you see signs of feeding fish."

Equipment used for tuna would include an 8 to 8½-foot salt water spinning rod, medium action, a salt water spinning reel, at least two hundred yards of twenty-pound line. Use No. 12 wire for leaders, with No. 3 McMahon swivels. Almost any hook will do, with single, double, or triples in 5/0 or 6/0 commonly used. When a tuna strikes he won't open his mouth unless the line goes slack. Even a barbless hook can be used if a taut line is maintained.

Fish on! Salmon anglers offshore

A standard salmon mooching rod can also be used for albacore, with a 4/0 Penn or equivalent and twenty-five to thirty pound monofilament line. If the boat is propelled by outboard motor, troll with lots of line out. Don't strike the fish with a tight drag. A tuna hits like a truck going the wrong way. He will close his mouth on a feather and head for the bottom. Work the fish hard, if he has headed away from you, give him some line.

The nice thing about offshore tuna fishing in the Northwest is that it comes during the salmon season, and if it's too rough offshore you can always fish for salmon. Charter boats usually run about two hundred dollars a day with up to ten people sharing. Tuna is best canned, and canning facilities for sportsmen are available at all ports.

On salmon charters, Jim also had a few words. In his opinion, there is still no spot on the entire Pacific coast where salmon are more abundant than off the mouth of the Columbia during late July, August, and early September.

"If a visitor wants to make sure he brings home some fresh salmon," he said, "he should pick a time in the last two weeks of August. Reservations on a good boat should be made at least six months in advance. The cost is usually about eighteen dollars per person, with charter boats handling from up to fourteen or more fishermen."

Most of the salmon will be coho, with an average weight of 8 to 10 pounds, going up to 18 to 20 pounds. Some chinook are still caught in the 40 to 50 pound class but they are getting scarce. The chinooks comprise about 15 per cent of the catch.

There are many other areas off the coast of Oregon and Washington where good fishing can be had, but not with the consistent high ratio as off the Columbia, Conway said.

Tackle is available on the charter boats, but experienced anglers bring their own spinning gear or conventional gear with star drag reels.

A spinning rod of medium action and 7½ to 8½ feet in length is a good size. Reels handling two hundred yards of twenty-pound line should be used. Mooching sinkers and leaders and hook-ups are available locally or from the skipper.

Mooching, trolling, and stripping are the most successful methods of fishing bait herring (also obtainable locally). If the fish are hitting easily but are hard to hook, try either a plug cut or strip bait. This will often outfish a whole herring.

More than half the fishermen strike a salmon too fast and lose the fish. When mooching especially, and a fish is working on a bait, pull off some slack line and let the fish get a good hold on it. Then set the hook. The salmon is biting because he's hungry, so why jerk the meal away from him as soon as you feel him touch the bait?

Trolling is more difficult as the fish can feel the heavier weight used. A little slack, quickly dropped back, will help get him hooked more securely.

The better charter boats will average as high as 2.7 fish per angler during the month of August. With a three-fish limit this is good fishing.

6.

Offshore Banks, Pelagic Predictions, and Intruders

The average citizen had no conception of what inhabits the continental shelf along the eastern rim of the North Pacific until the huge Russian and Japanese factory fleets began operating along Washington and Oregon in the late 1960's (as they had been doing for years in Alaska) sometimes as close as a mile offshore.

When the citizenry became alarmed at this intrusion, and public opinion forced bureaucrats to at least go through the motions and make some mildly indignant noises, the fleets moved off a little bit more, to about three miles—the international limit then recognized by the United States. Then, following Congressional action extending our jurisdiction over fishing to twelve miles, these intruding fleets moved a little farther out.

Meanwhile they ran their trawls and longlines around the clock, completely depleting such stocks as the hake and seriously crippling other stocks of demersals that inhabited the offshore banks and seamounts. As many as several hundred huge Japanese longline ships have been observed off the Northwest coast at one time.

The Soviet fleet commanders publicly acknowledged taking salmon while trawling for bottom fish. In fact, one of them, the skipper of the Soviet research vessel

Oghon, even recovered a tag belonging to the Oregon Fish Commission, taken from a marked chinook caught August 8, 1968, on the high seas north of Heceta Bank, about thirty-three miles off the mouth of the Alsea River. The tag was returned by Vladimir V. Fedorov of the Pacific Research Institute of Fisheries and Oceanography in Vladivostok.

The Soviets maintain they do not fish for salmon primarily, "even though they feel they have the right to do so." They have publicly called fishing for salmon on the high seas, "barbaric."

An unexpected result of this concentrated exploitation of offshore banks along the Oregon coast was a population explosion of shrimp which occurred when the hake, which feed on shrimp, were eliminated.

Shrimp fishing off the Oregon coast then reached major industry proportions. In a 1968 survey, forty-one shrimp boats landed a record eleven millions pounds in Oregon ports, an increase from about ten million pounds the year before. During the previous ten years, the average was about three million pounds a year.

It might even have been bigger in 1968 had not unusually severe weather hampered the operations, which was then followed by a cost-price squeeze in May, June, and July.

These shrimp beds are found in green

mud bottoms from four to twenty miles off the coast. In recent years the banks off Coos Bay have been most productive. In 1968 the banks off Port Orford set a catch record for the Pacific coast outside of Alaska.

Other shrimp beds are found in the banks off Brookings and Garibaldi.

The United States Bureau of Commercial Fisheries, operating the M/V *John R. Manning* in a series of exploratory cruises in Alaskan waters, has discovered and surveyed immense shrimp and scallop beds in offshore waters off Forrester Island, Dall and Baranof islands, and in Hoonah Sound; in waters adjacent to the westward coast of Alaska in the gulf, around Kodiak and off Prince William Sound.

The Forrester Island mentioned above, incidentally, is now a wildlife refuge, but once it was a remote and rugged spot visited only by an occasional troller. On one occasion when I came in there, a herd of "wild" goats was seen on the high cliffs that marked the island. It is located in latitude about 50°40′, some distance off southeast Alaska, and is a wild and forbidding place.

The Bureau has also engaged in exploratory cruises with the F/V *Viking Queen* in Alaskan waters, discovering and surveying some commercial scallop beds in the vicinity of Kodiak Island, Cook Inlet, and along the continental shelf between Cape Spencer and Cape Saint Elias, and other places.

Oregon State University scientists have discovered incidentally that North American Pacific salmon can be distinguished from Asiatic races by atomic radiation counts.

Dr. William O. Forster reported on experiments in which concentrations of zinc-65 from Columbia River reactors and manganese-54 and iron-65 from Bering Sea nuclear fallout areas, have been detected in sample fish by spectrometer analysis. The samples were taken at ten selected points between Bristol Bay and Eureka, California.

Chinook are north-south migrants. Those taken in Alaska waters had ten times the radioactive manganese and iron as chinook near the Columbia River mouth. Chinook taken south of the Columbia show forty times as much radioactive zinc as those in Alaska.

Unlike chinook and coho, the sockeye migrate east and west in the Pacific, showing little zinc but lots of iron and manganese. The Soviet variety shows a lot of brass, too.

Radioactive analysis could be one sure method by which the International North Pacific Fisheries Commission could equitably divide the Pacific fish stocks among the nations involved.

Sportsmen have long fished the offshore banks along the California coast, around the Farallon Islands, and the seamounts off northern California, going out in large party boats carrying up to twenty or thirty people.

This sort of togetherness has never appealed to sportsmen farther north, and particularly the method of taking salmon off the Golden Gate which involves the use of heavy gear and sinkers weighing three or four pounds.

The party boat concept, however, is being considered in the Northwest by many charter boat skippers who are finding it difficult to get customers willing to pay the price for the exclusiveness of a six-man boat. Many of them are planning offshore vessels capable of taking twenty to forty sport fishermen out to the banks for a day or even a weekend, and no doubt this will be a service of the future.

Actually, most of the offshore banks have never been fished by sportsmen. These are seamounts, or underwater rocks and reefs that rise up out of the ocean floor to within a few fathoms of the surface, and are populated by large numbers of demersal species.

Some of which come to mind are the Rogue Rocks off Gold Beach, the Heceta Banks, the Rockpile off Newport, Oregon, the codbank off Cape Kiwanda, Orford Reef off Cape Blanco, the reefs off Cape Elizabeth, Umatilla Reef and Flattery Rocks, Swiftsure Bank off the Strait of Juan de Fuca, on the edge of the submarine valley.

In British Columbia waters there are the La Pérouse Bank extending about twenty miles west and twenty-five miles southwest from Amphitrite Point where depths run from nineteen to fifty fathoms; and others along the west coast such as the banks off Cumshewa Inlet, the Bowie Seamount and the Hodgkins Seamount off the Queen Charlotte Islands, and the Ibbertson Banks off the Gordon Islands.

Offshore anglers (and commercial fishermen, too) who have had considerable experience with albacore tuna, have noted a correlation between environmental factors such as winds and temperatures and the activity of these pelagic species.

Wind forecasts have been used to predict upwellings of nutrient-filled cold water which brings game fish into range of the fisherman.

The albacore tuna migration off the Pacific Northwest fluctuates widely from year to year, depending upon the currents and water temperature, and upon other weather and oceanographic phenomena—especially the aforementioned upwelling.

This occurs in the summer and early fall when the offshore waters are warming and the tuna are moving northward. The predominantly northerly winds at this time turn the surface waters away from the coast

and they are replaced by cold water from the depths.

During such periods of upwelling, the tuna are farther out; when the wind changes to southerly, the inshore temperatures become warmer and the tuna move closer inshore after the food left over from the upwelling.

With detailed wind and temperature records, the tuna fisherman can learn to predict the offshore schools with astonishing accuracy. For example, during the midsummer, when the surface temperature offshore beyond the upwelling region is ideal for tuna (60° to 68°), the surface synoptic pressure charts available from the United States Weather Bureau should be examined daily. During this period a high-pressure pattern is usually found off the Pacific coast, with northerly winds near the coast. The coming of a low-pressure area, bringing southerly winds, can be predicted from the trend shown on the charts. The intensity and duration of the southerlies with the low will indicate the extent to which offshore temperatures will rise, bringing the tuna closer to shore.

If, to use an example, a slow-moving low could be predicted for a period during the tuna season, following a record of strong northerlies, fishermen could predict as long as five days in advance when the tuna would be moving close to shore.

This theory of wind and pressure gradients, affecting the albacore, worked out to an almost perfectly classic situation for an offshore run made by me in company with another boat in August, 1968.

The bluefin tuna fishermen have also observed this characteristic. When the water is in the range of 62° to 68° F., fishermen know the tuna will be most plentiful when sudden changes in the surface temperature or fronts occur. At these boundaries the surface temperature may change by as much as three degrees over a few yards, and are often visible as color differences in the water. These gradients can also be detected by thermometer, and even by putting a hand in the water.

Tuna fishermen off New South Wales, for example, are now using isotherm maps of the sea surface temperature. These are quickly and cheaply compiled by aerial surface patrols equipped with remote temper-ature-sensing devices. In this way the temperature gradients can be found readily and the large tuna boats do not waste time steaming endlessly around the ocean.

It is interesting to note that the Australian experience indicates that major changes in surface temperature will occur over a few days' time. One front of warm water observed, moved at a rate of seven nautical miles a day. Previous estimates by oceanographers were a movement of only two miles a day.

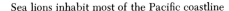

Sea lions inhabit most of the Pacific coastline

7.

Three Thousand Nights

An old college chum, Hoyt Barnett, now of Sausalito, California, operates a sailing school among other things. Sausalito is a most historic spot, incidentally, for this was where the early nineteenth-century whalers from New Bedford to the Bering Sea put in for fresh water and supplies. Hoyt probably knows more about the North Pacific and its whims than most men alive.

An ex-newspaperman, Hoyt was doing work for the O.S.S. in South Africa early in World War II. He walked aboard a United States Navy ship in port one day and enlisted as a seaman, spent the rest of the war seeing action in the European and Pacific theaters, and, like me, returned to civilian life to get a college education *after* the war. During the Korean War he again saw service. He has written several books, hundreds of articles, and is a regular contributor to magazines such as *Rudder* and *Sea and Pacific Motor Boat*.

But let him tell you about life on the North Pacific:

"When Vasco Nunez de Balboa first saw it in 1513 he was standing on a hill and looking at only a bay of this 63,750,000 square mile ocean when he called it 'the peaceful' sea. He didn't know a damn thing about it."

In the area from Conception to the Gulf of Alaska are some of the roughest seas of the world. The Tillamook Light, more than one hundred feet above the surf line, several times has been smashed by rocks hurled against it. The light, now abandoned, has been replaced by a moaning buoy, hard to see and difficult to hear when the weather report is screaming in the rigging.

In the more than three thousand nights I slept aboard my ketch while trying to resign from the human race after my tour of duty in the Korean bit, I have anchored in every cove and behind every rock between Astoria and San Diego. I have lost track of the times I have made the coastal passage.

In those years I have observed some who dabble in this area of the ocean in the manner of a small boy's toe-testing the water, for unwanted baths. I've seen others who, ill-equipped, have tried God's patience with their recklessness. Still others, and they are numerous, combine good judgment with their skill to distill a little peace for a fretted spirit.

Basically, this area provides no big game fishing such as the leaping billfish of warmer waters. The king is the big chinook. More spectacular is the quick-ripening coho, a surface fighter.

To compare is not to disparage. Those

Hoyt Barnett, Sausalito, author, adventurer, and sailing school master.

who go for trophies are a different breed than those who go fishing for fishing's sake whether they fish our lakes, rivers or the sea. As you observe the latter sort "mooching" for salmon off Winchester Bay, Oregon, or working lingcod in the fog-enshrouded reef area hard by the bleak, towering Farallones off Golden Gate, they give the impression of an eerie kinship with Pleistocene man scrounging for food on the fringes of a Cenozoic Sea.

The comparison is not 100 per cent poetic license, for each time a man steps aboard a small craft and stands out to sea north of Point Sur, he is moving into an area where winds sometimes build swiftly from eighteen to the area of fifty knots, or fog descends as quickly. It is then that these men

on their little vessels learn all at once that the twentieth century is where they left it: on the beach.

Three types of fishermen, each in his own way and purpose, take satisfaction from our stretch of ocean to the north'ard of Point Buchon. One group makes up the customers of the "puker boats" whose skippers take their clients on guided tours of the sea's butcher shops.

The second group own boats they can move on trailers. Some of these craft are up to twenty-eight feet, even more, and many are equipped with twin inboard-outboard power plants that produce twenty knots or more on a flat sea.

The third group, a smaller number, have seagoing craft that owners and a few guests can live aboard as they, for thirty days or so each summer, become coastal nomads along our shore.

I, as one of some three thousand commercial fishermen along this section of our coast, for eleven years treated the ocean as a bank on which to draw a check, if one is big enough to cash it.

Anything I have to say about how and where to fish offshore for salmon would be redundant. Every newspaper published in cities and towns along our coast has at least a weekly column filled with sound, carefully screened information which takes much of the hogwash out of the self-centered braggings by "puker" captains who, on Thursdays off San Francisco, take turns telling lies over their 150-watt transmitters beamed at the Sacramento trade.

But the fishermen for whom I feel a sense of rapport are of that larger group who go fishing for a change of pace in life. These men, and sometimes their wives, show up at odd places along our coast.

Working out of Morro Bay, they move

close in over the reefs near Point Buchon on the south tip of Estero Bay, or work the kelp to the north'ard of Estero Point below the big radar station there.

Lingcod is their usual catch, along with various rock cods and now and then a flounder or a "portside" California halibut.

The last is a mediocre fish by northern standards. In addition to having its eyes "on the wrong side"—port instead of starboard—the California flounder has a somewhat rusty color, its meat is coarser than the chicken halibut taken off Heceta Head, for example, and the flesh is darker.

The half-hidden reef off and below Point Buchon to Lion Rock is a dangerous place to fish, but many big ling still live there.

If you're going to fish that area, you must work the reefs that make a fathometer's recording line go crazy. It is in this region of less than five miles of coast that, over the years, seven men I knew well have died.

A little farther to the north, San Simeon is being used by an increasing number of sports fishermen. The seven-mile stretch westward from the anchorage to the rocks of Piedras Blancas is a meat fisherman's paradise. The same is true for half a dozen miles down the coast to the rocks off Cambria.

If you want big ling cod off Cambria, those that weigh fifteen pounds or so, you have to go where they live—where few other fishermen go for them. I've caught them there, at eighteen cents a pound head off, when I could look over the side and see rocks reaching for my keel. This isn't bad on happy weather days, but when the sea builds up a lump and the tops start falling off, I found that in the separation of men from boys, I was a boy.

In this area of the coast, where the sea goes into the land, or, as the perplexed Norseman once wrote, "two pieces of land go into the sea, I know not which," sea life seems pretty much in balance. The fry of various rock cod spawn, hatched by the million, provide good food for the ling.

Farther along the coast, between Piedras Blancas and Point Sur, lies a stretch of fishing grounds that is little fished because it is difficult to reach. A few hundred yards west of Cape San Martin a reef system begins just outside an eighteen-fathom patch of good anchorage sand.

These reefs, rarely shoaling to less than eleven fathoms, are murder for a professional's fishing gear as he tries to work the rocks, for here the reefs are a combination of lava, coral, and granite. Here, too, abalone divers have found huge chunks of jade, some of them so large they could be loaded only aboard a "dragger" equipped with hydraulic hoisting gear. Fortunately for the jade market of the world, it is almost impossible to work jade pieces of such size without sending blemishing fissures throughout the piece, and the divers' dreams of bright tomorrows became once more bleak yesterdays.

The big ling still available along this stretch of coast rarely are bothered by sports fishermen. They colonize offshore pinnacles whose peaks are more than twenty fathoms beneath the sea. This is too deep for the gear most sportsmen use, but the pros, with their power-driven gurdies, often harvest up to a ton a day when weather conditions let them work. And good working days for such gear on these reefs are fairly rare, for a consistent swell stands in from the northwest, and when lingcod gear gets hooked on the rocks while a boat is rising on a sea, something parts. It is not only the expense of replacing lost gear that drives a commercial fisherman toward poverty; it is the lost time during short winter days when he is fixing gear instead of fishing.

Not many fishermen frequent this stretch of the California coast, but it is there. Good anchorages exist, and if one is looking for a place to meditate and try his luck, there are no Keep Off signs.

Point Sur, like all major headlands along our coast, serves as a "spacer" in our variegated coastal climate. Also, northbound travelers often find Point Sur a witch to get around. But there is a flat anchorage at Point Pfeiffer, half a dozen miles below the point, where, behind the kelp one afternoon, I killed thirty-seven kelp flies before I missed—and while drinking a martini.

Several times I've laid in this anchorage, warm in the sun, while three thousand yards out a twenty-five-knot wind drove the seas like leaping sheep to the south'ard.

About midnight this wind usually subsides, and the time is then to up anchor and work around Point Sur for Monterey Bay.

I've never seen a "sportsman" fishing the reef area stretching southwest from Point Sur Light, but such pros as my friend Bob Tunison, a hard-nose Irish type, has taken his quest into those sometimes dangerous waters and brought out a good "trip" of ling and red rock that averaged out around nine pounds.

As one progresses northerly along this essentially lonely piece of shoreline to Point Pinos (which fishermen have trouble pronouncing properly), one comes to Carmel Bay.

Usually, moving north or south along this stretch of ocean, I follow the fifty-fathom curve. A sailor rarely gets in trouble where the water's deep. But once, like a minor-league Odysseus, I stood in close to shore, worked carefully past Point Lobos and into Carmel Bay.

The bay is a peaceful piece of sea, and for about an hour I cruised or drifted while, with binoculars, I tried to locate the house I once, in a moment of misplaced trust in real estate, had purchased.

Moving out of Carmel Bay along the jutting shore that is dotted with the homes of the wealthy who reside on the famous seventeen-mile drive from Monterey to Carmel, I encountered the treacherous current and unexpectedly heavy seas off Cypress Point.

As I labored my way to deeper water, throttling down as I hobby-horsed over the crests of seas that were as steep as the face of a cow, I had the feeling I was maneuvering across a vicious, ebb-tide bar. Several commercial fishing boats have been lost along this stretch of coast, and that afternoon I learned why. With care and prayer I kept *Bonnie* headed out to sea, and hours seem to pass before the depth indicator flashed twenty fathoms and the sine wave changed.

A similar current and short, steep seas exist at times close on the beach northward of Point Pinos when, on a normal course for Monterey, vessels are cruising in the trough.

Monterey Bay, heavily fished by sportsmen and, in some unusual seasons, by the commercial salmon fleet, is a beautiful body of water characterized by a deep sea valley and three good harbors: Monterey, Moss Landing, and Santa Cruz.

The sea valley narrows as it approaches Moss Landing, in what may be termed the center of the bay's shoreline, and it is so deep that a one-hundred-fathom depth indicator will not pick up bottom until you are a few hundred yards from the Moss Landing jetty.

Monterey Bay, like Estero to the south, has been heavily fished because it is so easy to reach, and today most of the sports fishermen, particularly those based in or working out of Santa Cruz, move around the corner to the north'ard and fish in the vicinity of the "cement plant" or farther along to the area off New Year's Island, or "Ano Nuevo" as most charts list that bleak anchorage and its protective reef.

In many years the commercial salmon fishermen make good catches offshore from Ano Nuevo and Pigeon Point a few miles still farther north. But sportsmen rarely get into this act. The fish usually are far out beyond the fifty-fathom curve, and lie so deep that only the heavy weights and steel gear of the commercial fishermen can reach them.

All along the stretch of coast from Pigeon Point to Half Moon Bay reef areas exist which are heavily populated by rock-cod types ranging from big "white bellies" weighing up to ten pounds or so, to the more numerous "yellowtail" cod which usually run about a pound and a half more.

The latter, considered a torment and a nuisance by commercial salmon fishermen, often feed near the surface. They are a fine fish to eat, and the fillet of a freshly caught "yellowtail," if cubed and soaked overnight in soya sauce can be eaten raw. But it is better, by my notion, to sauté the cubed fish in bacon grease and eat it with eggs for breakfast.

Offshore along this stretch of coast, in toward the Farallones lie Guide and Pioneer seamounts. Often, in summer months, albacore school above these underwater pinnacles, as they do farther to the south, above Davidson Seamount and San Juan.

Guide and Pioneer seamounts are closer to the shore than most of the others, such as Davidson and San Juan. Both Pioneer and Guide can be reached in about a forty-mile run from either the Santa Cruz or San Francisco salmon area, yet sports fishermen rarely go for albacore to these seamounts.

Now and then, when albacore are over the outer reaches of the Monterey Seavalley or a dozen miles to the westward of the Farallones, sportsmen do take a run for the longfins, but nothing like in the numbers that fish for albacore on the sixty-mile bank southwest of San Diego or in the waters just below San Clemente Island.

One of the reasons for sportsmen's lack of interest in the offshore fishery over Pioneer and Guide and beyond is the lousy weather. Often, when fishing out of Monterey or San Francisco, the albacore fishermen have forty miles or so of "ground swell" seas to traverse before they reach the albacore grounds. This rough, cold water—often in the low fifties—gets increasingly rough near the warm, blue water in which the albacore travel north each summer.

The reason for this roughness is simple. The Davidson current, close in to shore and cold, moves to the south'ard. The California Current, the summertime warm water of sixty degrees and better, moves to the north'ard. Where these two rivers of the sea rub together a very bothersome turbulence develops and the seas seem never to fit the boat.

Albacore fishermen are accustomed to this. They grit their teeth, stow the wine securely, and tough it out until they cross the temperature gradient that marks the California Current.

Although the summertime seas do whip up on the albacore grounds, built by the twenty- to twenty-five-knot winds often rotating around the characteristic offshore stationary high-pressure area, the seas on the fishing grounds do have a rhyme and reason, and if the going gets too sloppy for fishing, a boat will ride comfortably on a sea anchor.

For some reason I've never had explained to me the inshore seas along the coast from Half Moon Bay to the Golden Gate can be unreasonably large. This approach to the Gulf of the Farallones can be truly dangerous, particularly in the late autumn and winter months.

This past December (1968), two vessels were destroyed by these huge seas. The first was the schooner *Altura*, 47-feet L/A. She disappeared with all hands, including owners Douglas and Ruth Kewell of the San Francisco Bay area, their two children, David, 7, and Becky, 5, plus a crewman identified only as Mr. Borrotto.

A week after this tragedy a Spaulding 33, *Pirate*, was lost in the same area, but before she came apart her owners got off a "mayday" and a Coast Guard unit rescued them in seas estimated to run between twenty-five and thirty feet.

The size of the "lump" that often runs in toward Point Montara and the southern approach to San Francisco Bay often creates a real hazard to vessels using the South Channel into Golden Gate. Experienced fishermen avoid this shoal-water approach, and stand the longer course to San Francisco Lightship, make their turn there and take the characteristic weather on the port quarter as they run down the main ship channel to the harbor.

At times in the summer months sportsmen fishing for salmon out of San Francisco Bay create real traffic problems, particularly when the fish are schooling just to the north of Channel Buoy No. 1, or slightly farther to the north off Double Point or Duxbury Reef.

The distance to these areas from the Golden Gate ranges from six to a dozen miles. Often, particularly in the early spring months of the season, salmon are feeding near the surface as they consume large quantities of crab spawn as these creatures are completing their last larval stage and still are pelagic. Fortunately for the crabs, the salmon run barely is getting started before the crabs, in their life cycle, develop into recognizable crabs and, instead of floating helplessly, descend to the bottom and do whatever crabs do in the three or four years it takes them to develop to legal size. Then their hard luck starts again.

One of the enemies of "baby crabs" in the Gulf of the Farallones is the striped bass. These fish, introduced by man into San Francisco Bay about the turn of this century, have developed into a fine sports fishery, and to some degree have upset the balance of nature both in San Francisco Bay and in the nearby sea. Not only do these "aliens" eat huge number of salmon fry as they trek to the sea from the Sacramento River's spawning beds and hatcheries, but the bass do go out into the sea and eat quantities of baby crabs, those of about one inch and less in diameter.

I know this to be fact because a commercial fisherman friend, setting for white sea bass, unintentionally wrapped a net of stripers. As he emptied the catch on deck, the stripers started regurgitating "hats full" of baby crabs. He had to throw the stripers back into the sea since it is illegal to catch them with commercial gear or for commercial purposes. But he thought a couple were so badly injured they couldn't live, so in the interest of science he "autopsied" them. Each of these, he told me later, had stomachs filled with baby crabs—and nothing else.

One of the natural hazards to the fishermen working out of the Golden Gate is the infamous "Potato Patch," a four-fathom shoal area lying outboard of Bonito Channel leading to the north.

This shoal area got its name in the early days of San Francisco when coastal schooners, coming down from the north, would take on a deck load of potatoes at ports such as Bodega Bay. Then, in those days before adequate charts or established channel buoys, the schooners would cross this shoal area, get hit with a "sneaker sea" and roll the potato cargo into the ocean.

Although this shoal area is well marked on charts mentioned prominently in the *Coast Pilot*, and designated by the channel buoys, small boat skippers still goof off and try to cross it when they shouldn't. Not many boats are lost in this fashion, but a few curling, smoky breakers coming out of nowhere can turn a small boat every way but loose and make Christians out of skippers.

As the major bays on Mexico's west coast often resemble one another in their shape if not their size, the headlands—even the anchorages—of the California coast are often similar in their configurations and their dangers.

As Piedras Blancas juts some six miles into the sea to form a lee for San Simeon, Point Sur shelters Pfeiffer by about the same distance. And Point Reyes, the northern part of the Gulf of the Farallones, shelters Drake's Bay and turns that sweeping arm of the sea into a good summer anchorage. The same general setting characterizes Point Arena and its rugged Arena Cove where many a good vessel has been lost by dragging anchor.

The Point Reyes area is a windy one, and the seas off the lighthouse there often turn back fishermen trying to get around to Bo-

dega Bay. For often in summer months they are driven by gale-force winds clocked honestly at fifty knots on the surface and up to seventy knots where the Coast Guard maintains the weather station and the light.

These fierce winds usually go down with the sun, and basically are created by the co-location of the offshore stationary high pressure areas and a tightly wound up low-pressure area over northern Nevada. The winds swinging clockwise around the high-pressure area and the counterclockwise wind around the low get together at such places as Point Reyes and, in joining, build a wind velocity that combines the Weather Bureau's predicted 15 to 25 knots into a good fat 40 knots and often higher.

On bright summer afternoons I often have seen 150 to more than 200 fishing boats anchored close in to the sandstone cliffs with seven or more dragging anchor at the same time. In the parlance of the trade this is known as "anchor drill."

Salmon fishing often is fantastically good off Point Reyes, either directly north of the North Island of the Farallon group or over Fanny Shoal.

Sportsmen do not much frequent these fishing grounds, some twelve miles or so from the Drake's Bay anchorage. Instead, they work in the lee of the headland—between the anchorage and Point Reyes—and pick up a limit of good fish before noon.

Then, if they want to hit big ling, red snappers, and other bottom fish, including flounders, they move around the point and work the reef area magnetic north of the light until the afternoon wind starts knocking the tops of the waves. They then have a downhill run for a usually quiet anchorage.

Drake's Bay has one other favorable characteristic. The point that cuddles the western portion of the bay juts to the south'ard. This, and the extending reef area not far from Coast Guard dock and fish buyers' piers, provide the only lee I know of in a natural harbor to give a boat protection in southerly weather. Here, if one makes sure he isn't dropping his hook on kelp, a southerly can be ridden out in moderate comfort. But this is a small area, and if more than twenty boats try to share this area, things get pretty crowded.

Landsmen, particularly landsmen involved in politics, divide California into two sections, north and south, with the division hitting the coast in the vicinity of Morro Bay. But sailors know California as a three-deck deal: southern, central, and northern.

Southern California, to a sailor, ends abruptly at the twin points of Conception and Arguello. From there to Point Arena, north of Point Reyes, lies central California. And north of Arena is that climatically and psychologically completely different place, northern California.

Point Arena, a low-lying promontory jutting into the sea, is a bleak, foreboding sentinel standing guard at the approach to the northern California shore, its hills covered with green trees instead of summer-dried grass and vegetation, often no more than shoulder high to a small deer.

No one in his right mind rounds Point Arena close aboard, and many a hardy soul will not even enter Arena Cove. South of the cove, at Fish Rock, is a better anchorage anyway. In fact there are two anchorages at Fish Rock. The other one is about eight fathoms close to and under a huge rock that not only stinks but is inhabited by noisy sea lions. The inner one, approached more safely by hugging the cliffs to its northern portion, is quiet, warm, and flat. But there is a rock, barely awash at high tide, roughly in the center of this cove. In this respect it is quite like Fort Ross, just to the north'ard of Bodega Bay, and resembles Cuffey's Cove between Point Arena and the Noyo River to the north. Just why these rocks exist as they do in the virtual center of otherwise completely beautiful anchorage areas is a comment on God's attitude toward seamen.

The area along our coast from Point Arena to Shelter Cove (a doubtful cove and more doubtful shelter if wind and seas swing from the west) is a slow transition into what I think of as the truly Northeast Pacific.

Officially, the point forming Shelter Cove is Point Delgado. The area, served by a road leading in from U.S. 101 and an airport for light planes, is in the hands of real-estate developers; and, in these days of a growing leisure class of early-age retirees, this may not be a bad thing.

Shelter Cove marks the northern limit of such fishermen as the Yukon Gang, the Sicilian fishermen operating "Monterey Clipper Bow" vessels out of San Francisco. This group of fishermen make more noise on their radios than you'd hear from the USS *Enterprise*, but they do fish their little boats with both courage and skill and land a lot of salmon.

But they never go north of Shelter Cove. It is as though someone had torn the rest of the country off their charts. Or it may be the benevolent protection of Mother Mary, in whose honor they paint their bulwarks blue, they hate to leave, for beyond Shelter Cove, as you move north, you are getting into the rough country.

The first bastion to this area is Punta Gorda, backstopped by Blunts Reef and the lightship there.

The conflict of currents at Punta Gorda is

almost unbelievable. One day, working to the north'ard in air so flat that cigarette smoke went straight up, two seas hit me from different directions and filled my boots with water as I stood by the wheel.

No one in his right mind is going to move into this reef area to catch a few rock cod, flounders, or scaleless ling. But tough commercial fishermen, after salmon or crabs, have made a season in this general area.

Salmon fishing here is often good, and now and then an upwelling of warmer water—around fifty-two as contrasted to forty-eight degrees at the surface—occurs westward of Blunts Reef Lightship, out beyond the steamer lane of coastwise shipping and in turbulence that makes merely living hard work as big lunkers are brought aboard.

Blunts Reef is my personal black knight, although for downright vicious weather it isn't often as bad on purpose as Cape Blanco often is by accident.

It isn't absolutely necessary to go around Blunts Reef when working to the north'ard for Eureka. There is a crooked passage behind the reef, and fishermen who have intimate local knowledge—and good visibility —always run this channel. But you've got to see the landmarks and know the ranges, because the currents are so unpredictable that you can't, with any degree of safety, run a compass course.

About the third time I rounded Blunts Reef Lightship via the outside route, I encountered heavy weather. And a lapse of caution.

For the only time I can recall, I did not secure the hatch on the trunk cabin of my ketch. Close hauled on a starboard tack, working to westward to get sea room to round the lightship, green water now and then came over. Then, in complete unpredictable fashion, the hatch flipped open,

seawater came into the cabin area, and in the manner of the capricious gods who rule the sea, some seawater hit my fathometer, my loran, and radio direction finder—wiping them out in a matter of seconds.

I secured the hatch, and as I inspected the below-deck area, I didn't find more than twenty gallons of the lousy ocean. Hardly enough to bother about pumping over the side.

But now, all at once, I no longer was a twentieth-century mariner with sophisticated electronics gear, but on a par with the first sailor who stood into the night at sea with only a magnetic compass, a piece of string and a hunk of lead.

After I weathered the moaning, bobbing lightship and came to a port tack for Eureka, the fog fell on me—and the night. All at once I was moved back two generations, technologically, and I didn't like it.

Fortunately, once a sailor gets north of Cape Mendocino standing to the north'ard, he has a pretty decent sort of coastline until he reaches the jetties of the Humboldt River bar.

But in the fog and darkness my imagination fabricated jagged reefs clutching for my keel. I also recalled a line from Shakespeare's *Tempest* in which one character offered to trade "furlongs of this sea for an acre of barren ground."

Finally, I rigged a sounding line and cast the lead. I was in twenty fathoms somewhere south of the entrance to Eureka harbor.

By this time the afternoon's wind had died, so I furled my sails and lit off the diesel.

In this stage of my experience with our sea, I'd call it Mare Nostrum if I could spell in Italian, I'd learned two things: (1) if you want to find a port, head northeast magnetic, and (2) if you want safety, head the slab due west.

For ninety minutes at seven knots I stood to westward, shut down, and hit the sack. When morning came, I had a visibility of twenty miles.

In Eureka, partly because of the fishing fleet based there, but more importantly because logging companies use radio extensively, good electronics techs are available, and they fixed my damaged gear.

The next year, moving northward with all the purpose of a bewildered duck, I prepared for Blunts Reef by asking an experienced Eureka fisherman, then in Noyo River harbor, to mark my chart so I would have a reasonably good chance to make the inside passage when I approached Blunts Reef.

I hit the passage late in the afternoon. This area always is bleak. The mountains my friend had marked had disconcerting similarities to those he had not marked. But there is one called Table Mountain, not much like the Table Mountain I'd often seen at Capetown while covering parliament as political reporter for our Minister to South Africa. But it is a reasonably effective replica, and on it I took my bearing.

About halfway through the crooked passage, with twilight well upon me, fire broke out below. It was a lousy electrical fire, caused by a short circuit in the Mickey Mouse wiring lash-up I had added to each time momentary prosperity had enabled me to buy another piece of electronics gear.

The fire didn't amount to much, but even a little fire is a big thing at sea. The chemical extinguisher put it out. But it was on the starting battery side of my dual electric system, and I knew that if I shut down I'd never get the engine started without help. And the only help was a few sea gulls soar-

ing around waiting to make dinner of my eyes.

But this flap, like all others men survive, didn't really amount to much. The diesel engine kept banging away, the iron mike wouldn't work, but who cares about iron mikes in the wake of a fire?

Farther to the north'ard, north of Crescent City, is Oregon's southern gate—Saint George Reef.

Here, as at Blunts Reef, the voyager has a choice. He can stand the long way around Saint George Light, or cut through behind the reef to Pelican Bay and the sometimes good harbor at Brookings.

Between Eureka and Crescent City is Redding Rock, a bold stone jutting from the sea much in the manner of the North Farallon Island. I believe the base of this foreboding rock holds the secret to one of the minor mysteries of the sea.

About ten years ago, two young fellows stood out of Crescent City aboard the fishing boat *Toiler,* a converted landing craft powered by a Chrysler Royal with a leaking exhaust pipe system. They were going to Eureka.

About 2200 they hit the phone and reported to a friend that everything was working normally, the weather fine, visibility good, just north of Redding Rock. Since then, all has been silence.

Not even a life jacket, a piece of hatch cover, or a plank identifiable as part of *Toiler* has been found. I've often wondered if *Toiler,* with an unconscious crew of two, overcome by carbon monoxide, might not have rammed the Redding Rock, striking its north side on an inexorable course held by that mechanical helmsman that has a lookout capability limited to eighteen inches.

From Brookings north is the true green area of our coast. But the boatsman here runs out of anchorages, for the rain that keeps the forests green fills the coves with rivers, and north of Port Orford, which, Drake's Bay like, lies in the lee of Cape Blanco, every good anchorage area except South Cove below Cape Arago and the anchorage below Cape Lookout, seems to have a river in it.

While Blanco has never done anything bad to me except wear me out as I caught salmon in seas so high I sometimes jerked them downward from the tops of waves to the deck, this jutting promontory is a summer windhole to end all windholes. Sometimes the fishing there is truly fantastic, on tacks running northwest from Fox Rock in about twenty-five fathoms. The fish, when they are there, are the biggest of the chinook I've ever seen, some of them running to fifty pounds or better, gilled and gutted.

Port Orford anchorage, in summer's usual Northwest weather, seems large enough to accommodate the Pacific Fleet.

If the fish are lying chiefly north of Fox Rock, the salmon fleet uses the anchorage area directly south of Cape Blanco Light.

The way from outside into this anchorage is tricky, and the few times I've used it have been on days when the visibility was good and I could identify the various rocks shown on my chart and slide into the sandy bottom area without much fuss.

North of Blanco, in the Coquille River region, we have the harbor of Bandon. This is a sneaky-pete sort of place, with a long shoal area offshore that, in a heavy lump, can form breakers.

One afternoon, tempted to try for Bandon rather than Coos Bay because I was running short of oil for a leaking reduction gear, I nearly had my comeuppance. As I approached the jaws of the jetty, a sea broke behind me, another broke ahead. And then

one broke under me, turning my ten-ton ketch into a virtual surfboard as we barreled down between the jetties, traveling so fast the rocks that made the jetties became a blur.

In a case like that the only thing to do is stand still and pray, afraid even to shift a chew of snoose for fear it will damage the vessel's trim.

North of Bandon, off Whiskey Run, lies a fishing area out in the fifty-fathom country, that commingles coho salmon on the surface with good chinook lower down. There is a peculiar current pattern here that commingles uprooted trees with bait fish, and some of the most fantastic action I've ever seen with coho has occurred in this area, some dozen miles to the south'ard of Coos Bay. Yet with all this action here I've never seen a sports fisherman involved. This does not mean they do not frequent the area. I merely have not seen them.

North of Coos, on the twenty miles of ocean to Winchester Bay, is a fishing area that often is bare, but often in mid-June and a little afterward produces coho fishing that hardly will stop. Once on a single tack I picked up 168 coho and, quite by accident, three chinook.

Winchester Bay is a lousy bar. The Coast Guard maintains a range to guide the fishermen through the treacherous seas of this entrance to a harbor. But the channel shifts from year to year, and the Coast Guard ranges are permanent.

This man-eating harbor, a dirty piece of water, has killed at least one commercial fisherman every year since I have known the place. This is not counting sportsmen, and sometimes as many as three or four.

As one works northward past Winchester Bay to the vicinity of Florence and Heceta Head, he enters the southern boundaries of the true halibut, those with their eyes on the starboard side. Usually, below Heceta, they are pretty scarce, but after rounding Heceta on the way to Newport and Depoe Bay, they become more numerous.

The bylaws of international treaty covering halibut, the real kind, that is, set quotas for various regions. This can lead to trouble. If you catch a halibut below Heceta Head, it may be perfectly legal to take him ashore. But if you catch it above Heceta, it may be that the quota has been fulfilled, and you can go to Portland to "see the man" if you bring one onto a commercial fishing dock. Several times, because I couldn't prove just where I caught a few halibut, I've taken them to the Coast Guard boys at Depoe Bay as a "gift" of sorts.

And as for Depoe Bay: This is the narrowest, scariest, and often the safest entry to a harbor along the Oregon coast.

The first time I approached this refuge I was running a temperature with an early season case of flu. I had talked to many fishermen about this harbor; and I thought I knew how to approach slowly, drift in under bare steerage way, turn ninety degrees to port, and then ninety degrees to starboard— like moving through a light trap into the darkroom of a photo lab.

But when I stood in against that mass of bluff and looked at that little bitty hold, I thought that anyone in his right mind who tried to go there surely was crazy. So I made a 180-degree turn.

As I did, the skipper of a puker boat came along, laughing at me and waving for me to follow him. I did.

After that I used the port often, and once, when the breakers at Newport closed that bar, I mozied to the north'ard and without trouble stood into this deceptively scary harbor. Still, it lingers in my mind that this is the one harbor on the Oregon coast that, each spring, they have a festival in which flowers are tossed from boats to honor those fishermen who, somehow, failed to make it safely into port.

Often, in late summer and in the early autumn months, extraordinarily good albacore fishing exists so close in to the Oregon coast that twenty-pound albacore can be yarded aboard within sight of the green Oregon hills. These big fish, the Norskies call the "home guard" fish, live at this season where the temperature of the water breaks from around fifty-eight to sixty degrees on the surface. One year I moved out of Newport, working the gradient line, and entered Astoria with a good load that averaged better than eighteen pounds. This size fish, compared to the ten- to twelve-pound "school" fish that make up the bulk of the commercial catch, will give sportsmen out of any northern Oregon port some real action with the longfin and where in recent years, many commercial fishermen have landed as many as one thousand albacore in a single day. Tuna has paid the mortgage on many a salmon troller.

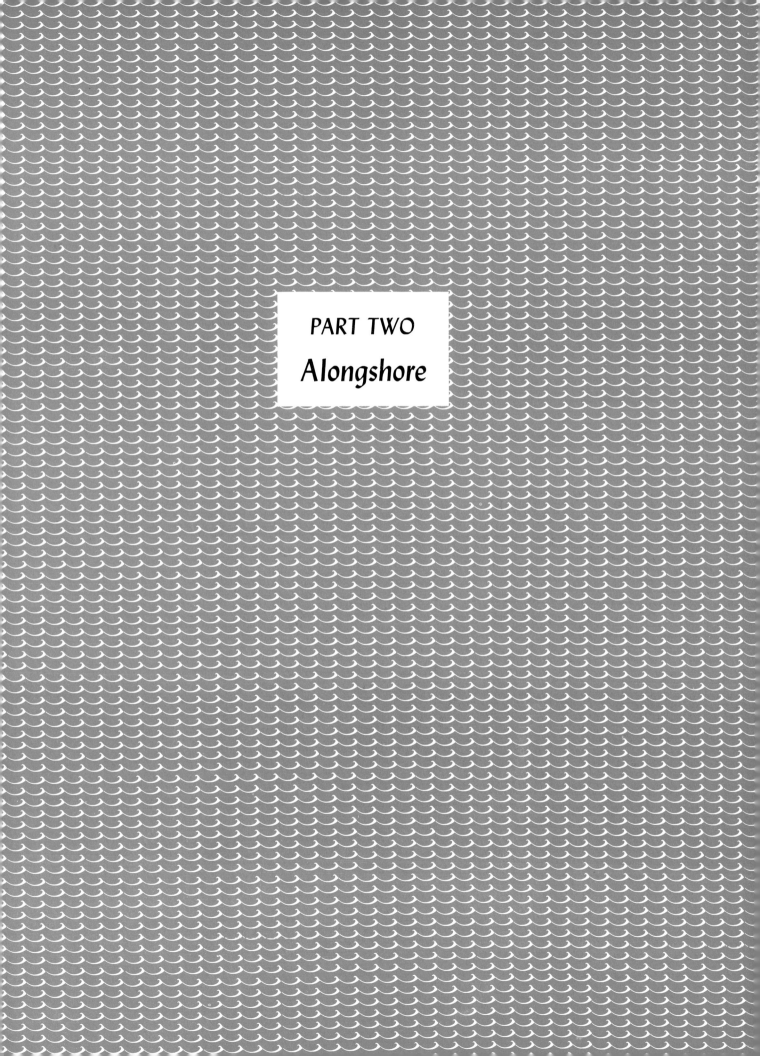

PART TWO

Alongshore

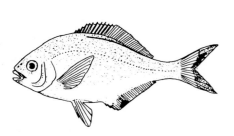

White Seaperch

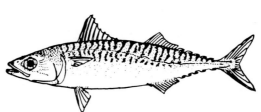

Pacific Mackerel

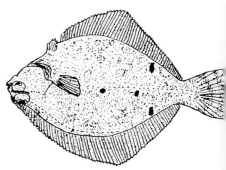

Spotted Turbot

I.

Chinook!

High on the western slope of the Continental Divide some scavengers wait.

They stand guard over a clear, cold pool of water at the head of a small creek that runs into the North Fork.

The North Fork is a respectable stream that flows into a roaring river called the Salmon, that joins an even more substantial one that has its head in Yellowstone Park and is called the Snake, but which was first called the Mad (because anyone was mad to attempt it), that flows into an international waterway called the Columbia, that eventually fans out into the Pacific.

In this clear, cold backwater pool there lie the remains of a fish slowly decomposing, its particles clinging to pebbles and enriching the surrounding waters so that life yet to be born will be nourished by it.

It is a big fish—or had been—weighing about forty pounds, tremendously rich in fats, oil, and proteins; in its system once flowed some mysterious elements that for one brief period in its life, gave it energy and stamina and recovery powers relatively far beyond those of most creatures.

This phenomenon, when triggered by some unknown biological means, had driven it from its feedlot in the rich Pacific, up the Columbia, then the Snake, then the Salmon, then the North Fork, and finally into

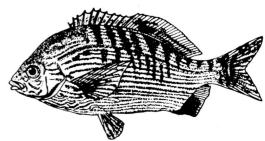

Rainbow Seaperch

Lingcod

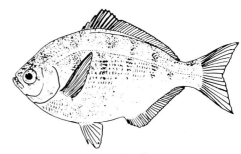

Silver Surfperch

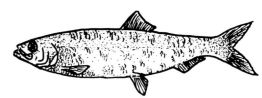

Pacific Herring

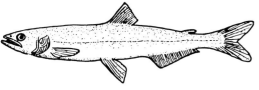

Caudlefish

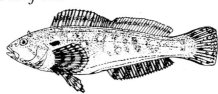

Rock Greenling

Yellowtail Rockfish

this small, pine-and-aspen-lined creek bed where redds were dug and eggs laid, a thousand river miles from saltwater. Then it died.

This rotten, ugly, decomposing carcass once was Columbia River Royal Chinook Salmon.

The Royal Chinook, spawned by the great Columbia, is the finest, most desirable salmon that swims. It is a beautiful, functionally symmetrical creature that sometimes reaches eighty pounds and attains four feet in length.

Its flesh is of the highest quality and of the finest flavor; unlike chinook salmon from other Pacific streams, its meat is not bright red and crumbling like those of Alaskan waters, for example, but it clings in close layers of rich muscles like the growth rings of a giant Douglas fir. Its flesh, unlike that of other chinooks, is the color which is generally described as "salmon."

It is called "Royal Chinook" because this race of salmon was the most prized by the gourmets of Europe and Asia—fit for a king.

Salmon, however, are not respective of international boundaries and political subdivisions. Marked hatchery releases from the Sacramento-San Joaquin system in California, and from coastal California rivers, once in the ocean, move northward along the west coast of Oregon, Washington, and Vancouver Island, and back again. Oregon-grown chinooks move southward off the California coast, and northward off Wash-

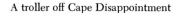

A troller off Cape Disappointment

ington and Vancouver Island, through Dixon Entrance and around the Queen Charlotte Islands, and even farther northward into Alaskan waters. Chinooks from the Columbia drainage, once in the ocean swim southward as far as Point Arena; and northward past British Columbia and Alaska. Puget Sound salmon swim out through the strait, then southward as far as Port Orford and return; and northward to the Queen Charlotte Islands, and Alaska. British Columbia born salmon, from the Fraser, Skeena, and other rivers, once in the sea, swim as far south as Newport, Oregon, and as far north as Alaska. Alaska salmon come down as far as the southern tip of the Queen Charlottes, and then move back.

The trend however, is most often northward by nature, until the time comes to return to the stream of birth.

The three principal chinook salmon producers are the Sacramento-San Joaquin, the Columbia River system, and the Fraser River drainage.

There is a difference in the behavior pattern of the lower Columbia River fall race of chinooks from the winter, spring, summer, and upper-river fall-run fish. They all react somewhat differently to the ocean environment, mainly in their growth rate and range of movement.

An escapement of from 100,000 to 600,000 annually is recorded for the Sacramento, that is an "escapement" from the chinook's principal predator—man. Similar preservation characteristics are claimed for the other major chinook rivers. It should be pointed out that a fishery resource is not necessarily propagated and sustained merely by the size of the escapement. Moreover, the primary rivers that contribute to sport and commercial fisheries might be a thousand miles from the "point of catch."

Columbia bar produced this chinook for Art Kohanek of Portland.

Fall-run chinook caught off Vancouver Island and in the Strait of Juan de Fuca, for example, in the most abundant numbers are more likely to be of Columbia River origin than chinooks caught off the mouth of the Columbia.

The winter, spring, summer, and upper-Columbia fall chinooks are caught by fishermen mostly off British Columbia and Alaska, only 25 percent off Washington and Oregon.

Juvenile winter and spring-run chinook usually stay in fresh water for more than a year, then move downstream toward the sea during the second spring. Fall chinook usually migrate to the ocean the first year. Summer runs do both. Freshwater growth is much slower than it is in the ocean, mainly because of the nature of the food. For this reason the various races of chinook differ in size for the same age, and results in many variable factors in the management of this resource.

Actually, considering that the Pacific salmon has been known to science since the mid-1700's, and has been the basis of a multi-million-dollar annual industry for one hundred years, you would think that everything that should be known about this crea-

feeding and trying to keep from being fed upon, and in its wanderings finds itself off the mouth of its parent stream system about the time for Nature to trigger the spawning urge.

Finally, to complete the cycle, the old idea that to maintain a salmon run all that is necessary is to provide a maximum amount of escapement, is now known to be nonsense. If, for example, one thousand

Part of the charter fleet heading into Ilwaco, Washington

ture's life and biological nature would be thoroughly documented. This, however, is not the case. Only in the past decade, in fact, has any real scientific progress been made in this direction.

For decades it was widely believed that once in the ocean the salmon disappeared into some watery limbo, never to reappear until time to spawn. Actually, it is now known they "don't go anywhere." The Pacific salmon simply enters the ocean and moves up and down the continental shelf which is rich in nutrients and forage food,

chinook salmon are assured of escaping the predators of the sea, the sport and commercial fishery, and survive the dams and pollution of their native rivers, to finally reach the spawning grounds, this does not mean that these one thousand fish will produce ten times as many offspring as one hundred fish would have.

The spawning grounds, like your backyard strawberry patch, can support only so many spawners, and any more will simply be "wasted" fish.

Thus, conservation of this unique and

fragile resource is concerned with the sum and total of all the factors that influence it —sport and commercial fishing, pollution by wastes and heat and insecticides, blocking dams, extensive irrigation, logging and road building in the upper watersheds, destruction of spawning areas, and by the many indirect and natural effects such as floods, droughts, and natural diseases.

The link in the chain can be broken at any place along the line.

The west coast of the Queen Charlotte Islands is everywhere rugged and indented with many inlets, some of which penetrate a considerable distance inland. Most of these inlets have not been surveyed.

The one-hundred-fathom line runs from one to three miles offshore, and then abruptly falls off to great depths. The current sets northward at a rate of about one or two knots.

From October until Christmas the prevailing wind comes from the southeast in heavy gales with drenching rainfall. From late December until February the offshore winds come from the northwest. In February, March, and April, the wind blows from the southeast again. In May come the westerlies; in June, July, August, and September the winds are southwest mostly. Sometimes these are interrupted by a williwaw which can lay a boat over on its beam, and even put its poles in water.

The coast is marked by wooded mountains rising higher than 1,700 feet (518 meters), with inland peaks to 3,000 feet (914 meters).

With this rain and windswept, wavelashed, rugged, and beautiful setting, it is sometimes hard for the stranger to find shelter even in fine weather.

It is midsummer. Off Cape Saint James a

During salmon season, trailer parks and camps around the mouth of the Columbia are full

large school of chinook salmon has been feeding for months on candlefish and herring, growing rapidly, losing some of their number steadily to sea lions, to prowling killer whales, and to the lures of trolling fishing boats and the nets of purse seiners cruising off the islands.

Then suddenly, as if on cue, their feeding tempo increases as they slash through schools of forage fish, herd schools of herring into ball-ups that boil on the surface. The salmon begin to put on weight and muscle at a rapid rate, and at the same time they move against the set of the current, pushing southward along the banks off Vancouver Island, past the tidal rips and strong currents of the Strait of Juan de Fuca, most escaping the lines and nets of the fishing fleet.

As they move southward, many of the commercial boats that had followed their movement, now haul in salmon gear and in late July and early August head southwestward into the broad blue Pacific, out where the water temperature reaches up to sixty-five degrees or more to intercept the pelagic schools of albacore.

This took much of the pressure off the school of chinooks, which is now dwindling in numbers, but still feeding in ravished frenzy.

The school reaches the rich, nutrient-filled upwelling of cold water from the immense undersea Astoria Canyon, just off the mouth of the Columbia. The waters are alive with marine life, and the changing tides bring a rhythmic changing of salinity and temperatures, some of which strike a strange chord in the metabolism of this particular school, which is now dwindling rapidly by predation of its enemies in the sea as well as on the thousands of boats moving about on the surface.

But the remaining chinook grow bigger, tougher, bolder, and possessed with increasing drive. They spend the last days slashing schools of feed fish, cruising back and forth through the changing tides, testing the periodic freshets brought down to sea by the mighty river, and tasting a strange but somehow wonderful and familiar element that strengthens an age-old longing.

Presently, one day when these freshets of fresh water taste and smell and feel just right, the school suddenly bunches closer together, some leaders take over and start through the strong swirling currents on the bar, enter the brackish estuary and move past Desdemona Sands, dodging logs, debris, rafts of sewage and pollution, and herds of hair seals that are feeding off the bars; upstream and onward, past long drifting nets of gill-netters, the remnants of the run now developing a slight hump, losing the bright iridescent silvery color of the ocean, and taking on a darker sheen.

Moving against the strong surge of current they pass out of the brackish water but still feel the force of the tides that come and go, but in lessening effect. They won't be out of the tidal rhythm until they reach a point more than a hundred miles away from the ocean.

Past islands, up underwater channels, escaping the nets and the thousands of sport fishermen who sit in anchored "hog lines" or are camped on the bars and beaches around the mouths of tributaries. The salmon have stopped eating as they move into fresh water, but they will attack anything that comes near them, and some of them even continue to grab and swallow other fish, including fingerling salmon from another generation that they pass on their way down to the sea.

About 126.3 nautical miles inland, the chinook encounter a major obstacle—Bonneville Dam. Here the chinook after some confusion find the stair-stepped pools or "ladders" that allow them to swim up around the dam and enter the sluggish impoundment behind the dam.

Above here the chinook come to the Indian nets which take a heavy toll. Then another huge dam is encountered, this one even higher. Then another, and another, until it seems the river is now composed of a series of concrete monoliths, each holding back a larger still-water pool.

About three hundred miles upriver the school reaches a point where the water suddenly has a different taste and temperature, and a vague familiar feeling. Unerringly they turn into this channel and enter the broad Snake River. The water is shallower, but colder and swifter, and the bottom is strewn with boulders. Another series of

Busy fish cleaning station at a Columbia river port

large dams, and the remaining school reaches another tributary with yet again a different taste and smell. This is the Clearwater, joining the Snake at Lewiston. In past eons many of them turned off at the Clearwater, but now its spawning reaches have been destroyed forever by man's obstacles. The run stays in the Snake and continues upward in a southeasterly direction.

The chinook school, or what remains of it, now plunges into mountains, through deep, swift currents and narrow channels, from which none will ever return. The chinook have already been in fresh water for about three months and have eaten nothing or very little, their digestive processes halted, and their bodies now sustained by the nutrients gathered during their years in the ocean. They are now dark-hued and becoming more misshapen, the jaws of the male most pronounced, the lower one curling up and almost around the upper. Chunks of skin and flesh are already peeling off.

Deep within the Grand Canyon of the Snake the chinook now come upon yet another tributary with a different and even more familiar taste and smell and feel. It is the Salmon River, the River of No Return—a descriptive name that was applied to it for a different reason, but which fits the salmon run most appropriately.

Up the boiling, raging Salmon River, the few remnants of the school that started this age-old odyssey months before, far north in the Pacific off the Queen Charlotte Islands, now finds the going tougher, the water shallower and sweetened with rains that bring sediments into the main stream and muddy the water so that they cannot see where they go.

(There is record of a chinook salmon,

two years old, returning to a hatchery in Orick, California, two and a half miles inland from the ocean, by means of a discharge outlet through a series of culverts, a drain pipe, and a wire net, after swimming up two creeks and a four-inch drain pipe with a ninety-degree turn, then leaping a two-and-a-half-foot-high pipe, and getting over a two-foot-high wire net. At one point the salmon had a choice of five pipes, four of which were dead ends and took the right one.

The salmon, which had been marked and released into an entirely different stream the year before, apparently was led back to its own hatchery by a sense of smell.)

Days later they have turned off into the North Fork, go onward and upward now, expending their last reserves of energy, now in water so shallow that often their dorsal fins stick out into the cold autumn air. Here and there a bear or an eagle or a prowling bobcat extracts a toll from the six or eight fish left out of the school that left the Queen Charlottes.

At last, reaching finally the branch creek, from which these chinooks had originally wriggled out of their egg sacs and up through the gravel to become fry, the returning adults now in the last stages of the spawning cycle, move over the shallow gravel beds washed by cold, crystal-clear water that started its flow not far away from some underground springs.

The vicious-looking hook-nosed male and the female move over a certain spot of gravel, with sweeps of their tails, dig a watery trench maybe a foot long and a few inches wide and deep. The female moves in over this trench and hovers there, taken by convulsive movements. The male stands by, keeping a wary eye on a squawfish hovering nearby under the overhang of a willow bush. As the female begins to deposit eggs the squawfish moves out and starts to circle. In one mighty burst, the male lashes at it and drives it off. Then, the trench now filled with perhaps five thousand bright pale-orange eggs, each the size of a pea, the male sidles over, edges the female out of the way, and lays a stream of sperm over them.

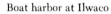

Boat harbor at Ilwaco

This sperm has astonishing qualities of tenacity. As it touches the eggs or anything else for that matter it clings immediately like the strongest glue.

The eggs laid and fertilized, the male and female now hover around the nest, stirring up the gravel with their tails, covering the eggs to protect them from preying fish.

Now, the spawning urge complete, the adult chinook are too exhausted to move. The flesh comes off in great chunks, rotting even as they still live. Their jaws and mouths are twisted out of shape, eyeballs are dropping loose from sockets. With one last spasm of his great tail, the male chinook expires and slowly turns over in the water, the gentle current sweeping his remains into a little backwater eddy. A few hours later the female also dies, her carcass caught in the current moves on down until it comes up against a rock, there it hangs until it attracts some watchful magpies.

Since the beginning of time this ritual of life has been repeated each year.

2.

The Mightiest Bar of All

Each year as spring rolls around in the Pacific Northwest a powerful and sensual pageant of nature begins again, as it has since the beginning. It begins the moment the great chinook, king of Pacific salmon, appears off the mouth of the Columbia River.

The sportsman who hasn't taken part in this living drama hasn't lived; and once he has experienced it he finds himself drawn back each year as irresistibly as the salmon.

Center of the stage is the Columbia estuary, where the second largest river in North America meets the long rollers of the open Pacific. Here the chinook first tastes its home waters again after a four-year journey in the depths of the sea.

The Columbia bar is the gateway to an inland empire, an escape hatch for a dynamic region and a bridal arch for the chinook's honeymoon journey upriver to the mountain spawning grounds.

No one can spend a day here on this living ocean mouth and not feel a sense of being close to the origin of things. The bar can be gentle and caressing, harsh and brutal, occasionally wild and violent; but it is always one of the most fascinating and sometimes challenging spots on earth for the sport fisherman.

There is no delta here. Nearing Astoria, the river widens out to a nine-mile expanse of sandbars and channels, then pinches together at the jaws into a forty-foot-deep half-mile-wide entrance that makes a long dog leg into the open sea.

Farther out at sea underwater currents flow off into a gigantic submerged canyon that would make Grand Canyon look like a drainage ditch.

Oceanographers and marine biologists know almost nothing of the mysteries beneath the surface at the Columbia bar, or for that matter, all along the entire coast.

The sportsmen, however, who come here each year, experience firsthand the power and force of nature and environment as nowhere else on the West Coast. Maybe it's symbolic that the lure that brings them back each year is the aristocratic Pacific salmon.

Beginning in February, the salmon appears off the mouth of the river almost as regularly as the tides and seasons. Gradually at first, in two main waves, the migration wells up in a crescendo that reaches a frantic climax for fish and for fishermen in the last two weeks of August.

The river draws the fishermen from half a continent. They come from Oregon, Washington, and California; from the Rocky Mountain states and the Midwest; from the prairies of North Dakota and the

Coast Guard aircraft and surface vessels patrol the Columbia bar during the salmon sport season

plains of Texas; and even from as far as Florida and New York.

They come by car, train, airline, and private plane. Some charter expensive private boats. Others share the cost of a crab boat for a day. Hundreds trailer in their own cruisers and outboard skiffs. They converge on Astoria, Warrenton, Hammond, Ilwaco and Chinook, the principal embarkation points.

Most of them have good luck. All of them come away awed by this river and its outpouring of life and strength; and once they've experienced it few are ever satisfied with the prosaic fishing back home.

The river itself is a primitive force that appears out of the misty heights of the Rockies hundreds of miles from the sea. It foams and surges down through deep-walled canyons, momentarily slowed by man-made dams, only to burst its bonds and plunge again toward the sea. In the lower reaches the river is often swollen by floods to ten times its normal volume.

Not even man's puny tampering with dams and channels has been able to tame the Columbia. It rolls on virtually unchanged, still the greatest salmon river in the world and probably the greatest all-around sport-fishing river.

Legendary even before it was seen by white men, the Columbia has a drainage system so vast that even today few can agree on its exact origin. One part of the system rises far up in Canada and is fed by such rivers as the Kootenay, Spokane, Okanogan, and Yakima. From eastern Washington the Snake River reaches eastward and south like a tenacle through Idaho to the high plateaus of the western slope of the Rockies.

On it have passed Lewis and Clark, the Hudson's Bay and Astor fur traders, mountain men and adventurers, Indian dugouts, frontier stern-wheelers, long tug and barge chains, freighters and tankers from all the seven seas. It brings the commerce of the world to freshwater ports hundreds of miles from the sea, to a four-state region and more than four million people. Truly a great river.

It is the home of the huge sturgeon, shad, smelt, steelhead and other trouts; carp, catfish, whitefish, bass and panfishes--and of course the several species of salmon.

To the Astoria estuary where the river meets the sea come the fishermen; as many as twenty thousand have fished here in a single day during the peak of the season.

The brackish water at the mouth is a maelstrom of life in the raw. The fisherman sees and feels the overwhelming power of it. Overhead gulls wheel and dip; compact flights of small birds dart in perfect for-

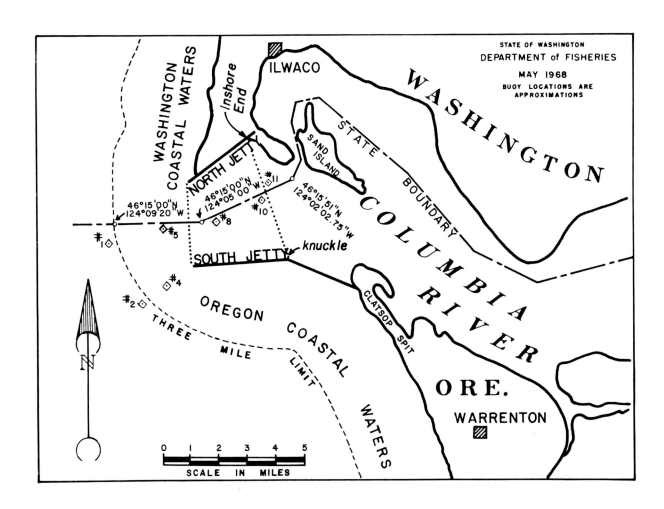

mation at wave-top height; loons, grebes, and diving ducks herald new food discoveries. Here and there is an orange and pink phosphorescent plankton bloom, or a surface boil where larger fish have herded to the surface, schools of herring, anchovy, and pilchard on which the salmon grows fat and prime.

Far out in the blue-water region there are passing schools of tuna, or albacore, but here inside the one hundred-fathom line the dogfish and soupfin sharks, sea lampreys, lingcod, sea bass, snappers, flounder, halibut, sea perch, sand dabs, sole, tomcod and other species merge. Herds of gray whale pass through here close to shore on the southward migration, and schools of blackfish and porpoise roll and play.

Occasionally the slick-whiskered head of a sea lion pops up for a breath of air. Floating on the surface are the glutinous creatures, unidentifiable iridescent masses of half-plant, half-animal life. Beneath the boat, living and reproducing, are the pelagic shrimp, euphausids, and other plankton forms on which the young salmon has fed during his journey to the sea years before.

Here, where the upwelling from the cold depths of the ocean meets and churns with the snow-born torrent from the inland continent, life gathers and the drama runs its course as nowhere else.

Were it not for the Pacific salmon most of the sport fishermen would never have the opportunity to witness and be a part of this breathtaking pageant.

The Pacific salmon is probably one of the most mysterious and exciting fish in the world. No one knows what inner forces control its exotic life. No one knows what prompts it to return to its own particular stretch of gravel far up in some mountain creek. Its life cycle is a delicate and highly selective process of nature, one of nature's most wasteful and frenzied phenomenons.

Even salmon of the same species have minor physical differences caused by subtle changes in the composition of water and its temperature from stream to stream and gravel bed to gravel bed. Something in the chemistry of a particular stretch of water fills the peculiar needs of the individual fish.

Once in fresh water the salmon stops eating, its body becomes humped and misshapen, turns a reddish color and finally darkens into a sickening hue. As he heads upstream he is possessed with a frenzied instinct that drives him through rapids, over waterfalls and man-built fish ladders until bruised, broken, and raw, he finds his destination, energy nearly spent.

Here in the clear shallow water the female spawns in one last convulsive act. The eggs—as many as five thousand from one female—are fertilized by the male. Then both die and their carcasses become food for the living.

From the five thousand eggs not more than fifty will hatch, grow strong enough to make the journey downstream to the sea. Of the fifty only two or three will survive the hazards of the ocean and return past the hooks, nets, dams and natural hazards to fulfill the perpetual call. The total catch of chinooks each year amounts to about twenty-five million pounds or about 90 percent of the total run.

The chinook is the largest and most numerous of the five species of salmon. It has a sleek, magnificent body. At sea it may reach a maximum of four feet in length and a weight up to eighty or ninety pounds. When ocean-bright its flesh is succulent, ranging in color from light pink to deep red. In fresh water the flesh deteriorates rapidly and in its final stages is unfit to eat.

On the trip downstream the young chinook feeds on mayfly nymphs and beetle larvae. As the long odyssey gets under way he reaches the brackish water of the Astoria estuary, pauses while he becomes accustomed to sea life and then heads out to sea on his mysterious course. He may drift south along the Oregon coast, but more often he follows the Davidson Current along the continental shelf as far north as Queen Charlotte Islands.

In the fourth year of his life he turns back, stirred by the sexual urge. By this time the chinook is a full-grown fish with thick layers of fat and full of fighting energy.

The return trip takes three or four months and he reenters the Columbia through the submerged Astoria Canyon ready to fight his way upriver to the place of his birth and complete the relentless cycle.

During the sport-fishing season the boat basins and launching ramps at Astoria and Warrenton on the Oregon shore and at Ilwaco and Chinook on the Washington side are scenes of excited activity. Everything from cruisers, sleek yachts, and sailboats to trawlers, trollers, and crab boats are pressed into service for the sport fishermen.

Most of the fishermen go out on ocean-size boats with professional bar-wise skippers, usually in a cooperative group of four to eight persons. On the average it costs a fisherman from twelve to eighteen dollars for a day's fishing off the mouth, which includes bait, coffee, and sometimes the Dramamine. Gear is also furnished if the fisherman does not have a suitable outfit.

Beginning at daylight the boats put out from the docks for the run down to the bar. The skipper judges the sea and its mood. If

Coast Guard tows in a distressed private sport fishing boat

it's too rough he may fish in the inner estuary along the Washington side from the bar upstream. The boats stay out until limits have been taken or darkness and weather force them in.

At times the bar may become still as a millpond under a soothing sun and gentle breezes; again a southwest wind may drive huge swells in against the outgoing tide and river current. Squalls come and go suddenly. Combinations of tide, wind, and long sweeping rollers from far out at sea can make the bar one of the most dangerous spots on earth. The ground swell at times is so great that ocean liners sink hull-down in troughs. Sudden storms and cross swells have been known to sweep clean the decks of ships, pilothouse and all. It is a place that commands respect from men who live by the sea.

The sportsmen take all this in stride and usually in good humor. However, one year a Portland nightclub owner became so seasick that he offered the skipper one hundred dollars to put him ashore. Since the salmon were hitting good at the moment the skipper refused. The man whipped out his checkbook, bought the boat on the spot for twice its value, and ordered the skipper to return to the dock.

At the peak of the season as many as five thousand boats of all types may be milling, bobbing and crisscrossing the bar; some trolling, most mooching—drifting with the currents. The Coast Guard rides herd on the congestion and not without reason. Each year the statistics mount. While most of the fishermen use good judgment and caution, there are inevitably drawn to the scene the spooks, the hairbrained and ignorant in ten-foot prams, leaky homemade monstrosities, and even small rubber rafts.

A sample of the traffic across the Colum-bia bar during the salmon fishing season, as recorded by Coast Guard lookouts, in one recent year showed 39,500 crossings. This was an increase of 6,000 over the previous year—or about 12 percent a year increase in sport fishing offshore. Of these crossings incidentally, the Coast Guard answered nearly four hundred calls for assistance. The "Bar" at the river's mouth is officially considered to be two miles wide and five miles long, extending from Buoy 12 to deep water at Buoys 1 and 2.

Some of these, especially those from the hinterlands who are just ignorant of the ways of the ocean, can be understood if not excused. The idiot element that tempts fate and the lives of innocent passengers—often members of the family—can neither be excused nor understood. The presence of the Coast Guard patrol boats in these cases at least helps to keep down the loss of life.

Sport fishermen are subject to the game laws of either Oregon or Washington, depending upon the embarkation and landing point, and license held.

Until recent years most salmon caught on sport tackle were taken on plugs such as the Lucky Louie or Pink Lady, many on wobbling spoons and plug-cut herring. Tackle was heavy and unwieldy because of the strain of trolling through powerful currents and tide rips. In recent years the Puget Sound method of mooching was introduced into the Columbia with spectacular success. Trolling with heavy tackle gave way to light saltwater equipment, including spinning gear.

A typical sport setup now is an eight-foot glass rod with a heavy saltwater reel and three or four hundred yards of limp monofilament line of from ten- to twelve-pound test. A mooching rig consists of two bait hooks tied to leaders of the same test and material as the line. One hook is passed up through the mouth and gills of a frozen herring and drawn back to hook through the backbone. The other hook is passed through the jaws to hold the mouth closed. A half ounce of lead is usually sufficient for mooching.

The fisherman lets out the bait, allowing it to swirl with the tide and current, the motion simulating a wounded herring. For chinooks the bait is fished deep; for the more active but smaller coho, just a few feet under the surface. The boat drifts freely, subject to wind and tide. If the weather is rough, or a ground swell is running, the boat plunges deep into a trough to rise again and teeter precariously. Drifting freely, the boat is pitched and shaken and yawed off at unpredictable angles. The fisherman tries to brace himself and anticipate the next move. He is thrown off balance, slammed against the rail or pilothouse, battered from one side to another. He reels and staggers like a drunken man. He gets queazy in the

stomach and dares not go below to the hot, close cabin even for the call of nature. He fixes his gaze on the horizon and tries to think of pleasant things, hoping if he doesn't think of the sea it will go away.

The salmon do not strike hard on mooched bait. Often the fish simply nibbles at it until hooked, or strikes at it with a passing slash of the tail. The fisherman waits until he's sure the salmon has the bait before setting the hook, then he sets it hard for the salmon has a tough mouth.

If it's a smaller coho, the battle will be short but spectacular, the fish leaping out of the water and threshing the waves. If it's chinook, especially a big one, he'll sound and sulk and no amount of coaxing will get him to the surface until he's ready—but there's no mistaking the power and fury on the other end of the line. A big one may take from half an hour to two hours to land. Meanwhile the boat must be maneuvered in and out of the congestion while the fisherman's arms ache from sustained tension.

Salmon fishing off-shore in the late 1940's was uncrowded.

A fish on always attracts the other boats, especially if the fishing has been slow, and soon the lucky boat is surrounded by others. At times the sudden excitement of birds will send dozens of boats to the scene hoping it is a school of herring or pilchards.

There is no predicting the course of a day's fishing. The boat may pitch and roll on the bar for hours and not connect with a salmon; or suddenly run into a feeding school in the last aching seasick hour of the day. Sometimes the fishermen start connecting as soon as the lines are in the water and take limits within a few minutes.

But this is all part of the sport and no matter how tired, or how sick, or how bruised and battered the fisherman is from being slammed around the deck all day, the sudden dip of the rod or thrill-loaded first tug of the line that signals a salmon, will jerk him out of his mood and pitch him up to the peak of excitement—the like of which occurs only when the chinook and fisherman meet the next year on Columbia bar.

3.

The Cruise of the "Question Mark"?

Two tall-poled salmon trollers cut a flat arc across the five-mile expanse of murky-blue river. The Megler ferry ghosted out of a thick fogbank in the direction of Point Ellice. A cannery whistle shrilled and the solemn tones of a steamership signaling for a pilot hung low in the air.

A fresh southwesterly beat against the surge of current as we put out from the oil dock in the *Question Mark?* and headed full speed for the bar. Behind us in our thrashing wake, three sea gulls dipped and swooped in anticipation. I was glad they were not buzzards.

"At least that's one good omen," I told the others. "If the sea gulls follow you're bound to have luck."

Joe Munson, our skipper, looked back at the thick fogbank now lifting in the breeze toward the crest of the hemlock and fir coastal mountains behind Astoria.

"It's liable to get a bit snotty outside," Joe said in one of those pearly understatements that strike exclamation marks in man's daily routine of quiet desperation.

By "outside" he meant across the roughest bar in the world, and onto the open Pacific off the mouth of the Columbia River. By Joe's standards the bar didn't get rough until a ten-thousand-ton steamship sank out of sight in a swell.

"We'll run down for a look-see," said Joe the Intrepid. "If we can't get out we can always troll up around Point Ellice."

This was not the first time I fished the open Pacific for salmon, but it was a typical trip. Over a period of nearly thirty years, offshore fishing trips have blended into a blurred scenario like one of those psychedelic posters.

So I wasn't embarking on a new adventure. Our sturdy craft, however, did not overwhelm me with confidence. The *Question Mark?* was a twenty-six-foot charter "cruiser" which had been built with two-by-fours for frames and shiplap for planking. Joe skippered it on shares with the owner, and since this episode occurred many years ago before the modern charter fleets reached the present state of sophistication, a sport fisherman wanting to fish the high seas didn't have much choice. During the peak of the runs the commercial trollers and seiners preferred to work their own boats alone rather than cater to a bunch of seasick sports.

I regarded the name *Question Mark?* as one of deadly insight and premonition, whoever suggested it.

One look at the others in our party told me they were of the same opinion. Besides Jack Moys, now a Seattle radio station exec-

Patrol boat on the Columbia bar

utive, there were Don Rickles, then an NBC-TV announcer from Hollywood; and Bill Tate, a Portland cafe entrepreneur.

It was 7:00 A.M. and the estuary was alive with fishing boats of all kinds. In those days the local mercenary chamber of commerce types sponsored abominations called "salmon derbies," which attracted hundreds of meat fishermen and similar subhuman species to the area during the salmon runs, and anything that would float was reserved for months in advance.

We passed Desdemona Sands Light, where the day before a fisherman had spent the night clinging to the superstructure when his outboard kicker conked out. Our boat shuddered and yawed as we hit the tide rips at the entrance.

Ahead lay the bar between the South Jetty and Peacock Spit. Five miles out, the leaden gray of the open sea merged into the dark overcast obscuring the horizon. An idiot in a sixteen-foot skiff headed out ahead of us. People like him make heroes out of Coast Guard sailors.

Joe cranked the bow around in the general direction of the Columbia Lightship just as we met the first swells. Looking over the top of the pilothouse, I got hit in the face with a bucket of water. The next moment I was slammed against the bulkhead and then tossed to the cockpit rail. My camera slid along the deck and smashed against the transom.

"It's pretty calm today," Joe said. "Might get kinda snotty when the tide changes, though."

We somehow had the foresight to rig up gear before we left the dock, one of the few smart things we did that day. We spent the five-mile run across the bar trying to keep the boat approximately under us. To be honest, however, the *Question Mark?* proved to be a surprisingly rugged and seaworthy little craft.

A mile off the end of the South Jetty we

Joe Munson, skipper of the *Question Mark?*

spotted birds and forgot all about the sea. We had made it, and the only damage appeared to be the mast which had broken loose and was flapping some. But there, following the birds, was the trolling fleet.

Joe cut the throttle and all hands got lines over. We used wooden plugs, Pearl Pinks, and Blues and Lucky Louies, and had a large assortment of spinners, dodgers, and wobblers along. This was in the days when mooching in this area was done only in the local beer joints.

The chart showed the water here to be about ten fathoms. We all tried different depths at first in order to find the fish. The current was so swift that my streamer bounded on the surface. (Always a rebel, which is a euphonism for "contrary," as my mother used to describe me, I was experimenting with a coho streamer fly.) Any more weight would have killed the action, so I started to reel in and change to a conventional plug or wobbler. Halfway in my streamer was attacked by a coho that came out of water and dove on it. He missed.

"Hey!" I yelled. "Here they come—get set!"

I dropped the streamer back just as Joe's rod bent and the line whanged as a comber came across the gunwale and buried everything. I grabbed for the wheel with one hand and held my rod with the other while Joe fought with a ten-pounder.

Jack dropped everything and rushed into the cabin for a lure like Joe's red fluorescent flasher. Joe landed his fish without a ruffle. "About six feet under," he announced. "Troll back about thirty to forty feet."

Ten minutes later Jack also has a ten-pounder on and thereby broke a jinx that had plagued him for five years of unsuccessful salmon fishing. He brought the fish in and admired it like a man in a trance, as if

Jack Moys (left) plays a salmon while Bill Tate watches

he'd just signed up a sponsor for a lifetime contract, while the coho tried to kick the slats out of the *Question Mark's?* cockpit.

"I knew I'd break my jinx if I went out with you," Jack told me and I knew he was putting the hex on me.

A few minutes later his rod again whanged into a sharp bend and a coho exploded out of the water just short of the stern, so hard it slammed against the transom. The swells now had steepened and the fish leaped from crest to crest flashing his brilliant silver sides. Jack hung onto his rod with both hands as the motion knocked him from one rail to another, and subsequently boated a twelve-pounder.

He slumped on a sea. "Man! This makes up for all those years!"

I ignored him. The sea now got into a serious mood. Between hanging on, trying to take pictures, and fish at the same time, I kept busy. I felt a slight strike and set the hook in time to miss a heavy smash that made the rod zing. I started to reel in to examine the lure, when Bill and Don both yelled at the same time. The boat dropped into a deep trough, throwing Jack and his tackle box, and Bill, Don, and the loose furniture against the main bulkhead, with me as the shock absorber. Bill and Don, amazingly, both had fish on at the same time.

The tops of the swells now curled over and broke in foam. I looked up from the confusion to find us alone with no other craft in sight. Then we lost the school.

"Looks kind of snotty out here," Joe remarked. "Maybe we better get back inside the jetty and see if we can pick up some chinook."

Halfway there we hit the kind of weather that even Joe considered worthy of comment. Passing a large steamship headed out to sea, we watched it go completely from sight in the troughs. One minute we'd be surfing along on an incoming swell, riding the crest as the *Question Mark?* poised on the edge of a forty-foot hole in the water, then Joe would ease the throttle and let it pass under the keel.

A half hour of this brought us under the lee of the South Jetty where the swells were only twenty feet deep, with a few cross-waves and tide rips thrown in. A Coast Guard boat herded some stragglers inside, but in spite of the weather I counted fifty boats in our vicinity, ranging from sixty-three-foot converted AVR to a four-man rubber raft.

We had our gear out in the wake again with plugs on and from eight to sixteen ounces of lead to get a depth needed against the current. I saw a diving bird fold its wings and rocket into the water from high in the air. A moment later it came up with a pilchard in its beak, and I was telling myself there ought to be some salmon feeding here, when Bill and Don yelled in chorus again. For the second time in an hour both were fast to fish simultaneously. At first I thought they were chinooks, but when the first broke out of a crest and hurtled into the air I saw they were coho.

Bill's topped the scale for the day at fourteen pounds and Don's went about six. While all this was going on, Jack had been unusually quiet. I thought he was still in shock from his double score and broken jinx. Then abruptly he set his rod down and dove for the rail.

"Well, boys," he gasped, "when you take something from the sea, you have to give something back."

In Jack's case, it was breakfast.

My own innards felt like a churn of sour milk, and when Don also headed for the rail, I felt my gills burning. It did not bother Bill, though.

"That reminds me," he said. "I haven't had a bite since breakfast." He hauled out

Sport fishing offshore among the commercial trolling fleet in the old days

his lunch box and spread himself a picnic on the hatch cover.

I stuck my head into the wind and stared off to the horizon and tried to work a problem in higher mathematics. About that time the Coast Guard surf boat came back with siren going, ordering everyone inside. We trolled upstream into the river and spent the rest of the day in the estuary without success.

Then a mystery developed that has never been solved: We landed seven salmon, but only six were aboard when we counted them up at the dock.

What I remember about that trip was that it turned my entire body into a mass of black and blue bruises from the violent slamming and banging around the cockpit all day.

I also remember I got skunked, the only one who did.

This for some sadistic motivation seemed to tickle Moys's perverted sense of justice. He had broken his own five-year jinx, and in the process put the hex on me.

Indeed, whoever had christened our ship the *Question Mark?* had been singularly inspired.

Rigging up gear for salmon offshore

4.

Action at Kiwanda

It rained during the night, but not enough to knock down autumn leaves, let alone raise the Nestucca River enough to pass salmon over the bar. This meant we'd have to hit 'em where they lived—and the Pacific Northwest coast in the fall of the year is one place that gives you second thoughts.

But veteran doryman Paul Hanneman—who divides his time between guiding fishermen and guiding bills through the Oregon legislature as a State Representative from Tillamook County—checked the surf in the lee of Cape Kiwanda again about midnight.

"It will be okay by daybreak," he said.

And soon after, God willin', we'd be out there just beyond the surf where there were hoards of coho milling around restlessly, feeding in preparation for their spawning runs.

You can't tell about the Pacific, much less predict what's going to happen hours in advance—unless you're an on-the-spot expert. The swells start five thousand miles away and build up all the distance to the West Coast. Then there are local winds and currents, shifting restlessly in the autumn.

But to Cape Kiwanda's dory fishermen, this is the best time of the year. The tourists are gone, the birds are flying, and the air is stimulating. Just outside the surf line the salmon are feeding, gorging on anchovies, smelt, and herring, surging in and out impatiently along the ten-fathom shelf, waiting for the fall rains and the age-old biological trigger.

It is during this brief period when the coastal rivers are still too low for the bank plunkers and drifters, when the late summer and fall runs belong to Oregon's most exclusive fishermen—the surf dorymen.

Their mecca is Kiwanda—the only place on the Pacific coast (at this time) where boats are regularly launched through the surf. The fishing folk who live in the quaint little village of Pacific City nearby developed their dory techniques long ago, first using oars and sails, and then outboard motors. Now they come from all over the Northwest, from California, and even fly in to the state-owned landing strip along the river from as far away as Texas.

Sure enough, the surf looked docile at daybreak. The three of us, staying at Hanneman's cabin a couple of miles upriver, rolled out before daylight and piled into his rusty, temperamental, totally air-conditioned beach buggy and headed down to the beach without even a cup of coffee to stiffen our backbones. Behind us we towed Hanneman's twenty-foot double-ended dory, the *Kiwanda Clipper*. Besides Paul and me, there were Elmer Donicht, an Albany, Oregon, storekeeper, and Robert Bauman from Eugene.

A light offshore breeze sprang up as we launched, bringing a sprinkle of rain and some low clouds scudding over the sand dunes. A flight of brant flew by, crabbed at an angle to the wind. Haystack Rock, offshore, loomed darkly out of a fogbank over the ocean. An ancient Aeronca Champion, probably carrying a couple of fishermen from Portland, a half hour's flight away, dropped almost silently out of the broken clouds over the Coast Range and glided

power-off down for a landing on the strip. The offshore breeze picked up, rocking and bouncing the airplane which ballooned as it was about to set down. The pilot gunned the motor and went around again.

"If the wind picks up any more they may have to shoot him down," Hanneman observed.

As we launched the surf turned cranky. You can't tell how bad the ocean will be until you get out on it. After a moment of terror, we rode over some unexpected breakers, shipped oars, tipped the ten-horsepower motor down in the well, and fired up.

This type of dory is no longer in general use at Cape Kiwanda

"Cheated death again," Paul said.

We couldn't wait. The outboard had hardly made three revolutions before we grabbed our eight-foot glass rods and rigged up ten-pound test line for herring hookups. The salmon were hitting bait now, putting on fat for the upriver spawning run. Out here beyond the surf line we would troll the ten-fathom line parallel to the surf, just barely moving, keeping only enough power on to maintain way. Sometimes this is called "motor mooching," as it is one of the most deadly ways for salmon.

Here, during the summer season, Hanneman went "outside" on sixty consecutive days for salmon and on only five of these did the party fail to take the limit. Which may be some kind of a record.

Suddenly the wind died down again. The sun broke through the overcast and the timbered coast mountains which dropped down into massive sand dunes just beyond the beach gleamed up brightly in the morning light. A momentary calm settled over the water, and even the fog began to lift. A mile back we could see several other dories breaking through the surf.

Hanneman turned the dory shoreward, riding a gentle swell until just an instant before it broke over into surf, then swung the boat sharply to seaward again. This playing-tag-with-the-surf technique works fine but isn't recommended for heavy weather.

On the second pass, Donicht hooked a twelve-pound silver. He landed the bright, frenzied salmon after a short aerial tussle,

Paul Hanneman (left) retrieves his dory from the surf

The view from a dory as you launch into the surf

and on the next pass connected again. At the same time I hooked into one out of the same feeding school. With two fish on and the dory spinning around to make for the open sea, the action took an interesting turn. Our lines tangled under the boat. But we loosened our reel drags and played it cool until safely away from the surf. Then we managed to land both fish—fat, prime silvers.

For the next two hours we played tag with the surf, hitting a school and losing it again. The silvers feasted on herring and anchovies one minute, and the next would not open their mouths for anything. They were restless, unpredictable, anxious to get up the river and keep their appointment with Destiny.

An onshore breeze sprang up now, blowing unhindered from the southwest right into the launching site in the lee of the cape. Suddenly I was aware that the timbered hills and dunes back of the beach were hidden in haze. A few drops of rain slapped us in the face, slanting down with the rising gale. A short chop developed, knocking the tops off the increasing swells. No more boats were coming out, I noticed, and two others had already headed back in.

We needed one more for a limit, but we already had enough salmon to smoke for a fair supply of snacks.

"One more pass," Hanneman announced, sizing up the sky and sea with a quick, practiced eye. He's a veteran of dorying and all-weather launches. But he doesn't go for this Gung Ho bit.

This time he ran directly toward the breaking surf, swerved sharply, cut the motor and we drifted and bounced expertly on the edge of the breakers. The motion of the boat was so violent that I could only hang on, so I missed the first pass at my herring. Then my rod suddenly became a U-shaped stick, and a heavy coho leaped three feet out of water, then headed seaward. Hanneman spun the dory and we headed after him. Ten minutes later he was aboard and trying to kick the slats out of the bottom.

Hanneman didn't waste any more time on conversation. We headed full speed through the swells toward the launch site. In a trough just outside the breakers, he shut off the motor and quickly shipped the oars, swinging the bow seaward, letting the swells ease us backwards toward the beach. One large breaker caught us and carried the boat along on its crest between two rocky reefs, then suddenly we were high and dry on the sand with the water receding away from us. We jumped out and pulled the boat beyond the water's reach.

It was raining in earnest by the time we'd cleaned the salmon and loaded the dory on the trailer. On the way back to the cabin we crossed the bridge and saw the river's surface dimpled with Oregon dewdrops. The wind had a strong set to it even here, protected by the dunes. A few hours of rain and the Old Nestuck would rise a couple of feet.

For most of the dorymen the season here starts in May and ends in late September. The more experienced, like Paul, fish all winter, going out on "flat days" for halibut, lingcod, red snapper, or sea bass. One way or another there's fishing all year around, as well as clams and crabs in the bay. It just depends upon how and when you want to go after them.

Once you've launched through the surf with a dory, though, you're hooked on Kiwanda fishing. You'll keep coming back—especially when the tourists are gone and the birds are flying.

Hanneman squinted up and down the river and then at the sea. "The salmon will be moving inside tomorrow," he predicted.

And we'd be waiting for them on the river. After all, it doesn't make sense to give up salmon fishing entirely just because you can't get out to sea.

5.

I Like Humpback Salmon

The sign over the door said it was a cafe. It looked like a wannigan pulled up on the beach and equipped with a flyspecked counter, some barstools and an ancient jukebox.

It was also equipped with a tall, leggy blonde who was pretty well equipped herself.

The joint was jumping. A scratchy record blared out, ". . . I like humpbacked salmon . . . !" It was midmorning on Lummi Island and the red-necked reef netters who jammed the wannigan were playing hooky from their salmon fishing. Either the runs had tapered off or they found their coffee break more interesting.

The snatches of small talk I heard concerned the salmon runs and lack of fish this year. A lanky fisherman, just back from Cape Flattery, said a humpy run had been going through the Strait of Juan de Fuca for a week. He couldn't understand what was keeping them. He had a theory about it, which I didn't catch.

The blonde who juggled mugs of thick coffee and soggy pie had a suggestive manner and a bold look. My clothes stamped me as an outlander and she tossed an interested glance at me from time to time. It didn't set well with the reef netters.

But I only wanted to rent a boat. I bought a cup of coffee to go with the free information and the blonde told me her Uncle Arthur was down at the dock now. He had one for rent. "Hurry back!" she called after me, in a neighborly sort of way.

Uncle Arthur had one skiff left and a five-horse motor. The salmon he said, were all on this side of the strait today. "Big school of dogfish moved in over there and ruined the fishing." He waved toward Orcas Island.

I didn't see any sport boats on this side. Off the cove and along the shoreline the reef net boats were anchored in a long double line. The tide was running out, and running out fast, boiling and swirling over the submerged reefs. I looked at the leaky skiff and wondered if I should chance it. The looks the commercial fishermen had given me indicated they'd gladly throw me an anchor if I capsized. But the county ferry back to Gooseberry Point in the mainland Indian reservation didn't leave for another hour. I decided to stick around. I'd heard the humpbacked salmon were running and I'd never caught one on sport gear. Also, I wanted to see the reef netters in operation.

Lummi (pronounced "Lummy") is a small island in Puget Sound a few miles south of the border. It's about eight miles

long and a couple of miles wide. Here at
the cove the island pinched together like a
long-necked clam, low and narrow, but on
the south end a peak rose 1,700 feet out of
the water. The island is heavily wooded except for the fishing village at the neck.

For hundreds of years it's been the site
of this unique reef-net operation, first by the
Indians in dugout canoes, now by both Indians and whites and mixed breeds. Lummi
is the only place where Pacific salmon are
caught in this manner.

The currents along the west side of the
island are treacherous. The strait is shallow and full of reefs. All five species of Pacific salmon pour through here during the
runs on their way to the Fraser River in
British Columbia.

The reef boats are anchored in pairs.
They are thirty-foot bargelike craft. The
bucket net is hung between two boats and
operates on the principle of the flap on longhandled underwear. Lead lines go out upstream from the boats to outer buoys to
which crosslines are attached. Tufts of
grass are tied on the crosslines so they sway
in the current. This fools the salmon into
thinking the water is getting shallower as
they approach the boats and they rise to the
surface. Lookouts on twelve-foot towers
watch for the schools approaching the net
and on signal the loose end of the net is
raised, closing the trap.

A commercial fisherman who had crossed
on the ferry with me had not liked my looks
or my sport gear. I could see why now. The
net operation is tricky and they don't like
amateur spooks chasing in and out among
the nets. But I like offbeat fishing expeditions and I like to prowl around this Puget
Sound backcountry. The characters, color,
and quaint little settlements fascinate me.
Besides, I'd never found another place

where the humpies could be caught on sport
gear so conveniently.

I rigged up my ten-foot glass rod with
eight-pound test limp monofilament line
and squirted a couple of drops of oil in my
big saltwater spinning reel. I had picked up
a silver wobbling spoon in Bellingham that
morning. It had a herring scale finish and a
big single Siwash hook. I tied this to a No.
0-0 chrome-plated dodger with sixteen
inches of monel wire and connected the
dodger to a half-ounce trolling lead with
thirty inches of wire.

The weather was improving. A hammer-
head storm cloud that had hung around
the summit of Mount Baker dissipated. A
chill breeze that chopped the surface of the
bay on the way across died down. A brilliant slant of sunshine broke through the
overcast as I left the dock.

The tidal rip caught me immediately and
almost swung the skiff into an anchored
cabin cruiser. I straighted it out and got

A bright humpbacked or pink salmon caught off Lummi

Reef netters in the strait off Lummi Island

the line in the water and trolled through the reef boats. The five-horse motor could just hold its own in the current. I had inched through the first line into open water when I got the first strike. Automatically I shut the motor off. This was my first mistake.

The current grabbed the skiff and hurled it back toward the nets. An anguished howl went up among the fishermen on the reef boats. Meanwhile the salmon on my line circled the skiff like a maypole, the line ripping through the water. I caught a flash of fish deep down, then concentrated on starting the motor. I swept past a reef boat

so close our gunwales bumped. The two Indians on the boat doubled up with laughter, but I was too busy at the moment to appreciate the humor. Also, as long as they were laughing they weren't shooting. I swept past the entire line of reef netters before I got the motor started again. Meanwhile my line went limp as the salmon shook loose.

A fresh wind came up suddenly and raised swells that made the skiff harder to handle, but a salmon on the line was all the encouragement I needed. I headed back for another pass, telling myself that the Indians had fished here for several hundred years and they shouldn't mind if I tried it for a couple of hours.

Again the rod whipped down suddenly. I left the motor running this time, throttled down slightly to maintain my position. This salmon also circled the boat crazily and I revolved with it, at the same time trying to prevent the boat from yawing off. The salmon fought hard, deep down in the manner of the chinook, but suddenly shot out of the water like a coho and finished his fight jumping and thrashing on the surface.

The salmon never let up the fight for a moment until I had netted it—a six-pounder that tried to kick the slats out of the bottom of the boat. It had wrapped the steel leader around its neck, a typical coho trick, but this was no coho. It was a humpbacked salmon, olive-green back and large black spots.

Old *Oncorhynchus gorbuscha*, otherwise known as the pink (by canners), or humpy (by old Alaskan salts), or humpbacked is one of the most important of the five Eastern Pacific salmon and one Asiatic salmon species to the commercial market from Astoria to Hokkaido, and one of the most numerous of all the salmon races and species— yet is virtually unknown to sports anglers.

The pinks, or humpies, as I prefer, spawn in streams as far south as Cape Blanco, although in most cases they go unnoticed or unidentified. In the Puget Sound and Alaskan waters, however, they are a popular fish and well known to many salmon anglers who await their arrival with the same anticipation as the tourists watch for the swallows at Capistrano.

In the Puget Sound area, for example, the Skagit, Stillaguamish, Snohomish, Puyallup, and Nooksack, among others, are famous producers of humpies. Most of them in this area come in through the Strait of Juan de Fuca, heading for the Fraser. Along Whidbey Island, in the Port Gardner and Port Susan areas, all along the strait close inshore, and even around the cape to La Push, all are popular humpy spots.

The humpies mature at only two years of age to an average size of six pounds. The spawning run usually takes place in late summer and fall, with August and September the best months. They swim far up into the river headwaters, spawning in the gravel beds. The young emerge in the spring and head for saltwater immediately.

The humpies in the Puget Sound area, and in other places, are "odd year fish"— that is, they return to spawn only in the odd-numbered years, such as 1969, 1971, and so forth. There are some large and important even-year runs, however, especially in British Columbia and Alaska and often they even mix with the odd-year fish. The average commercial catch of odd-year humpies in Washington state is five million fish, which gives one an idea of the importance of this beautiful salmon.

The humpy will take any kind of sport lure, including flies, and they hit with a bang at the time you least expect a strike. Sometimes they hit so hard they tear loose, a trait that other salmon do not have. Local anglers often use a rubber snubber to take the shock when trolling for humpies in fast tide rips.

The humpy as a "two-year" fish, is a small salmon because of its short cycle, but has been known to reach fourteen pounds— a hefty hunk of meat for only two years' growth. The flesh of the humpy is a delicate pink and is prized for canning. Although fresh hump filets beat anything in their class, they are rarely found on menus or in butcher shops. You want humpy steaks, first you find a humpy—or catch one yourself.

The wire leader was kinked and ruined. I replaced it and let out line again. It started to rain then, a sudden chilling squall, but the sun came out before I could get my jacket on. A short time later another squall hit, sweeping across the water in a swath from the southwest. After this the strait was placid as a millpond for a time. Weather, in the San Juans, is unpredictable, but always interesting.

I hooked two more humpies ranging from four to six pounds. Meanwhile the tidal current slacked off briefly and started in again anew. I made one more swing through the next line of reef netters.

As I rounded the outer buoy and headed across the channel on an angle, two things happened at once: A strike slammed the rod tip down and the motor ran out of gas. The silence sounded unnatural after the noise of the motor. Then the netters saw what had happened and set up a howl as my skiff swept toward a trap. I jammed the rod into the holder and grabbed for oars. One of the netters jumped into his skiff and jerked the motor into life to head me off, but he was too late. Shouted advice, charged with epithets, and even some guffaws assailed me.

As I approached the trap one of the fishermen shouted, "Don't come through here!" This went down as the most superfluous statement of the day. I was already at the entrance and there wasn't a thing I could do about it.

My salmon was still on, however, putting up just enough fight to yaw the skiff. The drag whined against the strain, but the limber rod took up most of the shock. Suddenly the tide caught the other end of the skiff and held it just enough to allow the bow to swing around. The skiff hit the outer buoy just aft of amidships, teetered sickeningly for a moment and then slowly fell off on the outside of the trap jaws.

Author photographs a reef netter close up while trolling for humpies

I grabbed the rod and again took up the battle with the salmon. By this time both I and the salmon were exhausted, but I still had him on—a fat eight-pound humpy.

Back at the dock a bystander spotted me unloading my gear and fish. "The humpies are in!" someone yelled.

While the reason for the excitement was lost on me, I noticed the wannigan cafe spilling out its crowd of reef netters. Even the blonde could not compete with the humpbacked run—apparently a long-anticipated event. I was glad they were glad; at least I didn't have to look over my shoulder to see if any harpoons were aimed at me, after messing up the morning routine with my tenderfoot antics.

I strolled past the wannigan carrying my gear and fish to the car. The blonde was standing behind the screen door. The juke-box was still cackling, "I like humpbacked salmon . . . !"

"Hi, Lucky," she called to me. "You missed the last ferry. Why not have lunch while you're waiting?"

I was kind of hungry at that.

6.

Those Amazing Dorymen of Cape Kiwanda!

We're rough, we're tough, we're coarse.
What then?
We're the salt of the earth.
We're dorymen.
OLD FISHERMAN'S CHANTY

Moonglow outlined the eroded sandstone headland of Cape Kiwanda as we bounced over the beach in the rust-encrusted buggy.

The sea lay flat at this midnight hour, a shimmering blue-gray slate stretching west to the horizon under a mackerel sky. A shaft of moonlight struck a path across the passage between the Rock and the Cape.

All dorymen do this—at least the old pros who know this ocean and this cape, where for nearly a hundred years they have been going to sea simply by launching their small boats through the surf in this unique and sometimes tricky sheltered cove.

"Looks quiet," said my doryman companion. "It's a good sign we'll fish at dawn when she lays like this around midnight."

We sat there awhile, watching the timeless sea, and feeling its power and allure and knowing what has tempted men from the first tick of time.

"Did you see that?" asked the doryman.

"No, what?"

"That white foam breaking through the Jughandle."

I looked then and saw it. The Jughandle is the natural hole in the immense sea stack, some 327 feet high, known as Haystack Rock, or, locally, simply as "the Rock." It's one of the secret signs the pros have of judging the sea.

"There's another thing. See the slick black face of the cape? Means it's wet. My guess is there's some big long swells rolling in from Japan. Could be dying or building. We'll know at daylight."

It's been this way since the beginning, in the middle 1800's, when the first settlers pushed over the Coast Range and down into the lush, moist valley where the Indians, who called themselves "Nestucca," lived in their towns.

Many of these settlers brought with them memories of their Eastern seaboard homeland, and came West with an understanding of the New Jersey type surfboats and the famed Gloucester or Banks dory. Naturally they began building boats about the same time as barns—in fact, both were enhanced by the wreckage of some heavily loaded lumber schooners along the beach and thousands of board feet of prime lumber were available for salvage.

It was all sail or oars in those days, and the coastwise traffic was astonishingly busy. A commercial fishing industry developed at the mouth of the Nestucca, and, incredibly, sail-powered vessels regularly crossed the bar which nowadays has only about three feet of water on the flood tide, and sailed right up to a cannery dock in the estuary. There was much trade in canned and mild-cured salmon. Most of the settlers also looked to the sea for supplies.

Clyde Hudson, who still lives on the family homestead near Cloverdale, came here as a boy in 1892. His family built their barn with lumber from the wreck of the *Pioneer,* and Clyde acquired as a youth one of the first cameras in these parts. One of his first photos was of the *Della,* a steam launch of about sixty feet, built also from the *Pioneer's* lumber, tied up at the wharf at the head of tidewater.

He and others fished with the boats and sold their catch for five cents a pound over in the valley. There was Bill Raleigh, who had a college education but preferred the life of a fisherman. Others, like Vic Learned, Lloyd Kellow, Herman Miller, Will Glick, "Doctor" Hans Brooten, and, later, his sons, Harry, Tomm, and Dolliver; Brick Gilman—all family names still found on the mailboxes, road signs, and land plats.

Brick was probably the first regular dory-man to also guide sportsmen. His sons, Warren and Jack, are also guides. Jack was a top commercial fisherman as well, often bringing in a catch worth eight thousand dollars during the short summer season.

The first dory launched from the lee of Kiwanda was the small version of the Banks type, probably a twelve-foot bottom size, with the typically sharp rake of bow and stern and the tremendous sheer and rocker which help lift them over the breaking waves. In those days they had to haul the boats a mile down the beach from the end of the road by hand.

Although this is the only place on the West Coast where dories have been launched regularly, at this writing (1969) there has never been a drowning or even a serious accident to the dory fleet.

At first the dorymen rowed, sometimes all the way to Cape Lookout, fished all day, and then hoisted a rag of canvas for the run back to Kiwanda before the prevailing northwesterlies. Sometimes the wind changed and they rowed both ways.

In the late 1930's, when outboard motors became relatively dependable, the dories increased to fifteen and sixteen feet along the bottom and the outboard "well" came into use.

After World War II, with better roads and even an airstrip nearby, the dory fleet increased to about twenty boats. These were built along the same lines, but up to twenty-two feet in length and with more

A dory fisherman unloading his catch

powerful motors. There was even a twenty-five-foot double-ender troller, built by an ingenious fisherman named "Wild Horse" Smith, equipped with retractable airplane landing gear drive with engine power and a belt takeoff. But it was always falling into potholes as it waddled in out of the surf.

A war surplus DUWK showed up at the beach, too, and its hulk is still out there under the breaking surf where it capsized and drowned several people, but this was some outsider's scheme and not a part of the dory fleet.

As late as 1950 the dorymen still had to drag their boats a mile down the beach, but they had developed a beach buggy too, by then, to haul a trailer. The road to the cape was built later, followed by a new stretch of loop highway from the cape to Tierra Del Mar, and public facilities were installed by the county and state. In 1959 the first Dory Derby was staged by local fishermen as part of Oregon's Centennial.

The regular fleet now included Paul Hanneman, whose family once was nationally known as Jersey cow breeders and diarymen. They moved to the area in the 1940's. Paul became a state legislator from Tillamook County in the 1960's. L. C. (Pink) Schulmerick, a long-time county commissioner; the late Dutch Schermer, a retired wrestler who ran the sporting goods store; Jim Imlah, son of the former game warden, a World War II Navy and Coast Guard veteran and commercial fisherman—all were well-known dorymen.

To this group add a number of dorymen who did not live on the beach, but came over from the valley or other parts of the Northwest, and regularly made up the fleet. These included W. O. Van Meter from Salem, who is said to have brought in the first square-stern dory.

There were others such as Vic and Terry Learned, Clint Bailey, Robert Beutler, Ted (Shorty) Howe, Jim Coon, and young Bill Coplen, a Portland student who loved to fish and quit college to move to Kiwanda where he could drop a line and get paid for it.

Then came "Barefoot Charlie" Hollis, a transplanted Oklahoman who says "sallmon" for salmon, in 1960, and provided the corps with enough adventures to make him a reputation.

On one of his first sport charters, Charlie hauled a young boy and an aged grandfather who had to be helped into the dory. They fished off Pillar Rock until they caught a limit, but when they started back a dangerous surf was running, which was not discernible from seaward until too late. Charlie quickly stood the old man against the stub mast and told him to hang on, whatever happened. Near the beach a sleeper broke over them, sweeping Charlie overboard. The kid thought this was the signal to abandon ship and dove over the side, too. The last thing Charlie saw was the old man standing erect in the middle of the dory clutching the mast, like a George Washington crossing the Delaware, riding the crest of a wave right up onto the beach as pretty as a sea gull.

"The old man never got a drop of water on him," Charlie recalled.

Another newcomer, Victor Ferrington, arrived about 1960 from California with his wife and two hundred dollars capital. He began building skiffs on a shoestring, switched to dories, then with the advent of the big outboard motors, experimented with extending the run of the dory from just after amidship to a square transom in order to carry more power.

This development, carried on simultaneously by several dory builders, was a happy one. It made possible dories up to twenty-five feet or more in length, capable of being launched on almost wet sand, and of speeds up to twenty or twenty-five knots. It changed the entire technique and tradition of the Kiwanda dory fleet.

These boats were so successful that the fleet boomed to between three hundred and four hundred boats within a couple of years as sports from all over the Northwest fished off Kiwanda and became infatuated with these craft, and had to be dorymen. Besides, they had also learned that just offshore there was some of the finest salmon fishing on the coast.

The "outsiders" increased the fleet to about seven hundred boats at this writing, and perhaps even one thousand. The Oregon Marine Board about this time reported dory registrations to outnumber all other types combined.

Dory builders found themselves swamped with orders, and some were working up to two years behind. One large firm began selling these craft to other parts of the country as the word spread to areas where a large, roomy, inexpensive, and superbly seaworthy sport craft was needed.

The new craft also permitted an extension of the traditional dory season from May until October instead of July through September as in the past. Some of the old-timers were fishing all summer long, missing no more than a day or so because of weather. In one of the first years the ten top commercial boats averaged five thousand dollars each during the season.

So now we come back to Kiwanda at first light. A number of other dorymen are there, and a few more arrive at the same time. We all stand shivering in the brittle

End of a successful dory trip. The Rock is in background

chill, straining through the mist at the ocean, looking at each other for a sign or suggestion. White spray can be seen slapping through the Jughandle, but the swells are breaking fairly regular and easy.

"Well," says my doryman, "we can't catch fish up here on this sand."

So we launch, needing only a couple of inches of water. A deft punch at the starter button and we leap over a breaker, the sharp graceful bow pointed at a forty-five-degree angle. A couple of moments of stark terror, and then we are out and planing over the swells.

Unlike the old days, we are on the grounds off the Boy Scout camp at Cape Lookout in a few moments and the lines are in the water smack dab in the middle of a school of coho. We have limits before we even break out the morning jugs of hot coffee. In the old days it would have been a long row or sail back. Now we had six to eight hours of fuel, a fast boat, and nowhere to go on the biggest ocean in the world.

Just then the sun bursts over the Coast Range to the east and splashes against Cape Lookout. It is one of the most beautiful and rare sights on earth.

"For two cents," said my doryman, "I'd head out for the offshore banks."

"For two cents," I said, "I'd go with you."

The author (left) and companion with a limit of salmon

7.

Port Alberni in the Dark

In my more carefree youth, when time seemed slower and patience was thinner, it was considered the *in thing* to fly to British Columbia for a weekend's fishing and return in time to be at the office Monday morning. I owned and flew an airplane admirably suited for this sort of gay holiday.

It was a four-place Navion single-engine low-wing craft, originally designed by North American Aviation Company, the firm which had produced the P-51 Mustang of World War II fame, and the lines of this postwar attempt to enter the civilian market looked remarkably like the Mustang. The only difference was the Navion was some two hundred miles an hour slower, carried four passengers, and was about as hot an airplane to fly as a cargo parachute. It had, in addition to the four spacious passenger seats, a generous baggage compartment and the ability to waddle off the ground with and safely carry as big a load as you could stuff into it.

We used to fly frequently to British Columbia, and often to the San Juan Islands or to the Gulf Islands, during the summer months; and as a matter of practical expediency, if we did not bring back a load of fish, we at least loaded the baggage compartment with cases of Canadian beer, the equal of which is not found south of the

border. Sometimes this load of beer was such that with all four passengers and the supercargo aboard, the tail skid would scrape along the runway as I fought for life, sending sparks flying into the dry grass. But once the wheels came unglued, and folded up under the belly, the old Navion would climb upstairs, if not like a dove, at least like an earnest shitepoke.

The only trouble with the Navion was its wheels. There were very few landing strips in British Columbia where you could put wheels down. Most bush planes were on floats and thus could go just about anywhere. But with a wheeled ship you could get there in a hurry all right, but once you got there, where were you? I'll tell you: usually stuck on a deserted landing strip, miles from the nearest habitation, and, worse yet, miles from the nearest fishing water.

Moreover, most of the out-of-the-way strips were located in places where few navigation aids and weather services were available. If I had a dollar for every hour spent stranded on some lonely airstrip waiting for weather to unsock, my misspent youth would not have been so misspent.

A typical trip occurred late one autumn weekend. Three friends and I took off for Powell River to sample some "fabulous fishing" we'd heard existed in that area. After clearing customs and immigration at the Vancouver airport, we flew north along the coast, across Horseshoe Bay, along Texada Island and past Prince of Wales Reach, arriving in due course at Powell River's short dirt strip, and made our way into town to find quarters for the night.

Powell River was a company town, and the hotel was company-owned, old but sanitary and comfortable. The weather, however, had closed in behind us and even before nightfall we knew the next day would bring some problems. After local inquiry, we learned there was no fishing in the vicinity worth speaking about. So during and after dinner we discussed the situation, and all hands agreed that if we could get off on the morrow, we'd cross over Georgia Strait to Vancouver Island and fish Campbell River, and if this was not feasible we'd take a crack at the west side of Vancouver Island, which none of us had seen.

The following morning a dense, soggy fog hung over the strait and the town. We checked out, went to the airstrip, and waited. The strip was located on a bluff overlooking the town, so if it was clear enough to see the end of the runway you automatically had an eight hundred foot ceiling once you got off the ground.

About 9:00 A.M. the overcast lifted so we could see the strait. We cranked up the Navion and soon were airborne. But immediately after takeoff, the overcast moved in on the strip, preventing our return and forcing us down lower. About that time I figured we were going to swim before morning was over so I headed out toward a group of trollers working in the strait, buzzing through them so low I could look out the side window and see the tips of the poles.

Continuing on across to Vancouver Island, we made the Canadian Air Force station of Comox looming out of the overcast a bluff ahead. A quick twirl of the channel selector to the emergency frequency and we got permission to put down there. We gassed up and rented a car in Courtenay and drove north to Campbell River, still under a soggy overcast. There was nothing going on there, so we returned to Comox.

Turning the car back, we took off again in a break and flew south to Nanaimo, this time determined to go to Port Alberni and fish the west coast. At Nanaimo we rented another car, drove back to Parksville and took Highway 4 over the wooded hump of the island and down into Port Alberni.

It was dark by this time and much as I wanted to do a little sight-seeing in a bustling lumber and fishing community of about 25,000 people, we hurried to find lodgings for the night. This turned out to be the oldest hotel in town, and probably the quaintest, but only a block from the sport dock. The desk clerk, who was a ravishing-looking redhead, incidentally, at first assigned us to a single room. We objected strenuously without seeing it. She gave us one of those looks, then assigned us to two separate "double" rooms. We should have looked first. The rooms were "family" rooms, as they call them, each about the size of the grand ballroom in Seattle's Olympic Hotel.

We were up the next morning about 4:30 A.M. and down on the dock in the dark by shortly after 5:00 A.M. It was a rainy, soggy, cold morning but we decided we'd come this far and might as well give it a whirl for an hour or so. The old Scotsman at the boat livery fixed us up two to a boat (row type without motor) plus bait and rental gear.

We shoved off into the dark, Al and I in one boat, Jack and Hugh in the other. We lost them immediately in the dark as we rowed along a log boom, following a cluster of local fishermen.

The fishing is all done at the head of the inlet, in among the log booms and debris from the mills. The inlet shallowed out at its upper end where Sproat Lake entered the saltwater. A number of fish were hooked here as we trolled through the shallows, all of them dark spawners. Back again in deeper water, Al latched into a huge chinook along the log boom, and by the time we boated it about forty-five minutes later, the tide had taken us several miles down the inlet. The salmon turned out to be black, but was a monster that probably would have weighed fifty pounds or close to it.

Unnoticed until hunger pangs and fatigue had dragged us down, was the fact that it was again almost dark. At this time of the year, and with the heavy overcast in the canyon, the lights were already on when we returned to the dock, arriving there about the same time as Jack and Hugh. They had hooked several, too, but all dark spawners.

Back at the hotel, we loaded up our rental car and drove back across the island to the east shore where we found a modern motel and spent another night at Qualicum Beach. The next morning we rented boats and fished the strait for coho, and ran into a heavy school of dogfish which we could not keep off the hooks. The presence of dogfish always means no salmon, and some time later when a pod of killer whales came cruising through the channel close aboard, I suggested we go ashore as rapidly as possible.

We then drove south to Nanaimo, checked in the rented car, and flew to Victoria, took on a cargo of Canadian beer and cleared officialdom for the flight home.

While the airplane had stood on the airport at Nanaimo, someone had broken into the cockpit and lifted a couple of expensive instruments, including the compass. We also returned to the States without any fish to show for our weekend, and I never did see Port Alberni.

But we did return with a prize catch of Canadian beer—which is more than many fishing trips end up with.

8.

Juneau Striptease

There I was, rummaging through an old junk box, and I came upon this monstrosity of a fishing reel. Not really junk, because when I wiped away the grease and grime of thirty years it shone like a brand-new Hoover dollar. They really made them in those days. Reels, I mean.

This one was a Pleuger Pakron No. 3180, single action, 6-inch diameter, with a 1¼-inch-wide spool, and two big man-sized knobs on the handle.

It once held two hundred yards or so of the finest Japanese gut in twenty-pound test. Let me tell you about this here reel:

It was in Alaska, before the Big One, up around Juneau way where everybody's sport is salmon fishing among the straits, channels, and waterways of the Inland Passage.

This was in those days when all you had to worry about was where the next meal was coming from, and where salmon had to be pretty big to get a commercial troller to go fishing on his day off, which many did for sport.

Fishing was to Juneauites what skiing is to people in Steamboat Springs, Aspen, or Sun Valley; and what quilting bees were to folks in Aroostook County, Maine. During the season everyone went out, the kids and their teachers, the banker, tailor, the bull-dozers in the mine, the governor, the town loafers, the legislators, the office girls from the Federal Building, the pearl diver from the local hash house, an ancient sourdough who swamped out the pool hall, and even a *fille de joie* from Squaw Town.

The salmon came big, all right, a chinook (called "king" there) weighed up to sixty pounds or more. Most of the sport fishing was done by the "stripping" method. This is not the same type of stripping they talk about in Puget Sound or off the coast, which merely means fishing with strips of bait.

The true Alaska-type stripping got its name from the way the line was stripped in after letting the bait down to the bottom. Because those big Icy Strait hogs cruised right on the bottom and could not be enticed up like a coho, to get down to them you had to drop your bait through several layers of "trash" fish like halibut, flounder, lingcod, and even worse, that hideous, four-horned repulsive sculpin called the Irish Lord.

As soon as the bait hit the bottom, you started a fast retrieve, hand over hand, stripping the line in with big loose coils on the deck at your feet. The stripping imparted a wounded herring action to the bait, and no matter how fast you stripped, if a big chinook took after it he'd get it before it broke water. If you stripped too slow, you got a trash fish, and if it stayed on the bottom too long you got an Irish Lord.

Some fishermen did not even use a reel. They used a gallon strawberry jam can, and the line was simply attached to the can and wound loosely around it. When a chinook took the bait, he immediately charged back down into the cold depths, and often as not headed off in the direction of the Pribilofs. The line whizzed out so fast that burned fingers were common and slices to the bone frequent.

If you could not stop the salmon by the time all the line was out, you simply tossed the can, rod, and all into the water as a buoy and followed it by boat.

The more sophisticated angler used a large-size single-action reel and played the salmon in the gentlemanly way, but both methods used a six-to-eight-foot rod in up to twelve-ounce weight, of Tonkin cane, which had enough whip to tire the fish and enough power to horse him in when you did.

Mostly herring was used for bait, and either a pennant-shaped filet was cut and used as a shimmering strip of black and silver, or the usual plug-cut herring was hooked on. At that time we also used whole herring with two-hook rigs and this was where the so-called salmon "mooching" originated.

There were variations to this rig. Some used two hooks in a way to engage the whole herring, but first cut off the tail and slit the stub back an inch or so. One hook was inserted through both lips to keep the mouth closed, and the other just abaft of center under the backbone so the herring was held in a curved position. When adjusted right the bait darted from side to side as it was stripped in.

Some fishermen obtained this curve by pushing a four-inch sliver of cedar lengthwise into one of the eyes, twisting it over and under the backbone. In this way the curve was adjusted for proper action.

My first expedition cost me a half week's pay for an outfit, including the new reel, and the price of the passage on the halibut schooner converted into a party boat. On the run out to Marmion Island we all rigged up. The gut lines were soaked first in saltwater held in a one-gallon can, and when limber were ready for use. The easiest way, after the line was once spooled, was to throw the whole reel in a pail of water.

Anchoring off the point in a tide rip in about twenty fathoms, all lines went over the sides before the boat even coasted down on the anchor. Since this was my first time out stripping, I watched the others and then followed suit.

On my second cast and strip-in, I felt my head buzzing and a giddiness swept over me. Sweat beaded out on my face in spite of the raw wind sweeping off Taku Glacier. Just as my herring almost reached the surface, the biggest, meanest-looking chinook salmon I had ever seen on the prowl shot up out of the depths and hooked his jaws on the bait.

The next thing that happened was two hundred yards of expensive Japanese silkworm gut burned through the agate guides and spinning my new reel which didn't have the brake on, like an outboard motor. On each revolution those two big knobs cracked my fumbling knuckles.

When the salmon reached the end of the line he just kept going, taking everything but the rod and reel with him, and leaving me with a sick look on my face.

The sick look was real. It was later diagnosed as food poisoning contracted from some tainted pork sandwiches, but everyone thought I was just seasick and so I had to suffer through four hours of excruciating convulsions before we got back to port and medical attention.

Don't talk to me about "strip fishing."

9.

A Seagoin' Cheechako*

It was my first year of fishing, and like most cheechakoes, I had come to Alaska in the spring of '38 inspired by those hundred-dollar days I had heard so much about. But unlike most, I had been fortunate enough to secure the *Midget*, a twenty-four-foot troller.

My worst experience in the *Midget* was off Snail Point on Noyes Island, twenty-five miles from Craig, in southeastern Alaska.

The hull of the *Midget* was so rotten you could almost poke your finger through it. The pilothouse and deck were so full of holes you could almost (as Halibut John said) throw a cat out through it. I had a large bilge pump on her, and it was necessary to use it every two hours to keep from sinking, even at the dock.

When the blow hit, it was seven o'clock in the evening and we were eight miles out to sea. It was, according to the natives the worst storm in years.

I hadn't caught a thing all day, but suddenly one of my poles jerked violently. A fish at last! Almost simultaneously a strong gust heeled the boat over. Then there was a dead calm. In my excitement, I paid no heed to this, and landed my fish, a fifty-pound king salmon. Being a greenhorn, even when the rest of the fleet pulled up gear and started for home, I did not become alarmed.

While standing in the trolling cockpit, working the line in on the gurdies, the full storm hit. The boat shuddered and shook. A big wave washed over the deck, nearly taking me overboard. I clung to the coaming and waited for the boat to right herself. To my great relief she did, and I managed to pull myself on deck and make it into the pilothouse.

My poles were still down and my fish still trailing astern. I had no time for that now. The waves broke over in great sheets of spray. One moment I would be high on the crest and the next deep in a canyon-like trough, almost enveloped by green-gray water.

* Appearing in the January, 1940, issue of the *Alaska Magazine*, "A Seagoin' Cheechako" was the first story I ever sold. Prior to its appearance on the newsstands, the editor-publisher, Albert Taylor, wrote me on December 19, 1939, from the Pioneer Hotel in Fairbanks:

"Dear Don—Ask at the *Press* (in Juneau) where the supply of my magazines is and show this note and get five copies. Your rewritten story as published is not nearly as good as the draught lost at the *Press*. I think that that is my fault. I suggested some refinements, and you refined a lot of life right out of the story. Watch for this fault in later work."

The fact that the first story I ever sold was lost by the editor and a rewrite from memory was necessary, is ironic enough, but the purpose in reprinting here is mainly to illustrate what teen-agers were up to in the pre-World War II days.

The little stamp mill of an engine danced on its bed, missing a lick frequently now and then. The water crept higher above the cabin floor, as we shipped water with each wave that broke over the boat.

On the crests I scanned the sea for anyone I could hail for assistance, but the rest of the fleet had pulled almost out of sight.

I left the wheel and sprang out on deck to man the pump, just as a huge wave hit the boat broadside and nearly spun her around. I retreated to the wheelhouse again. Just then one of the poles broke and the end of it hit the water as we rolled. It swung across the deck, pinning the wheelhouse door shut. The bilge pump was outside. I was inside, locked in the cramped quarters with the water now nearly knee-deep.

Cold sweat broke out all over me, but I had little time at the moment to ponder the predicament. The flywheel was throwing water like a fire hose. The battery tipped over and the engine began to miss. I left the wheel again and waded down to the cabin to fix the engine. Just then the generator fell off into the flywheel. At the same time the grates fell out of the stove and hot coals rolled across my bunk.

Madly I dashed water on the blankets. Then the pots and pans fell off the shelves, cracking me on the head and shoulders. By this time my fear had turned to angry frustration. Cursing a blue streak, I returned to the wheel.

Something had to be done about the bilge, so I wrested the door open enough to squeeze out. I pumped until red in the face, but made no headway. The water poured in faster than I could pump it out.

I thought about making the beach in my six-foot skiff, but gave up that idea. It would have been fatal even to attempt it.

Even had I made it ashore the surf would have battered us to bits.

Next I tried to get my gear in and found the salmon still hooked. I brought him into the cockpit and tried to stun the fish with the billy, but missed and hit the backbone instead. Then I had a real battle on my hands. I finally gave up and left the salmon beating on the deck and went back to the wheel.

After hours, it seemed, I finally made the Hole-in-the-Wall, between the San Lorenzo Islands. But my troubles were not over. I negotiated the entrance, which was only fifty feet wide and dotted with rocks. The waves were breaking up into the trees on both sides of the entrance. Salt spray cut into my face and nearly blinded me. But I made it.

I didn't even attempt to take the fish to the scow, but dropped the pick in the middle of the channel. The anchor didn't hold so I pulled it up and dropped it again. Three times I did this, and each time drifted farther back toward the entrance—and those rocks.

I couldn't make it hold so I went over to the scow and tried to make a landing. The tiller chain broke, rendering the rudder useless, and I began drifting behind the scow toward the beach. I kicked her astern and bucked wind and tide until I got near enough to the scow to throw a line and tie up. No sooner had I accomplished this than the fish buyer rushed out and chased me away because the cannery tender was due. I backed out again, and then, with the help of the wind, ran head on into the scow!

Drifting downwind, I just missed the bow of another boat, passing to port. But my skiff, trailing astern, took a notion to pass to starboard, with the result I found myself hung up on another man's boat.

Maddened almost to despair, I hacked off the rope and let the skiff drift away.

How I finally maneuvered the *Midget* to the float and a safe landing, with no rudder, is a miracle I cannot yet comprehend.

Stranger yet, how I ever managed to stay afloat in those seas outside. But to be a fisherman in Alaskan waters, one needs more brass than brains, I decided.

My fish? You bet I got him!

PART THREE

The Tidal Shelf

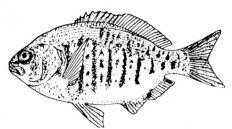

Barred Surfperch

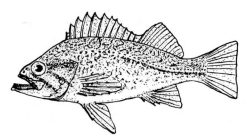

Orange Rockfish

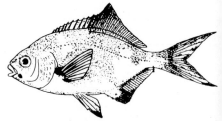

Pile Perch

I.

Salmon in the Surf

The air had an autumn smell and a crisp bite in spite of the sparkling sun. I parked behind the dunes and walked over to the group clustered on the beach. I saw that they included a number of surf casters, with long sticks and big reels pitching bait and lures with heavy pyramid sinkers in the general direction of Midway and Wake. Curiosity began to torment me. In all the years of fishing up and down the Pacific Northwest coast, I'd never seen anything quite like this. Maybe I was missing something.

I had stumbled upon this scene on a lonely stretch of Oregon coast—beach fires, picnic spreads, tents and bait flying oceanward toward the diving squadrons of birds. Scenes like this are not supposed to be in these parts—especially this time of the year.

An Old-Timer with a cherry-brown skin covered with wrinkles and crow's feet shouldered a gunnysack and headed for camp.

"How's fishing?" I asked.

"Fishing?" he repeated, raising his shaggy brows as if he'd never heard of the sport.

"You know," I said. "Whatever it is you do with that rod and reel you're carrying."

"Oh," he snorted. "Naw, not much doin' today. I think I'll go grouse hunting."

Surf fishermen must talk about it, I suppose; but if they do they talk to themselves.

Anchovy

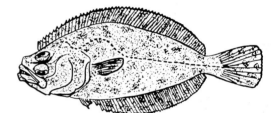

Bigmouth Sole

Humpbacked (Pink) Salmon

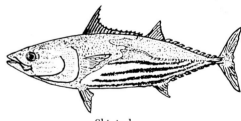

Skipjack

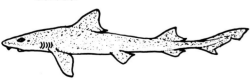

Brown Shark

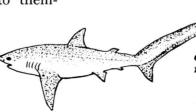

Thresher Shark

Tomcod

I watched the others for a few moments and then walked back to the car. On the way I passed the Old-Timer's camp and found him cleaning a collection of sea bass, snappers, lingcod, halibut, and a striped bass.

"I hope you have as much luck grouse hunting," I said pleasantly.

I stopped on top of the dunes and held my hat against the wind. Autumn clouds scudded by low and dark. Offshore the birds were dipping, wheeling, and screaming. I wasn't on a fishing trip primarily, but this could not but fascinate me. The coastal rivers were still too low from lack of rain for the late fall runs of salmon and steelhead to enter. Trout fishing had fallen off and sportsmen were thinking of deer hunting and bird season.

I had driven down from Portland without anything particular in mind except to kill a weekend. On the way I crossed over the hump of the Coast Range and through the Tillamook Burn. This time of the year it was splashed with spectacular fall colors. I watched for deer and spotted several herds along the Wilson River. Then I spent the rest of the time just prowling the back roads along the coast.

While surf fishing isn't new to the Pacific Northwest by any means, it's at least obscure and in a class by itself. Here salmon and steelhead get all the glamour and publicity. Most fishermen stick to the rivers and lakes, or go offshore in expensive chartered boats. With a few exceptions, such as at the mouth of the Siletz, to fish for salmon or steelhead in saltwater from anything but an oceangoing boat just never occurs to most of us.

Actually, in spite of its rugged coastline, the Pacific Northwest has some of the finest surf and jetty fishing to be found anywhere. And it's virtually unknown. There are hun-

A surf and rock angler on the Northwest coast has all the fishing to himself

dreds of small beaches—and some long stretches—in between the sheer cliffs and storm-lashed rocks from Brookings near the California line all the way to Cape Flattery.

There are more than two hundred varieties of saltwater fish, including sea bass, striped bass, lingcod, flounder, sea trout, halibut, sea perch, sand dabs, sole, kelp

Even salmon can be caught in the surf, if you know where and how.

greenling, and tomcod. This is all year-round fishing; no closed season, no bag limit and no license required, except for salmon and steelhead.

The salt chuckers use anchovies, clams, shrimp, mussels, kelp worms, and the usual jigs, spinners, and wobblers. Most of the surfers use conventional surf rods and reels and heavy tackle. Only an occasional maverick invades this clannish group with modern glass rods and light tackle; and usually it's some inland fisherman who doesn't know any better or isn't equipped with saltwater gear.

I studied the wheeling birds and wondered. The late fall runs of salmon had not yet appeared in the rivers. *Do you suppose they could be milling around out there waiting for the fall rains?* I thought. Once I began reasoning like this I got excited.

My salmon spinning outfit was in the car. It was a two-piece ten-foot glass rod with a saltwater spinning reel that held 275 yards of eight-pound test limp monofilament. It had a twenty-seven-inch cork handle and weighed seventeen ounces. It was tough but whippy and I used it primarily for mooching for salmon from charter boats off the mouth of the Columbia. I rigged it up and tied on a two-ounce silver wobbler and headed back for the beach.

My strange gear marked me as an outlander, but I was too busy watching the birds, studying the wind and surf, to pay any attention. I walked farther down the beach to a bight where I found a comparatively calm and protected spot. I spotted a boil of pilchards about one hundred yards offshore. This really excited me. The pilchards were leaping and threshing about in a frenzy the way I've seen them do from a boat. Schools of coho salmon attack the pilchards by rolling under them, forcing them to the surface. And when he is feeding on the surface the coho salmon is one of the most spectacular of Pacific game fish.

I cast out into the middle of the boil. The undertow caught the lure and straightened out the line. I began retrieving immediately to keep the lure from sinking. Nothing happened—that is until I had all but twenty yards of line in. Then a coho slammed into the wobbler so fast I forgot to set the hook. The momentum of his savage strike carried him almost out of the water. With a mighty swirl he caught the next swell and took off for the thirty-fathom curve.

On the next cast the line jerked just as I started the retrieve. I knew a salmon had swatted it with his tail and would be back for another run. I slowed the lure down slightly and gave it more motion with the rod tip. Then a coho blew a hole in the water and took off in a shower of spray. In the same instant he had the lure and I set the hook hard. He made a couple more jumps and headed north. I followed, trying to gain a little line. Finally he stopped

Surf casting for salmon in the Georgia Strait near the Canadian border.

For a surf fisherman, it's the lonely sea and sky

and I maneuvered the coho into shallow water. He was still full of fight when a swell caught him and carried him up on the sand almost at my feet. It was a bright eleven-pounder.

By this time the wind had risen and the Pacific swells were rolling with great force offshore. I lost the school of pilchards and as I looked back at the surfers' camp I saw that they were calling it a day. But I didn't mind. The weekend was well worth this one moment when I stumbled on a little-known method of salmon fishing that produces when the season is supposed to be dead.

In the weeks that followed I tried many of the other likely spots—near Florence, Yachats, Newport, Taft, Neskowin, Pacific City, Barview and in the vicinity of the Salmon, Nestucca, Siletz, Nehalem and

Umpqua rivers. When I found the birds flying, and the pilchards boiling, I found coho. Most of the time I never saw another fisherman even though the fall weather was at its best and the Pacific in its nicest mood.

It's a paradise for the light tackle caster, this saltwater spinning in the Pacific Northwest. The standard seven- or eight-foot glass rods with corrosion-resistant fittings and reels are ideal for light lures and lines up to six-pound test. Two-handed rods or longer lengths with fairly stiff tips are excellent for casting heavier lures. Large guides properly spaced are very important, and the reels should be of large capacity.

Hunting season almost forgotten, I discovered that fall is the finest season of the year on the coast; its crisp, tingling weather, the birds wheeling in the breezes and the white-laced Pacific waiting with its hoards of untapped inshore fish—including salmon. Then the rains came and the salmon and steelhead moved up the rivers and fall surfing ended for me.

After my first brief encounter that day, which opened up for me a new dimension in fishing, I picked up my prize coho and paraded past the Old-Timer at his beach camp. He looked at my bright fat salmon and the light tackle and almost dropped his pipe.

"That the first time I've ever seen a fish catch a fisherman," he said. "And a salmon at that."

The author spinning for salmon in the surf

2.

Coho Go for Flies

The scene: Bellingham, Washington, and vicinity, including the American side of the Strait of Georgia.

The time: Shortly after World War II.

Conjure a vision of an ex-Navy man trying to get used to civilian life again and enjoying the effort; driving slowly down a lonely beach road scouting the fall run of coho which pours through these narrows on the way across Roberts Bank to the Fraser River.

Imagine then, his outboard motor—without which no self-respecting fisherman in the Pacific Northwest would be caught—left in a Bellingham shop for a transfusion. In the back seat of the car is a two-piece ten-foot hollow-glass surf rod, of a type then almost in the experimental state, and a new-fangled saltwater spinning reel loaded with two hundred yards of eight-pound test limp monofilament.

The spinning outfit is brand-new. It has yet to be exposed to the tang of salt chuck —and so far as this fisherman was concerned, never would be. Nothing had yet been encountered on this trip to give this awkward-appearing outfit any credit. Indeed, it was an irritation and annoyance whenever the car had to be packed or unpacked.

Ahead, through the afternoon haze, there is a flock of gulls wheeling and diving offshore about one hundred yards, maybe less. Their excited cries sound like a run on nylons at a wartime bargain basement sale. An area of about ten or fifteen yards in diameter boils with frenzied candlefish. Here and there a hump of water wells up as predators feed upon the close-packed school.

In the Pacific Northwest waters this means salmon—in this instance, coho salmon.

Looking south I saw another school moving inshore. Far out in the strait I could make out the vague white blurs of the trolling fleet. Up on the point was another flotilla of sport fishermen—in fact, practically every rental motorboat within fifty miles was in use today. Which was precisely the reason I was on the beach instead of out there, too.

Either the boats were trolling deep for chinook, I thought, or they were unaware that coho had moved inshore after candlefish. It wouldn't be long, though, before someone with binoculars spotted the birds. Meanwhile, here I was within one hundred yards of them and helpless as a bug in a bass pond.

I could have launched a light cartop from the sandy beach just below the bluff and rowed out through the kelp—if I'd had a car-top boat. Or if I'd had my motor I could have dashed back to the nearest resort, laid hands on a skiff, and still beaten the mob to the scene. Having neither, I could only watch until the agony became unbearable, then head for home.

Typical coho flies tied with polar bear hair

But if you think this was my unlucky day, you're wrong. I count it as one of the luck-iest in twenty years of fishing for Pacific salmon. This was the day I discarded the last of some deep-rooted notions about coho fishing and sampled an even more exciting *modus operandi*—if that is possible.

But this great awakening actually began in a cow pasture, not there on the beach, and it involved that spin fishing monstrosity with its awkward length and huge fragile guides that I'd been cursing for two weeks. It also involved a type of lure that fisher-men would have laughed at when I first ar-rived in the Northwest. Even today only a few enlightened salmon fishermen know of its wonders. But first the business about the rod.

Driving home that day, thinking about my misfortune in being at the right place at the right time and not being able to do any-thing about it, a thought suddenly occurred to me just as I was entering my friend's ranch yard. I pulled up the car and slapped my forehead. There in the back seat I had the means to reach those cohos, but I had been so busy bemoaning my bad luck that it had never once occurred to me: the new surf-casting spinning gear.

I lost no time breaking out the gear for a closer look. Not being a bait caster I was bound by no preconceived ideas, and after what I'd seen that afternoon my imagina-tion ran wild. First of all, I thought, could I reach out that far with this outlandish outfit? I was a bit dubious, even with spin-ning gear. After all, a hundred yards does-n't seem like much just kicking the idea around, to the inexperienced caster it might as well be a mile. The world's record for bait casting, I remembered, was only a little over four hundred feet.

I put the rod together and tied a one-ounce sinker on the end of the line. Posing in my best surf-casting stance I tentatively aimed the rod at a clump of apple trees at the other end of the two-acre pasture. Across the fence the neighbors, who were eating in their patio, stood up to watch me. I couldn't see the expressions on their faces, but to tell the truth I felt a little silly myself.

I took aim again and made a self-conscious halfhearted cast. To my amazement the sinker sailed completely out of sight. I thought the sinker had snapped off the line, which was still going out.

Finally the line stopped running and I reeled in, walking along as I took up the line. By the time I got to the end it seemed like I'd walked halfway across the county. Just short of the apple trees I found the sinker, still tied to the line. I couldn't believe it. I looked back at the house and saw my friend standing on the back steps, a spot of color in the distance.

I still thought it had been a lucky cast, but to play safe I waved my arms and shouted for my friend to get out of sight so as not to get brained with a hunk of lead. Faintly on the light evening breeze I heard derisive laughter.

Again I took aim and this time used some body English. The line spiralled out and after what seemed like minutes I heard a faint yelp and saw my friend jump like as if jabbed with a needle. Walking back I found the sinker lying among the flowers beside the back porch. The sinker had hit the porch a foot above the door.

Having marked the limits of the first two casts I now paced them off. The first cast had tossed that sinker 333 feet; the second cast, somewhat longer, measured 346 feet. Supper forgotten, I practiced with the new outfit until dark. Toward the last, when I got the hang of it, I could stand in one corner of the two-acre pasture and reach any part of it with that one-ounce sinker.

My sleep that night was interrupted with dreams of standing on Lummi Island and casting a candlefish so far that I had to call a Coast Guard plane to trace it down. There was also a second feature wherein I stood on Cape Flattery and reached every

fishing spot on the West Coast. The next morning the bags under my eyes would have held all my fishing gear.

Bright and early I was again cruising the beach road watching for birds—and my interest wasn't in ornithology. The tide was coming in, bringing with it some fair-sized rollers. The sun came out hot and the smell of tidal flats lay heavy and pungent on the air. I must have covered several miles without a sign of a school. I retraced my route impatiently and finally stopped the car at a likely spot and walked down to the beach for some practice. And here the second factor entered into my great awakening: I had forgotten to bring bait.

While rummaging through my box of spinners, wobblers, and plugs, I came upon some coho flies which I had picked up on the trip just in case I got a chance to try some trolling for hooknoses off Whidbey Island. At home in Oregon coho flies were unobtainable—and besides these were pretty enough to lure the most discriminating fisherman.

Why couldn't you surf cast for coho? I asked myself. They will take trolled flies with reckless abandon at times. It seemed to me that it didn't matter how you got the fly to them as long as it did its business when it got there. And with a rod that you could cast a nautical mile, there seemed to be no good reason why it wouldn't work.

To appreciate fully the heresy I was contemplating, you need a working knowledge of Pacific salmon fishing. Pacific salmon have been caught on artificial lures for at least fifty years, and probably longer if you count the Siwash bone lures. All of these are made to resemble herring or candlefish—the staple diet of the salmon.

The accepted and time-tested method of catching the two most popular salmon—coho and chinook—in saltwater is by some form of dragging a weighted lure or baited hook, such as in mooching, spinning (not to be confused with the use of fixed spool gear), stripping or just plain trolling. The salmon in saltwater is a school feeder and a voracious eater who will often double his weight in a month's time where the feed is plentiful. The king or chinook feeds in deep-water channels, sometimes strikes hard and sometimes just nudges the bait gently. Often when hooked he latches onto the bottom and sulks. Fighting a chinook can be something like bringing up a water-logged hemlock—compared to the coho, at least.

The coho is more often a surface feeder, herding the schools of candlefish inshore or cruising along the surface at the edges of kelp beds. He's a mean customer who will go to any lengths to bust your tackle. The coho weighs in much less than the chinook, averaging ten to twelve pounds. The early runs in the spring and summer average

around six to eight pounds, growing heavier until, by the middle of September, twenty-pounders are often taken.

Because of these peculiarities, over the years certain kinds of tackle had become standardized. Because of strong tides and currents, weight needed to reach the bottom and the popularity of fishing from power boats, this tackle often approached the size of logging rigging. Forty- to sixty-pound lines and thirty-pound test leaders were not uncommon, and many rods could support a fair-sized pole vaulter. But down through the years this kind of gear was found to be best suited for boating salmon in saltwater. After all, when you lose a forty-pound chinook worth fifty cents a pound on the hoof, you're losing a sizeable chunk of mazuma, to say nothing of a couple dollars' worth of gear. Losses like this mean nothing to the well-heeled sportsman, but it does mean something to the thousands of us peasants who enjoy this sport.

The author landing a 15-pound coho caught on a streamer fly

Since the war, however, the development of light strong monofilament nylon lines that sink rapidly and don't require as much weight, as well as improved gear such as light glass rods and better reels, have caused a trend toward lighter gear. The popularity of spinning tackle, particularly, has helped this trend. Spin fishermen regularly catch 20- and 30-pound salmon and steelhead in the Columbia on 5- to 10-pound test line and 4½-ounce spinning rods, even trolling from power boats.

With the coming of lighter gear a few salmon fishermen got the notion of combining it with a streamer fly and after much experimentation a few patterns were developed. These include the Fire Fly, Blue and White, Silver Killer, Coronation, Candlefish Fly and Purple and White. They are all tied on No. 5 or No. 6 tandem hooks. Polar bear hair which has a silvery effect in saltwater is used mainly for the streamers. The most effective flies are those with small spinners ahead of them and the best color seems to depend on the time of day and light conditions. One thing that could not be changed, however, was the salmon's feeding habits, and the simple secret of these fly patterns is that they resemble candlefish when properly trolled.

Coho flies are trolled just under the surface about fifty yards behind the boat. The edges of kelp beds are the most productive spots but it depends on where the candlefish are. The flies are trolled fairly fast but not fast enough to cause them to skip. In rough weather they are trolled deeper, finding the right depth by experimentation.

This sport seems to have originated in the northern waters of Puget Sound and it is gradually spreading southward to other salmon-fishing areas.

All of which brought me back to the question: Why won't a coho take a cast fly? The answer seemed to be that there was no reason at all why he shouldn't. Accordingly I lost no time selecting a Silver Killer and rigging up for a practice session. The problem was to use enough lead to cast out where the salmon would be and yet not

The Siletz River "Jaws" near Taft, Oregon, is an ideal spot for salmon fly casting

enough to pull the fly too deep. After a half hour or so of trial and error I finally came up with a rig that wouldn't snap off the sinker when I cast and yet was light enough to give the fly a good action when reeled in fast. This consisted of a weird arrangement including a one-ounce sinker, a plastic bubble and thirty inches of five-pound test leader, all properly swiveled.

I couldn't get the distance I did the night before, but managed to put the fly out about three hundred feet. Retrieving worked out fairly well, too, when I got the knack. In the midst of this experimentation I thought I felt a light strike and when I reeled in I had a twelve-inch herring!

I didn't have long to wait for bigger game. About this time the tide started to turn. Glancing down the beach I spotted a flock of birds about a half mile away and just offshore. Quickly I gathered up my gear and drove to the spot. The dust in the road had hardly settled by the time I was at the water's edge and ready to cast.

Just offshore at this point was a thick kelp bed lying parallel to the beach. It was useless to cast across this, but a few yards on there was a clear channel through the kelp about ten yards wide. At this spot the rocks and the background partly obstructed my casting, but there was no choice.

The first cast fell in the kelp and I was able to jerk it loose by quick action. The next fell clear but far short of the feeding fish. I made several more casts without success, but I noticed that the candlefish were moving in closer as the coho took their toll. On one cast I felt a hefty strike which could have been anything, including a snag.

Then, just as I started a retrieve I saw a V-shaped wake heading for the fly and a dorsal fin sticking out of the water like a small shark. I watched it fascinated—then

it hit the fly. The surface boiled for an instant and then a coho made a spectacular leap that took him four feet into the air.

But the ecstacy was short-lived. The coho shook off before I could set the hook. Reeling in the stub end of my gear I saw what had happened. He hadn't thrown the hook; he'd pulled a typical coho trick—rasped the leader across his sharp gill covers and cut it. Rigging up again, I tied a length of cuttyhunk between the fly and leader.

By now the school had moved into the opening in the kelp bed, and the birds even swooped on my lure as it sailed out on each cast. I paused to wipe sweaty palms. Then, as relaxed as possible, I took another try at it. This time the fly sailed out almost effortlessly in the longest cast of the day. As the fly fell right in the school I felt a quick surge of excitement.

Just as I started the retrieve, with all the slack taken up, a coho sliced through the water and hit. The rod tip jerked sharply a couple of times and then he came out of the water in a shower of spray, scattering the birds and fighting like seven devils.

A coho is a tricky guy and he never gives up the fight. Often the first thing he does when hooked is to wrap the leader around his head several times making it tough to play him with his head down and mouth closed. This time, though, the quick retrieve of the spinning reel and the whippy action of the rod must have confused him. I was able to keep the line tight even in his rushes. The lively rod enraged him so much he grew reckless and sapped his own strength. In ten minutes, before he knew what had happened, I had him on the beach —a nice, bright eight-pounder. And in less than an hour, when the candlefish disappeared, he was joined by two others ranging from five to fourteen pounds. I was almost glad it was over. I couldn't have stood much more excitement in one day.

Feeling somewhat like Marco Polo returning from the Orient with exotic spices and loaded with wealth, I left for home the next day in time to meet the coho runs in the coast streams with my newly acquired technique and bag of coho flies.

At home the biggest run of coho in twenty years had piled up off the coast rivers, waiting for the first rains. But as the hot dry weather held on past the normal time, Oregon fishermen grumbled and stewed impatiently and hoped they'd never see that damned sun again. Millions of salmon milled offshore all up and down the coast, but the only fishermen catching them were the ones who went out into the open sea after them.

It was an ideal situation for my new bag of tricks and, not being able to keep a good thing to myself, I called Bill Osborne, my fishing sidekick, whetted his interest with the news that I had an inside track on something, and picked him up on the way to the coast. At the mouth of the Siletz, where reports indicated one of the biggest

concentrations of coho at the moment, we stopped. The river inside the bar was lined with fishermen. Some coho and a few chinooks had been taken but apparently the fishing was sporadic. No one, though, offered to leave and give us a place because at any moment the tide might bring a school inside the bar. We finally found elbow room farther out on the spit.

When I tied on a coho fly I heard a couple of snickers and caught the nearest fisherman grinning at my equipment.

"What are you fishing for?" he asked casually. "Fur-bearing steelhead?"

If he would watch closely, I informed him, he would witness a new and spectacular method of salmon fishing that could possibly revolutionize the sport—providing there were any feeding coho within striking distance.

He didn't bat an eye, but when the fly sailed out and fell just short of Guam a look of approval appeared on his face. Nothing happened on this cast, nor during the next hours. Then suddenly I saw just beyond the breakers what looked like a fin chasing the fly in. I yelled and Bill looked just in time to see the coho hit, roll savagely, and

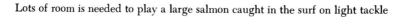

Lots of room is needed to play a large salmon caught in the surf on light tackle

take off for the clouds. The battle that followed gathered a crowd down from the riverbank and no one was more intrigued than Bill.

The coho, a fat, shiny beauty weighing exactly fifteen pounds, never once gave up the fight, but I gained line on him steadily with the big spinning reel and finally a long roller caught him and brought him onto the beach without the aid of a gaff. When it was all over Bill's face was alive with interest. He took over my rod and examined the gear in detail as if there was some trick to it which was not readily apparent.

And his interest in the gear was more than academic. You see, the rod and reel that I had cursed for two weeks on my trip north before I discovered a use for it, belonged to him. He had bought the outfit in a weak moment six months before and, I suspect, loaned it to me for my trip just to get it out of his sight. Right then and there he repossessed it.

And, what was worse, I had to give up one of my precious coho flies to pay the rent.

3.

Admiralty Island Clambake

Rain slopped down steadily on the pilot-house deck, as only rain can in southeastern Alaska. Sid and I listened to Johnny swearing in sort of a falsetto grumble, as only Johnny could, while we got ready to shove off in our thirty-foot *Peter B.* Sid and I exchanged glances and grinned.

"Let me tell you," Johnny said, "if this blessed engine conks out and we pile up on the rocks, I'm gonna make you both swim all the way back to Juneau."

Oliver Inlet, on Admiralty Island, was noted for its delicious butter clams. Sid and I had reasoned, toward the end of an evening in a waterfront bistro, that if we could convince Johnny of the commercial demand for these clams perhaps he would contribute his share of the boat to the trip. Then, while he worked the mud flats with a profit motive, Sid and I could do some fishing for a change.

Johnny had been skeptical. First, he knew better than to trust us. Second, he had an abiding distaste for any activity wherein the profit was in doubt. Third, he had an almost neurotic fear of the treacherous Inland Passage waters.

A chronic worrier, his pink cheeks grew pinker and his soprano voice higher pitched the more worried he became. We'd sunk all our dough into a scheme for making a couple of fast bucks commercial fishing and wound up the worst season in Alaska's history without enough gas to get us back to the States. Some of the boys had had to sell their skiffs to get fuel for the return trip. Ours was so beat up we couldn't even give it away.

It looked like we were stakebound for the winter and so Sid and I decided to make the most of it. After all summer on a fishing boat, neither of us had wet a sport-fishing line—which is like saying that bacon doesn't agree with eggs. Neither of us had much use for commercial fishing, especially after the summer fiasco. On the other hand if we had been marooned on a desert island with Marilyn Monroe and a fishing rod we'd have put her to work tying flies.

If Johnny had suspected our real reason for this voyage he would have blown a gasket. Sid and I chuckled gleefully and scurried around loosening lines and moving other craft out of the way. The *Peter B.* had been one of the first boats in and we were tied up next to the dock. The late arrivals had tied up outside of us until the rows of boats were stacked five deep. It was not only difficult to get a thirty-footer free of this maze, but Johnny also made loud noises about losing our place next to the dock.

After we pulled out, incidentally, our

move upset the boat harbor routine for days. It was the custom for those living on outside boats to reach theirs by crossing the decks of the others. Most of the boats looked alike in the dark so you had to count the boats as you crossed them until you came to yours. When we pulled out it left the last boat one berth nearer the dock. We later learned that when Halibut John's Thlinget bride returned late one night from a nearby pub she, though her arithmetic was generally accurate even under full sail, walked across her own boat and stepped blithely into the bay.

We got free from the boat harbor with only one mishap. Sid accidentally dragged a heavy spring line across the Charlie Noble (stovepipe to you) of a small troller. The pipe disintegrated in a puff of black soot. Johnny would have quit right then if the irate owner had not popped up on deck waving his fists and demanding we come back and talk damages.

Finally we put the dock behind us and rounded the buoy off the rock dump. Immediately we hit dirty weather and a heavy head wind funneling down Gastineau Channel. To Sid and me this was escape from stifling boredom. The rainy season had begun in earnest and our recreation had simmered down to a walk to and from the post office on mail-boat days, and to and from the employment office on other days. Since Johnny shunned any unnecessary recreation we had cooked up an appeal to his fiduciary instincts.

Sid was the exact opposite of Johnny. Bubbling over with energy and with an appealing disregard of consequences, he was always cooking up some sort of deviltry. I fell in easily with Sid's schemes; when I was alone with Johnny I found myself borrowing some of his troubles. We three,

however, were buddies and had been through enough together to make all the normal allowances.

None of us had ever been in Oliver Inlet. In a rare moment of caution Sid and I had sneaked a look at the *Coast Pilot*. The description of the place left little to the imagination:

"Oliver Inlet has its entrance on the south side of Stephens Passage . . . through a narrow neck one mile long and 200 yards wide. The inlet is accessible only at high water to boats and small craft, the narrow entrance being barred at low water by a natural dam of rocks, over which the water pours like a waterfall except at slack water. At high-water slacks, small vessels drawing not over six feet can enter. Tidal currents in the entrance have a velocity of 6 to 8 knots, forming heavy swirls. . . ."

We hid the book under the seat cushion and once under way we slyly adjusted our speed so that we would arrive at the entrance on high-water slack.

Off Marmion Island Light I relieved Johnny at the wheel and pointed the bow toward the inlet, four miles across Stephens Passage. When Johnny got off the seat to go below he accidentally knocked the cushion to the deck, exposing the *Coast Pilot*.

"So that's where that blessed book is," he said. "I've been looking all over for it."

He took the *Coast Pilot* below with him. Sid and I exchanged glances and I advanced the throttle a little. Once out in the passage we ran into even dirtier weather blowing down from Taku Glacier. To make matters worse the run across put the heavy seas on our beam. Spray slapped viciously against the pilothouse windows as the *Peter B.* threatened to dip her trolling poles under as we wallowed along.

I could hear dishes and pans rattling to

the deck in the cabin below and I had hopes Johnny would be too busy at the moment to look at the *Coast Pilot*. Off our port bow I could see a familiar landmark—a graveyard of ships bulking in the shallow water just inside a small cove. An object reminder to the foolhardy.

As I approached the bottleneck entrance to the inlet, I saw that we were right on time. The tide was high and slack. We had to go through now before the tide turned or we would never make it. I aimed the boat directly between the rocks on either side of the opening and advanced the throttle.

At this point Johnny fought his way up from below and grabbed for the wheel. "Turn this damn boat around!" he yelled. "I've just read the *Coast Pilot!*"

Sid made an effective block, keeping him away from me and at the same time trying to reason with him that we would make it all right since we drew only three and a half feet of water.

"You can't depend on that. Turn around before we pile up!"

For a long moment the three of us seemed suspended in action like a motion picture suddenly stopped. Johnny was still swearing in his peculiar soprano voice and poised to spring his big bulk at me. Bald-headed Sid had his wiry little body braced between us. I had my frame draped around the wheel as if I were afraid it would jump out of my hands.

Just then the *Peter B.* rocked sharply fore and aft.

"We've hit a reef!" Johnny cried.

Sid and I turned about the same pasty shade of green. But the boat surged on merrily and we were inside at last. Our collective sighs of relief sounded like a steam exhaust.

We ran to the far end of the inlet and anchored in three fathoms just inside a small cove. The inlet itself was long and narrow, shaped somewhat like an extended gourd. Densely wooded mountains rose all around us and high peaks at the far end extended upward out of sight in the overcast. The inlet was a perfect harbor, we thought.

No sooner had we anchored than the gale broke. Fortunately our hook was buried in the mud. But we were to discover that, far from being a perfect anchorage, Oliver Inlet was like a funnel through which the williwaws shrieked down from the inland mountains on the island. Under the force of the wind the boat yawed violently and then heeled over on her beam. The three of us took refuge in the pilothouse until it had blown itself out.

Afterwards we went out on deck and launched our six-foot skiff. Whitecaps were kicking up.

"You and your blessed ideas!" Johnny said to the world in general.

At that moment I discovered we had lost one of the skiff's oars in the blow.

"That's fine," Johnny commented. "Here we are, after jumping a reef to get in the place and we can't even get ashore!"

"Maybe I can make it with one oar," I volunteered. I dropped down into the skiff and as I did so Johnny shoved it away from the *Peter B.* with a calloused laugh.

"All right, start rowing, wise guy!"

I might as well have been on a pumpkin seed. The waves tossed me about at will and when I tried to use the oar it only made the skiff spin around in circles.

Finally I hit upon the idea of clamping the oar to the transom with one hand and sculling with the other. It was only a few yards to the beach and in this manner I eventually made it.

On shore I pulled the skiff out of the water and started looking for a piece of driftwood suitable for making an emergency oar. On the other side of the cove I spotted a familiar object. I waded out and retrieved the lost oar.

When I returned to the *Peter B.*, Sid was overjoyed. "It's a good thing you found it," he said. "Johnny's growling around like an onery bear. If the tide had been right he'd have pulled out without you. If we're going fishing we better get him ashore with a shovel before he changes his mind and sneaks off without both of us."

"Maybe we'd better lift the distributor rotor," I suggested.

"Good idea, I'll get it while he's cooking supper."

Johnny was in a bad mood but after a good meal under our belts we all agreed things could be worse. Tomorrow, Johnny told us, we would go up on the tideflats, load up with clams, and go home. Tomorrow, Sid and I told ourselves, we would hike across to Seymour Canal for some real fishing.

Sitting in the pilothouse smoking after supper, Sid wondered out loud if there were any fish here in Oliver Inlet. We decided there must be, so Sid dragged out a skate of halibut gear.

"What'll we use for bait?" I asked.

"Shucks, I forgot about that," Sid said.

"Try some sourdough batter," Johnny piped up. "They claim it's good for everything from hot cakes to hooch."

He was only kidding, but Sid took him up on it. "It's worth a try," he said cheerfully.

He went down to the galley and got a wad of sourdough from the starter behind the stove and molded it around a halibut hook. Then he dropped the line over the side and secured it to the rail.

Johnny, still worrying about the williwaw we had encountered that day, insisted we take turns on anchor watch that night. We turned to willingly enough, but as the night wore on the man on watch would barely wake up in time to wake up his relief, who promptly fell asleep again when he reached the pilothouse.

I was sleeping on watch about midnight when awakened by a violent pounding on the side of the boat. Thinking we had drifted onto some rocks I turned on the deck lights and rushed outside. Sid's hand line was snapping and twitching along the side of the hull as if bewitched. I grabbed the heavy line and heaved in, but it took all my strength with my feet braced against the rail to budge whatever was on the other end. It was like trying to pull the bottom out of the bay.

I yelled for Sid and Johnny and they came running out in their skivvies. All three of heave-ho'd on the line and slowly brought it in until the mysterious thing on the hook broke the surface.

"It's a devil-fish!" Sid cried. But then the fish turned sideways and we got a better look. It was a huge halibut. "Holy mackeral—er—halibut! It'll go 150 pounds at least!"

"What'll we do with the bloomin' thing?" I wondered.

"Cut it loose," Sid suggested. "I hate halibut."

"If you blessed guys cut that fish loose I'll cut your blessed throats," Johnny threatened. "That there halibut'll bring us two cents a pound at the cold storage."

We got the monster aboard and on ice in the hold. Sid and Johnny went back to bed and I went back to my watch. But the night was not over. No sooner had they gone back to sleep when I began to imagine the boat was in motion. I peered through the pilothouse windows at the dark wooded shoreline and I could have sworn we were drifting. Alarmed I switched on the spotlight and swept it across the beach. It turned out that we had only been swinging at anchor. Just then I saw a movement on the beach. I focused the beam on it. There a few yards away, was the biggest bear I had ever seen.

Again Sid and Johnny came a-running in their scanties. As they crowded into the pilothouse the brownie reared up to his full formidable height and made a couple of passes at the light beams.

"Golly, look at that brownie!" Sid breathed. "Hold the light on him while I get the gun."

But Johnny drew the line there. Digging clams was one thing, but wrestling with the carcass of an eight-hundred-pound Admiralty brownie was another. Thinking of our projected fishing trip, Sid and I said nothing.

At daybreak the next morning we had breakfast and rowed ashore. When Johnny saw us unpacking our fishing equipment, he swore.

"So that's why you blessed guys wanted to go clam digging. Now I suppose you'll leave me here to do all the work."

"We'll be back in an hour," Sid said lamely. "We're only going a little ways up the trail."

I got Sid aside and whispered: "Did you get the distributor head?"

He nodded with a wink. Leaving Johnny to the clams, we headed up the trail over the portage to Seymour Canal. We were so glad to get off the boat and out into the woods on a fishing trip once more that we fairly ran the half mile across the portage. Once down on saltwater again we followed the shore of the arm until we came to a fair-sized creek.

"This looks good to me," Sid said.

I was already jointing my rod. I rigged out a four-pound test leader with a hook and split shot, and baited up with single salmon eggs, stringing them on the hook and pushing them up on the leader.

I heard Sid yell and rushed down to the water. "Look, there's a run of dogs coming in!"

The creek was alive with a late run of dog salmon, their fins poking out of the water. The dog was considered a trash fish by most residents. In fact the fox farms trapped them for animal feed.

"There should be some Dolly Varden in among 'em looking for spawn. There always are."

I whipped my line out among them and drifted down through a fan. Instantly the water exploded with a Dolly on the end of my line.

"Wow!" yelled Sid.

I shot a side-look at him and saw that he had one on, too. After a few moments my fish ran into shore and I beached it—a fat fifteen-incher. Sid was still working his and not making much headway. I moved down to give him room and caught two more about the same size. When Sid finally landed his it proved to be a bright six-pounder.

I hooked and landed the next one, a twenty-incher that I had to chase down to the bar at the mouth of the creek before I could work it in. Sid hooked into another small one or two and then grew tired.

He took off his leader and tied a treble hook to the line. "Watch this," he said.

Sid cast almost across the creek and dragged the hook back in short jerks. About the third jerk the hook stopped as if snagged and then the explosion came. A large dog salmon took to the air, hooked near the tail. The salmon zipped back and forth across the creek, up- and downstream like a balloon with all the air suddenly released, with Sid yipping gleefully at every jump. It was hard to tell if he had caught the salmon or if the salmon had caught him. When the fish was tired Sid removed the hook and released it again.

Toward noon our creels were full of eating-size Dollies and Sid had strung several large ones on a short piece of cord. The Dolly Varden was a despised fish at the time, with a bounty of ten cents on their tails, but to my mind this fighting member of the char family was and still is one of our finest freshwater game fishes. Also, a good deal of hokum about their destructive tendencies has been disproved.

"Let's go upstream a ways," Sid suggested. "Maybe we'll get a crack at some steelhead."

I bent down to get my gear and heard Sid gasp.

"We got company!"

I straightened up and saw three brownies working the creek about a hundred yards above us. My muscles turned to glue as I thought of all the Alaskan bear stories I'd listened to. We heard a series of grunts and roars in the dense undergrowth on the other side of the creek and presently two more crashed into view and continued what seemed to be a grudge fight.

Suddenly they got our scent and all five stopped what they were doing and stood up for a better look.

"I think I've had enough fishing," Sid gulped, white-faced.

I was already backing downstream. Sid caught up and passed me, his short legs moving like a pinwheel. When we reached

saltwater again we headed for the portage at a dogtrot. After about a mile we risked a backward look. One of the bears was still following us, ambling along behind at a respectable distance. When we slowed down he slowed down, when we speeded up he did likewise. Farther back two more brownies were in sight.

I remembered the fish we were lugging with us. I emptied my creel on the run. "I hope he likes fish better than flesh," Sid said and dumped his too. We looked back again before we disappeared around a bend and the brownie had stopped to collect our ransom.

It was almost dark and a fog had rolled in when we reached Oliver Inlet. There was no sign of the skiff. Sid gave vent to some strong language, murmuring what he would do to Johnny if he ever caught up with him. "Leaving us stranded like this on the beach," he muttered, "pursued by wild animals."

Johnny had for a fact taken the skiff to the *Peter B.* We walked around the beach until we came to a point directly ashore from the boat. A minus tide had left the *Peter B.* nearly on dry land. The anchor was out of water and she floated only by virtue of a small tidal basin left when the water receded.

Sid motioned me quiet and dragging a long piece of driftwood we waded out across the mud until we came to the edge of the water. The skiff was tied alongside and we were able to reach it with the driftwood and work it ashore. Then we stepped into the skiff and crossed the short distance to the boat. Once alongside we counted three and then pounded violently on the side of the hull with the oars.

We heard a startled crash inside and a second later Johnny rushed out on deck gripping the shotgun. When he saw us he spat disgustedly and went back below. Sid and I laughed until we were so weak we had to hold each other up.

Sid stood up suddenly. "Do you smell that?" he gasped. I did. We scrambled aboard, tired, wet, bedraggled and half starved, and followed the smell down to the galley. Sid grabbed for the oven door and jerked it open. The aroma that escaped was one so savory, so delicious, that it left nothing on earth to be desired.

In the oven, in a steaming pan, were two dozen butter clams, spread with chopped onions and buttered bread crumbs seasoned with pepper, salt, and paprika, practically swimming in butter and browned to a turn. There was also a hot cheese sauce to go with them.

Johnny pushed us out of the way gruffly and served up our supper. After stuffing

ourselves until the seams were splitting we stretched out on the bunks while Johnny got up and cleared the dishes.

"I hope you blessed guys are satisfied," he grunted.

"We got what we came for, didn't we," Sid murmured. "Oh, those beautiful, sumptuous clams!"

"No thanks to you mugs," Johnny reminded us. "Come on, I want to show you something."

We dragged ourselves up and followed him to the hatch cover. He shoved it aside and we looked in. We saw at least three washtubs full of butter clams.

"It's a good thing somebody on board thinks about paying for the gas and oil. Especially when he's got a couple of shiftless sportsmen to put up with."

And that blessed, wonderful guy was looking straight at me and Sid.

Bank plunking for striped bass on the Coos River

4.

Dozin' for Stripers

It was one of those sunny days with a chilling wind, so common to the San Francisco Bay area. It was a weekday, but my neighbor in the same duplex where I lived on Lake Merritt in Oakland—ex-Oakland Oaks pitcher, Lefty Darrow, and I were taking it off to go fishing.

We were off because we couldn't wait to try out the little twelve-foot Penn Yan that Darrow had borrowed from a friend on condition that he paint it. We had spent the past two weeks in our spare time scraping and repainting the boat in the garage.

Then we had loaded up our fishing gear and lunches and driven to Richmond where we launched the boat under the lee of Point San Pablo.

The wind kicked up quite a chop and we took spray aboard as we headed out into the channel. I never had fished in the bay area before, and had never even seen a striped bass on the hook. Darrow was my guide, skipper, and, hopefully, savior if this dinky boat capsized. It did not, however, and an hour later we were bobbing under a placid sun and half dozing contentedly in the main

Tidal rivers, meandering through coastal lowlands, are ideal waters for shad and striped bass

ship lane leading to Vallejo Navy Yard. Every time a destroyer or cruiser sliced by, the bow wake sent us into some wild gyrations, waking us up.

Suddenly my rod doubled and I came awake with a shock—only to find Darrow had reached over and jerked my line as a joke. Now he was doubled up with mirth. After checking my two bait hooks and letting the lead out to the bottom again, I settled back down, tipped my hat over my eyes, and dozed off again. The next time the rod bent double, I sat up angrily to tell Darrow to knock it off.

This time, however, the line, bait, and everything were headed for Vallejo, and Darrow was dozing himself. My wild tussle woke him up, however, and I pumped the fish in—a twenty-five-pound striper. Just as I netted it, Darrow also hooked into one, a twelve-pounder.

This was my first encounter with the magnificent imigrant from the East Coast —for stripers are not native to the Pacific. The first stripers were brought west by rail

as young fingerlings and released into San Francisco Bay in 1879. Another planting was made in 1882. Like the shad, also brought from the East and planted in the Pacific, they spread northward to Coos Bay and its tributaries, and the Umpqua drainage. Some have been taken in the Columbia.

The first recorded catch in Oregon was at Coos Bay in 1914, and the runs have increased steadily since then. By 1945, a quarter million pounds of striped bass were landed commercially from Coos alone. From 1941 to 1960 the annual average was about one hundred thousand pounds.

The striper fishery in northern waters, however, has never been considered important to commercial fishermen. In the Coos Bay area, millions of pounds have been discarded as waste by gillnetters after salmon and other species—in that area the striped bass is considered a "trash fish" for some inexplicable reason—and the annual wastage, plus the increasing pollution of those waters has damaged the striped bass sport fishery severely.

Such news must be shocking to fishermen from the East where the striper is king. The native range of this species in the Atlantic extends from the Saint Lawrence River to Florida. In 1879 when some homesick pilgrim brought the first 125 out to the bay area by tank car, no one knew whether the transplanting would take or not. An anadromous fish, a thirty-pound female will lay as many as 1,500,000 eggs, probably one of the most prolific of all fishes. Within ten years after the San Francisco planting, the striper was supporting a commercial fishery. In 1935 the California legislature made the striper a game fish.

Stripers like brackish water of bays and estuaries. They feed on sea worms, crabs, shrimp, squid, eel, forage fish, usually in a

Part of the salmon fleet in the Seattle area

school. They seem to start biting on cue and stop the same way, all at once.

Perhaps one of the reasons the striper is held in such low regard north of the bay area is the impression they deplete the salmon and steelhead. There is no scientific basis for the assertion that stripers prey up-on salmon and steelhead to any unnatural degree. As a matter of fact, salmon and steelhead also feed upon young stripers if they get the chance.

The real enemies of fish life, stripers and salmon included, are unabated pollution and too much commercial pressure.

Bill Roberts, Coos Bay angler, plays a fighting shad on the Millicoma River

5.

Aquavit on the Millicoma

The Millicoma River—or North Fork Coos, if you insist—rolled swiftly under pressure of an August freshet. Rain came down so hard it splattered against the muddy surface. Besides the clumps of floating debris there were enough stray prime logs floating toward the sea to put a couple of kids through college.

A tug, its running lights glowing in the dusk, appeared around the bend, moving at unusual speed with the fast outgoing tide, towing two block-long rafts of logs to the Coos Bay mills.

"That's why this is a good striped bass hole," said Bill Roberts, from under his Aussie Digger hat. Bill is the proprietor of Penny's Tackle Box in Coos Bay, and lives for little else but fishing. "The tugs have to throttle hard to swing around this bend, and the prop wash keeps digging away at this hole."

We were bank fishing for stripers one evening during the late August rains, a few miles up the river from the bay, and in one of the few places on the West Coast you can plunk for stripers.

In addition to Roberts there were Ira Sturdivant, a local guide; Dr. Al Buck, an ebullient Coos Bay dentist-sportsman; and I. We were hosting some crew members of the M/S *Parrakoola*, a Swedish mo-torship on the Australia-Vancouver-Coos Bay-San Francisco circuit. The ship arrives here every four months, and each time it is a signal for a series of "fishing parties" for crew members. This time we had along Bob Perrson, fourth engineer of the *Parrakoola*, and Jan Aronsson, the radio operator.

Bob had brought on this trip a supply of authentic Digger hats, so this expedition to the Millicoma had a jaunty, if water-soaked, appearance. Bob was a Swede who had migrated to Australia about twelve years before and had finally gone back to sea after a time surveying in the Outback. Jan was still a Swedish national, having just completed his military service.

As is the custom in exotic places such as Australia and Sweden, the expedition was supplied with superb Aussie beer, some French cognac, and a Scandihoovian variety of nuclear reaction known as aquavit.

But the real purpose of this excursion was scientific research into the habits of another exotic visitor to the West Coast—*Roccus saxatilis*, otherwise called a rock bass or a rock fish, but more often a striped bass. Unfortunately outglittered in the Pacific Northwest by the more glamorous salmon and steelhead, it has few followers, but those it has such as Bill and Dr. Buck, are devoted ones.

We rigged up heavy saltwater spinning gear, twenty-pound test line (a heavy line is needed to break free from frequent snaggings), sliding swivels with three to four ounces of lead. On a large single hook are impaled chunks of frozen sardines, which in this instance were imported from South Africa.

Casting out from a muddy ledge cleared from a tangle of blackberry and willow, it was possible to throw the bait almost across the ebbing current. All of us snagged up on the first cast, which added to our confusion. But it was fascinating to listen to Bob, a Swede with a heavy Australian accent, react in a colorful dialect impossible to reconstruct.

The North Fork, or Millicoma, is only about eight miles long from tidewater to the forks. There used to be excellent striper fishing all along this stretch, which is easily accessible from the bank. The late fall or early winter is probably the best time, but there is also an excellent spring run. The shad come up this stretch in May and June, the harvest trout (sea-run cutthroat) from August to October; steelhead, chinook, and coho in October and November. So you can see, the Millicoma is a fisherman's river.

We fished the big bend hole until 10:00 P.M. without much luck that time, losing quite a bit of expensive tackle in the process, and finally stumbled back up through the bramble and undergrowth to the cars, drove back to the waterfront, went aboard the *Parrakoola* to Bob's luxurious cabin and told lies the rest of the night about the big monsters taken on other night expeditions.

With hot Swedish coffee, laced with aquavit, all such stories become believable.

Fishing the Millicoma for shad in the evening. Dr. Al Buck holds up one he just landed

6.

Harvest's the Time for Cuts

The August doldrums—or "dog days," as we used to call them back in North Dakota where I was born and raised—have different meanings for those to whom it has any meaning; but for me it means old *Salmo clarkii lewisii*, or *S. clarkii*, depending upon who the authority is, the sea-run cutthroat trout of the Northwest coast.

Actually these sea-runs (also known as harvest trout and bluebacks) start moving in from the salt chuck in late June, but it's usually around August before I get to doing anything about it. By that time the salmon season is peaking and to tear one's self away from that requires some strong motivation.

The coastal sea-run differs from the native Montana or Rocky Mountain black-spotted cutthroat mainly in the layman's eye, in not having the familiar red slash and deep scarlet sides. Instead it is ocean bright like a newly minted dollar, with an iridescent greenish sheen on its back.

The sea-run is native to the coastal streams, spawning in the upper reaches, but moving down into the food-filled tidal pools to grow muscles. There he quickly learns that just outside the mouth of the river, in old Mother Ocean, there is an incredible fecundity of food and life. There are also more predators, so although he's called a sea-run, actually it's more a case of moving in and out of the ocean at will until it's time to go up and spawn.

An adult reaches an average size of sixteen to eighteen inches and is a tough, scrappy bundle of energy. And there is no finer eating fish in the world than a fresh-caught sea-run cutthroat.

His habits are quite different from a salmon or steelhead. He likes to cruise close to shore, especially under the overhanging brush and trees, waiting for goodies to drop in the water, feeding on the changes of tides when the water is enriched again. He hits hard on light tackle and is frequently caught close in on short line, which tends to inhibit his natural tendencies.

Because there is also much food in the tidal reaches, he is best taken on bait such as crawdad tails and spinner and worm combinations. However, he will take conventional flies and artificials and this is a great unexploited sport.

Not being much shucks with flycasting gear, about twenty years ago I had a one-piece, 6-foot, 2½-ounce spinning rod made to order by a Vancouver rod-maker, to which I fitted a miniature Italian-made ultra-light spinning reel loaded with half-pound test line. With this outfit you can cast the tiniest spinning lure a country mile. You can even cast streamer flies with it.

Floating a coastal river for sea-run cutthroat on a languid autumn day

With this outfit you can stand on one bank and pitch a tiny lure across a river and under the overhanging branches on the opposite side. And you'd be surprised how effective this is.

But the main advantage of this outfit is that an eighteen-inch sea-run cutthroat gives you the same kind of action as a fifteen-pound steelhead on heavy tackle.

Picture then a day in August and sneaking off by yourself in the middle of the week

for a day or so harvest trouting. The lower Kilchis and Miami rivers are full of bluebacks, although the latter is posted with new signs along most of its best stretches. But where you do get the line in the water (or if you have a boat and come up from the bay) the action is fast and hot, and there is scarcely another fisherman on the river, most of them being elsewhere salmon fishing.

Move on to the Nehalem and rent a boat

and troll a Flatfish for a while in tidewater, waiting for it to turn, seeing only two other boats and they are fishing for salmon. On the other side of the dunes that hold the ocean back from the bay, the surf is crashing with great force, but all is serene on the river and more so as you move on up out of the estuary and into the lower river. Here and there a jack salmon rolls, and the surface from time to time boils with small fish, upon which some swooping plover are feeding in frenzy.

At the mouth of a creek you see an otter also busily feeding on them, rolling up once to look you over, then going back to his smorgasbord.

You pick up a fish here and there, then tie on a tiny spinning lure and as the tide changes, shut off the motor and drift as you cast inshore plopping the lure under the branches. You can see fingerlings chasing the lure in on the retrieve but outrun them. Meanwhile you've drifted to a backwash under a sandy cliff and see a school of blue-

backs now leaping two and three feet out of water into some overhanging branches.

You throw everything at them, including some chunks of crawdad tails, worms, and grasshoppers, and nothing works although they keep leaping. Then turning your head you see some small red berries, perhaps manzanita, hanging on low branches and see them bobbing up and down in the gentle breeze.

On a hunch you rig up a tiny spinner with red beads, and pitch it across. It hardly hits the water before you have a strike, a sixteen-incher, and the next one hooked is almost identical in size. This goes on until the tide turns and goes slack and the action quits like turning out a light. You are all alone and it is so quiet you are suddenly conscious of crows calling to each other.

The incoming tide brings with it the usual moss and debris and makes fishing difficult, so you quit. After all, it's been a most enjoyable interlude during dog days of August on a tryst with harvest trout.

Fishing writer, Francis Ames (left) and Bill Osborne, with a catch of harvest trout

7.

Nugget Goes for Sea-runs

Sea-run cutthroat (and Dolly Varden, too, in the water of British Columbia and Alaska) are to be found in most coastal streams all the way from California to Bering Sea. In Puget Sound and the waters of the Inland Passage north to Icy Strait, heavy concentrations of both are readily found in saltwater. The usual places are around points of land, close inshore in deep water under steep cliffs, and around the mouths of tributary streams. The only practical way to reach these is by boat, and since most boat fishermen in these waters are primarily fishing for salmon, most sea-runs caught are taken on heavy tackle. Thus they do not excite much sporting interest.

Actually, would they only know it, sportsmen would find unbeatable action on both Dollies and cuts if the proper tackle and lures were used—and one of the most satisfying of all is fly-fishing for sea-runs. For many years only a few experts like Enos Bradner, outdoor editor of the Seattle *Times,* and a few dedicated fly-rod men, knew what sport this could be. Today, however, fly-fishing is growing rapidly in popularity and such tackle should become commonplace around saltwater in future years.

Some of the old conventional patterns used on sea-runs include the Conway Special, the Yellow Hammer, the Royal Coach-

man with hair or feather wings. In British Columbia the best-known are the Black-O'-Lindsay, Teal-and-Red, Roderick Haig-Brown's Brown-and-Silver. Many of the old steelhead patterns, dressed on Nos. 6 or 7 hooks, work fine, too.

The lower Quinault River on the ocean side of the Olympic Peninsula is a famed cutthroat stream, as well as a steelhead river. Most of Quinault Lake and all of the river which empties into the ocean after a wild run through the forest are on the Quinault Indian Reservation and an Indian permit is needed as well as a state license. The Indians regularly take sports on guided trips, however, in their dugout canoes equipped with outboard motors. And this is an expedition that is well worth it just for the boat ride.

The canoes, hollowed out of cedar logs just as was done in prehistoric times, are about twenty to thirty feet long, amazingly light and seaworthy, and with just a ten-horse outboard motor hung on the stern will make speeds you wouldn't believe. The Indians practically live in these canoes from an early age, and their seamanship or canoemanship, if you will, is famed far and wide.

The strangest cut fishing I ever did was from the bank on Rich Passage near Bremerton years ago when I owned a young and untrained female golden retriever named Nugget. The tide was turning and the water boiled through the narrow channel at a speed of six or eight knots, with upwellings, boils, tide rips, and other ominous-looking conditions. I was glad I wasn't out in it with a small boat.

But the cuts were feeding on something and as soon as I started casting a small wobbler into the rips, I began getting violent strikes. Hooked, the cuts would leap two feet out of the water and cause all kinds of commotion. Nugget watched all this nervously, whining and running up and down the bank growling. I didn't pay much attention at first, being rather busy, and knowing that all my efforts at training Nugget to jump in the water and retrieve sticks had so far been unsuccessful.

Suddenly, as I hooked another one, Nugget leaped out into the boiling tidal rip and with powerful strokes headed right for my fish. I didn't know whether to drop the rod and try to save her, or land the fish and hope for the best. As a matter of fact, neither one would have made much difference. I landed the fish while Nugget, caught in the strong rip, was swept far out into the channel. Then I did forget my fish, fearing I was watching my dog lose her life right in front of my frustrated eyes.

Nugget, however, rather than being in trouble, seemed to enjoy the swim. She kept going right out into the middle of the channel, swam around for a while chasing sea gulls, and then swam back through the race to shore, landing some distance below me. Then she trotted back, wringing wet, head and tail high, panting happily, and looking up at me for approbation while she shook water all over me.

After that, I never worried about whether or not Nugget could swim. But I had lost a bird dog and gained a fishing pal.

Indian dugout canoe

8.

Winter Steelheaders Are a Breed Apart

A raw, frigid wind swept out of the coastal range of mountains, bringing with it tapioca snow flurries, scouring the river with erratic gusts that started rigor mortis setting in. I had just hooked a bright ironhead buck on the second drift through a slick at the tail end of this hole, using an Okie Drifter and a sliver of pencil sinker.

It was just before Christmas, on one of the famous coastal rivers that empty into the North Pacific. At this time of year, and under these circumstances, a visitor from elsewhere on this continent would surely think that this was the craziest Yuletide scene ever dreamed up.

Actually, he would be witnessing one of the greatest of Western sport fisheries—winter steelheading.

Most major coastal streams from Cape Mendocino to Cape Saint Elias have one or more runs of the seagoin' rainbow trout called the "steelhead." In fact, in many parts of the Pacific Northwest this trout, which reaches salmon size, is even caught and sold commercially—a practice that aggravates many sport fishermen who consider the ironhead the finest game fish that swims, on the order of the Atlantic salmon, a close relative.

These steelhead runs are divided into two general "races"—the summer and winter fish. It is the summer runs of steelhead that make up the famed fighter of the lower Rogue River and the "half-pounders" of California's Klamath, Eel, Smith, and other streams. Actually these are not half-pounders, but are immature fish averaging about two to three pounds which, if allowed to grow up a little, would turn into some real trophies.

The winter fish generally run larger—along the Oregon coast from nine to fifteen pounds, and up around the Olympic peninsula and Puget Sound tributaries, into an average of about twelve pounds, with an occasional trophy running up to twenty and even close to thirty pounds.

But most of these so-called "trophy" steelhead exist only in the imaginations of outdoor writers. The mathematical chance of catching a steelhead over twenty pounds anywhere in the Northwest, based upon actual creel counts and tag returns, is about one in five thousand. Now, if you like that kind of odds, go ahead and wish for a "trophy" steelhead.

Steelhead caught in British Columbia water are harder to classify from a sportsman's standpoint, because an enormous number of these game fish are caught commercially and go into cans—sometimes as "pink" salmon. But it is known that the steelhead along that stretch do run into the twenty- to thirty-pound size frequently. In Alaskan waters the steelhead is important, too, but not to the extent it is in southern waters.

Depending upon the river, the winter run starts in November and reaches a peak about Christmas, then declines slowly until March or April. After they run in from the sea and begin the spawning cycle, they gradually change color from the mint-bright, steel-backed, firm and solid sea runs to a gradually darkening rosy brown with blotches of bright red on the sides of the head and body. The flesh becomes soft and turns from a delicate pink to a sickly-looking white. The steelhead spawn much the same as salmon, and after spawning do not necessarily die as salmon always do. A steelhead may spawn four or five times, but this is rarely the case. Probably not 10 percent of spawned steelhead survive another spawning cycle.

For years the winter steelheader was a breed of angler unto himself, a unique and special clan, the members of which dis-

Rigid and frigid author holds an 11-pound winter steelhead on the Nestucca, caught on Christmas Eve.

dained the warm winter fireside, preferring to endure the biting winds and freezing cold of unfriendly rivers in barren winter dress. Their badge of honor was the frozen rod guide and the rigid fingers covered with the stinking, greasy, clinging fresh salmon roe which was once used almost exclusively by winter steelheaders.

Their gear was perfected especially for winter steelheading, and as evolved it includes a fiber-glass rod of eight to nine feet length, with a strong butt for handling big fish, and a light limber tip for sensitivity in feeling the bottom in the drift. Nowadays saltwater spinning reels are used a lot, but the experienced steelheaders prefer a free-spooling level-wind conventional casting reel of enough capacity to hold a couple hundred yards of eight- to ten-pound test monofilament.

The use of fresh eggs is fast dying out among steelheaders, not because it isn't effective, which it is, but because the eggs are becoming harder to get and keep, and the new artificial lures are nearly as effective anyway.

Some of these artificials are the Okie Drifter, which consists of plastic roe clusters threaded on a two-hook harness; Spin-N-Glo, a bottom floater with two little wings on it that give it the proper motion; and Okie Bobbers, which are merely round red cork floaters. Sometimes fresh eggs are hung on the above lures, and sometimes pieces of red yarn or flannel. The sinker or weight is usually a piece of pencil sinker which can be pruned off to the proper weight for the circumstances.

The basic technique is to cast into the current above a hole or "lay" and bounce the lure along the bottom as the current swings it into an arc. The lure must be on the bottom, because that's where the fish

are. The water, usually about fifty degrees or colder, makes the fish sluggish. They do not strike hard, but instead seem to just mouth the bait as it goes by their noses. For this reason the drifter must be alert to the slightest tug or unusual action of the bait and set the hook hard immediately. Nine times out of ten it will be a snag or a hang-up, but the tenth time the river will explode.

I once witnessed the behavior of a steelhead in the act of taking a lure. It was in a shallow run in water so clear I could see every detail of the bottom. I could not see the big eighteen-pound steelhead lying there just below me, however, because he blended in so nicely with the bottom. I made a routine cast, and as the lure swung out at the bottom of its arc, it went right past the steelhead's mouth. I suddenly saw it, without hardly turning its head, open its mouth and clamp down gently as the lure went by. I was so fascinated I almost forgot to set the hook.

In recent years, there has been a strong trend toward lighter gear and the use of steelhead fly patterns especially designed for the winter steelheader. All of these patterns are devised to simulate a cluster of fresh eggs bouncing along the bottom. It is an interesting and almost unexplored field of research for the serious student of the angle.

But to get back to my steelhead, which I have just hooked—just as he made his first jump, the morning sun breaks over the top of the mountains to the east in a dazzling, blinding flood of light that is reflected off the river and turns the ice crystals hanging on the trees and brush into a million spectrums of color.

At a moment like this, even the rankest amateur becomes a dedicated, unreconstructible winter steelhead addict.

9.

Those "Other" Fishes

It is astonishing how many people in the Pacific Northwest turn up their noses at those "other" fishes that inhabit the saltwater environment along the continental shelf.

These are the "demersals" (bet you never heard that name before, but I looked it up), or marine species, or bottom fish, or "ground fish" as commercial fishermen call them. Included in this classification are the many kind of rockfish, greenlings, lingcod and true cod, flounder, sea bass, sculpins, red snapper, and even the aristocratic halibut.

In appearance, contrasted to the glamor species like salmon and steelhead, the demersals to the uninformed seem to be creatures that God forgot when He was passing out beauty—indeed, some look as if they have been created with leftover parts. But don't let looks fool you. Beauty, in edible form, is always more than skin-deep.

In the North Pacific, there are more than two hundred demersals classified as food-game fishes, although only about twelve or fifteen of these are regularly sought by anglers, and, as you might surmise, these are the best eating as well as being the most readily available.

Lest I give the wrong impression, there is a substantial group of sport fishermen who

regularly go after bottom species, some of whom even prefer these to salmon and steelhead. An old fishing buddy of yesteryear, Don K. Bagley, a Bend, Oregon, bulk-oil distributor, always fished the bottom even when we were out on the high seas on top of a new salmon run. He simply put on enough lead to get to the bottom of things, and was always the first man with a fish on— a lingcod, flounder, or halibut. These he carefully cleaned and fileted and took home with him. And I noticed he never invited anyone to dinner when he had fresh filet of snapper or halibut steaks.

Another happy thought about the marine bottom species is there is no closed season on them, no license is required, and in only a few places is there any limit placed on the sport catch. (The halibut are strictly regulated to commercial fishermen by the International Fisheries Commission, a treaty organization of the United States and Canada.)

Commercially, bottom fish and sharks are caught with otter trawls, longline gear (heavy lines sometimes several miles in length to which are attached at intervals baited hooks on short leaders), and gill nets. The otter trawl accounts for 95 percent of the catch. This is a tapered, baglike net open in the front like a huge scoop, which takes in everything on the bottom as it is towed along.

The most numerous species landed are Dover sole, English sole, petrale, the rockfish, and in recent years, hake. Other important species are lingcod, gray cod, arrowtooth sole, rex sole, and dogfish shark.

The continental shelf off the Northwest coast shelves gradually to the one-hundred-fathom line, then the bottom drops steep to as much as one thousand fathoms. The shallow shelf varies in its outer limit from ten to thirty miles off the coast.

Halibut, the season for which is set in the period May through September, depending on location, is caught commercially by longline methods. Along with halibut are taken sablefish, sole, rockfish, and shark. The longlines are used in depths up to two hundred fathoms.

The sport fisherman, however, needs no such elaborate gear, nor any special time (or excuse) to bother the demersals. Most use whatever kind of tackle happens to be handy, and do their casting from the beach, from rocks, jetties, piers, barges, party boats, skiffs, kickers, cabin cruisers, and rubber rafts. Not infrequently they even hook into

Young Puget Sound angler with a catch of assorted "bottom" fishes.

a salmon, steelhead, or cutthroat which grabbed their herring or kelp worm.

Figures put together by people in the Washington State Department of Fisheries, who like to put figures like this together, show that in those waters, bottom fishermen catch 2.44 fish per angler per trip, compared to salmon fishermen who average half a fish per trip.

Emmit A. Glanz, Jr., of that agency, recommends a medium weight rod of six feet or so with a fairly stout line, of twelve- to twenty-pound test, on either a conventional or spinning reel. (Saltwater reels should be used, but freshwater types can be if washed thoroughly afterward in fresh water.)

"Most non-salmon species are not the dainty type," he said, "so an ultra-light rod tip isn't necessary."

A rental boat or the family kicker is ideal for protected waters. Rocky areas, kelp beds, and just about any type of cover are productive spots. The Strait of Juan de Fuca and the San Juan Islands abound in good holes. Piling, reefs, docks, piers, jetties—all are good spots to fish.

The more adventurous types like the swift tidal areas such as Tacoma Narrows, Point Defiance, Partridge Bank, and Deception Pass for rockfish and lingcod. Many good holes can be discovered even by the stranger with the use of Coast and Geodetic Survey navigation charts (or the equivalent Canadian publications). Look at the soundings, which are in fathoms (except in the shaded shoreline areas which are in feet). A fathom, friend, is six feet.

Jetties at places like Ilwaco in the Colum-

A typical catch of Pacific marine game species

Washington jetty fishermen returning with a catch of rockfish

bia Estuary, Westport in Grays Harbor, La Push, and Neah Bay are excellent places for rockfish, ling, and greenling. The docks are Point Defiance Park, Twin Harbors, and other locations draw a lot of bottom fishermen.

The shoreline at Shilshole Jetty, along Alki Point, is recommended for flounder, sole, perch, and bullhead. Surf fishing from ocean beaches will net you perch, rockfish, and others, as will the rocks and ledges along cliffs (be careful of getting trapped by incoming tides).

In Puget Sound you will find at least ten kinds of rockfish, sea bass, and snapper, and along the Northwest coast some fifty or more fairly common varieties of rockfish. Anglers using the conventional salmon mooching gear with whole or plug cut herring, on or just off the bottom, do well. A live herring on a single hook with a three-way swivel and enough lead to get to the bottom works wonders.

Jigs and spoons or wobblers work well, if you know how to jig. You can make good jig lure from three inches of pencil sinker lead, bent into a shallow "S" and pinched onto the line at the end just above a 3/0 hook. Bounce this off the bottom in quick irregular jerks and you'll be pleasantly surprised. The Canadians really know how to do this, and have many variations of this technique.

Jigging or bait fishing in a school of black or yellowtail rockfish in a tide rip or along a kelp bed can't be beat for sport fishing. Lingcod will also take to the same lures in the rocky bottom regions where the water is deep. Flat fish, of course, can be picked up off the bottom readily with tidbits. They are more often found on sandy or muddy bottoms. Throw the bait out and let it just lie there on the bottom. They'll find it.

Perch are not only good eating but provide more hours of sport than all the other species. You find them in the surf, around pilings, under piers, practically everywhere. A No. 4 or 6 hook with a two-foot leader and a sliding sinker works well. Scrape mussels off piling, pry them open, and string the meat on the hook. You'd better hide while baiting up as this really brings them in.

On the ocean beaches, a rather long lim-

ber rod with lots of line and a good reel will allow you to cast a three-ounce rig a nautical mile. Unless you like to be cold, wet, and clammy, I'd recommend waders, or hip boots. Or even a swim suit. Best bait includes clam necks, shrimp, kelp worms, pile worms, even pieces of kelp. For sinkers use the heavy pyramid types. Most surf casters also use a two-hook setup with both baited.

True cod, pollock, sablefish, greenling, sculpins, cabezon, pogie, and even dogfish are included in the marine grab bag.

Marine species will also take various kinds of flies and streamers on flyrods, yet. And herring can be taken jigging with bare brass hooks, a half dozen at a time.

Many bottom anglers, trying it for the first time, are alarmed by the color of the flesh of some species. Some lingcod, for example, have a greenish flesh. But this disappears with cooking, and in no case is it unappetizing or inedible.

A variety of rockfish caught in Puget Sound, including perch, sea "bass" and a quillback.

10.

Winter Blackmouthing

One reason why Washington sport salmon landings exceed the combined sport catches of California, Oregon, British Columbia, and Alaska, according to Frank Haw, biologist of the Department of Fisheries, is because of winter "mooching" in Puget Sound, and particularly the winter "blackmouth" fishing—much of which is done right in Elliott Bay within sight of Seattle's downtown loop.

The many protected bays, inlets, and waterways in Puget Sound, which permit year-around boating, and the presence of large numbers of feeder salmon all year around, are what make up this winter fishery.

While I don't agree that the deadly form of mooching originated in Puget Sound (I think it started in Alaska), there is no denying that the art form was perfected here.

Mooching is the lazy man's form of trolling. You just put your lure or bait in the water, let the swirling tides and currents take it, and you're in business. No trolling. No casting. No jigging. Just mooching.

There has been a lot of nonsensical stuff written about mooching by imaginative fishing writers looking for new leads, and even such variations as "motor mooching," invented to enhance the tales. But there is only one kind of mooching, and that is mooching.

And here's how you do it.

The ideal mooching grounds are in waters from 50 to 120 feet deep, over ledges and holes, and in channels close to shore, around points, and in tide rips and along kelp beds. The presence of birds in any numbers is a good indication. There is no secret about all this: Such places provide concentrations of planktonic creatures, which attract forage fish such as anchovies, pilchards, herring, candlefish, which attract birds and foraging salmon, and which attract moochers.

As Shakespeare once wrote:

THIRD FISHERMAN: Master, I marvel how the fishes live in the sea.

FIRST FISHERMAN: Why, as men do a-land; the great ones eat up the little ones.

Coast and Geodetic Survey navigation charts are ideal for finding good fishing holes, underwater ledges, channels, and other locations. It is not true that the best way to find a good location is to look for spots with the most fingerstains on charts hanging in waterfront sport shops. After all, there are some clean salmon fishermen.

Another good sign experienced fishermen look for—indeed, it is hard to forget—is the herring "ball-up."

A ball-up occurs when the feeding salmon or the screaming birds, feeding upon a school of bait fish, panic them into crowding together in one big, tight, terrified mass of little fish. Those inside the ball escape, but those on the outside are picked up by the fish ducks, slashing salmon, and dogfish from below. Sometimes a big salmon will charge right into a ball-up scattering them in all directions. Other times, when danger is past, the little fish will unwind and form into a regular school.

Rod and reel used for mooching are sometimes referred to by imaginative merchants as "mooching outfits," but this only means the conventional light sporting tackle, either spinning or casting type. The rod should be about eight feet, with a medium action tip. A good steelhead rod works perfectly. The reel is of the saltwater large-capacity type, either spinning or surf-casting style. Line should be from ten- to twenty-pound test. Usually a crescent or beaded swivel sinker is used—just enough to get down through the current. The terminal tackle can be a standard herring hookup, or strip bait, or plug-cut bait.

You are drifting along with the current, or usually the motor is in idle or trolling gear to maintain position in fast rips. You strip off enough line to let the bait plunge fairly rapidly to the level you wish to fish—generally on the bottom for chinooks, down a fathom or two for coho. Then checking to be sure the drag is set properly, relax. The first warning will be a pronounced strike. Then nothing. Wait. Do nothing. Presently you will feel a little pulling. Give up some slack. Then, when you feel a positive heavy pull, set the hook!

"Crackers"—beginners—are confused by all the different names for salmon. The chinook, king, blackmouth, tyee, and jack (chinook) are the same fish. The tyee is one generally over thirty pounds. The blackmouth is an immature feeder. The jack is an immature fish that makes the spawning run for nothing. King is merely a local name for a chinook.

Blackmouth winter salmon fishing begins in November. The best areas are the Strait of Juan de Fuca, from Waddah Island to Port Townsend, inside Neah Bay and Port Angeles Harbor along the log booms, inside Sequim and Discovery bays.

West Beach near Deception Pass is a good spot. Camp Casey, Bush Point, Point No Point, and Possession Bar are popular. The oil docks off Edmonds and Richmond Beach, the "Trees" just south of Richmond Beach, Camano Head, Baby Island in Saratoga Passage, are well known, and so is Holmes Harbor.

The highest catch-per-fishermen record remains in the Ballard-Jefferson Head, Elliott Bay, and Manchester-Bremerton areas in winter. Elliott Bay is best early in winter.

Winter anglers also go to Point Defiance and Point Evans in the Narrows, Wollochet Bay, Hale Passage, and the "Sand Spit" at the northwest tip of Fox Island. Off the town of Purdy, Anderson Island, Johnson Point, and Steamboat Island are producers later in the winter season.

Hood Canal is an excellent winter fishing area, with Jackson Cove best. Hazel Point and Oak Head are late producers. Pleasant Harbor on the west side of the canal and Bald Point, and the Sisters Point area, where the Hood Canal is narrowest, are all popular spots.

II.

Digging for Trout

Commander George Jessen, a retired skipper with long service in Alaska, loves to tell dudes about catching trout out on the tundra with a shovel instead of a rod and reel.

"You don't believe it?" he always comes back earnestly. "Well, now, tundra is actually a layer of vegetable matter, several feet thick, on top of real terra firma. You also know that live trout can be shipped across the country in a semi-frozen state without harm or injury. So, like bears hibernating, the trout in the smaller creeks up in the Aleutians bore themselves into the honeycombed tundra before the creek freezes over solid and remain in a semi-frozen state 'til springtime."

Come springtime when things start thawing out, you take your shovel and go down to the edge of the creek and start digging.

"There's nothing fantastic about this," he says. "It is just natural, and furthermore, in Alaska anything is possible."

During World War II, Commander Jessen commanded a Navy supply vessel on the Aleutian run. "I had one of the handiest little ships you ever saw for getting in and out of all the holes up there. Just 317 feet overall, A/G 66, the U.S.S. Besboro, we supplied the bases with everything from pork chops to bulldozers and also had ac-

commodations for 402 troops and 12 officer passengers."

Sometimes, the skipper said, he had too many passengers, and then had to put some enlisted men up in the brig, which was never used anyway. Actually, these enlisted men would be the only ones aboard besides the captain who had a private "stateroom" but there would always be some clown who would write home to his mother that he had been brigged on the Besboro, and the captain would eventually hear about it, via the chain of command from the lad's mother's Congressman.

I call Commander Jessen the "Poor Man's Mr. Roberts," which is one of my own little private jokes that I sometimes indulge myself.

Actually, Commander Jessen blames Bob Ellis, Sr., a veteran Alaskan bush pilot out of Ketchikan for the tundra trout story.

"Bob was a Navy commander in charge of the air station at Attu. On the run north we generally stopped at Ketchikan and dropped off a few things at the Coast Guard dock, where I usually put the ship's Jeep ashore and drove to Ellis's house where Mrs. Ellis would hand me some boxes of goodies for Bob, including smoked king salmon, which I would deliver.

"Well, it was one day when we were sitting in his quarters having a drink of (censored) and I asked him about the fishing on the island. He answered that he didn't know about how it was just then, but the week before the trout were so hungry they had to go ashore to eat.

"Since this seemed like an Alaska story I had never heard before, I sipped my (censored) and remained silent. Bob then continued that when they had caught and opened the trout they found field mice in their stomachs. If they didn't go ashore to eat, then where did they get the mice?

"Since this was an unimpeachable statement, stated soberly or reasonably so by an officer of the United States Navy and a gentleman in command of a Naval Air Station, I had to agree that this was, indeed, logical.

"I remembered then that I had, myself, dug trout out of the tundra with a shovel over on Great Sitkin Island, and only then did the coincidence occur to me."

But Commander Jessen's favorite place was not in the Aleutians, but Pleasant Island, by Excursion Inlet, across from Hoonah in southeast Alaska.

"On the starboard side going into Excursion Inlet, is Strawberry Point. If you go there with a .30-30 and sit for several minutes a buck deer will come up and look at you. You like clams? Big ones, bigger than coconuts? I can tell you where to find them. They are always big because it was impossible to dig them all out. They are in Yakutat Bay. They are, I believe, of the geoduck family and are tender and sort of sweet-tasting like the bay clams of Nestucca, and have the same black and white shell.

"I say they are *good*, and I am an old Alaska man who doesn't like lousy seafood!"

12.

Let's Go Clamming!

Long periods of minus tides along the Oregon and Washington coasts in summer bring out the clam diggers and revive that old mystery: What's a clam gun?

Originally it was simply a shovel with a long narrow blade. But a relatively new device for capturing these meaty shellfish actually looks like a gun.

It's made of a section of steel tubing about four or five inches in diameter and two feet long. The bottom end is open, while the top has a cap welded on with handles. There's also a hole about the size of your finger in the cap.

When you find a clam's blow-hole or "show" you quickly shove the pipe or tube down into the soft sand around the spot. Then you stick your finger in the cap hole and pull up on the handles. Out comes a core of sand, hopefully with the clam.

Object of most clam diggers is the Pacific razor clam (*Siliqua patula*) found from California to Alaska, and usually abundant on surf-pounded beaches as well as on sheltered flats. As anyone who has tasted them knows, the razor is delicious. In one year on the Washington beaches alone, 682,000 diggers took 13,166,000 clams—and certainly a half million diggers can't be wrong.

The razors reach maturity in about two years and spawn in April or May. Just before this the clams are the fattest and best eating. The females lay anywhere from six to ten million eggs, being incredibly productive. The young clams reach a length of a half inch the first season, and 3½ inches the next year. The two-year-olds will average four inches and some three-to-five-year-olds will reach five inches in length. The life expectancy is from eight to fifteen years.

The main problem these days, biologists say, is that too many young clams are taken and, worse yet, millions of clams are destroyed each year by diggers and left to rot.

Because of this the Clatsop beaches in Oregon from Seaside to Point Adams are closed during July and August, and in Washington the beach from Cape Disappointment to Westport is closed to digging until September 15.

Minus tides are best for clamming, simply because the beds are more exposed, but clamming can be done anytime. Hunting is simple. Walk down the beach slowly, keeping an eye open for "shows"—tiny holes left in the wet sand by the clam drawing its neck in.

"Surf digging" (grabbing the neck while digging at the same time) is most productive in the spring and fall, while "dry digging" (excavating) pays off in the summer.

To hunt clams, you need a "clam gun," and sharp eyes

Once you start digging, speed is essential because the clam can often outdig the digger.

Push the blade of the shovel straight down, removing sand with a lifting motion. Be careful not to touch the clam with the shovel or you'll break the shell. Broken clams not only are wasteful, but the shells are sharp and can cause injury.

To clean, remove the meat from the shell after submerging in boiling water for a moment, or pouring boiling water over them.

CLAM DIGGING

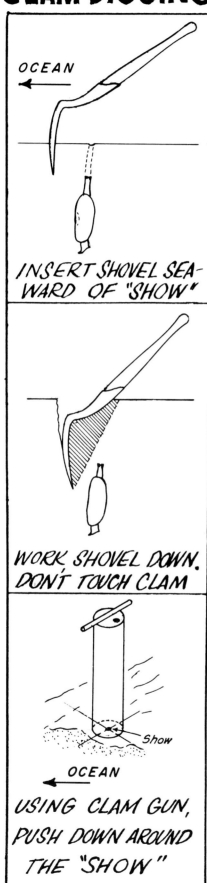

OCEAN

INSERT SHOVEL SEA-WARD OF "SHOW"

WORK SHOVEL DOWN. DON'T TOUCH CLAM

Show

OCEAN

USING CLAM GUN, PUSH DOWN AROUND THE "SHOW"

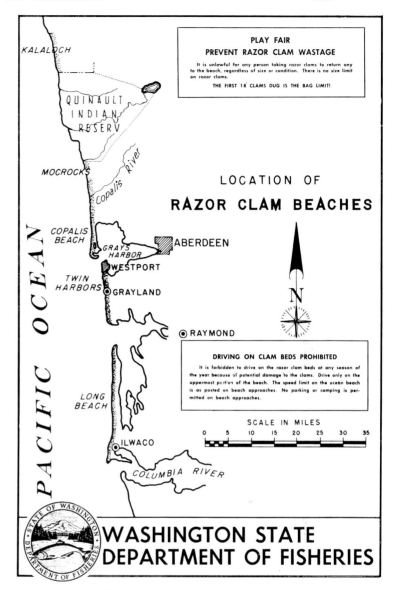

KALALOCH

QUINAULT INDIAN RESERV

MOCROCKS

Copalis River

COPALIS BEACH

GRAYS HARBOR

ABERDEEN

WESTPORT

TWIN HARBORS

GRAYLAND

RAYMOND

LONG BEACH

ILWACO

COLUMBIA RIVER

PACIFIC OCEAN

PLAY FAIR
PREVENT RAZOR CLAM WASTAGE

It is unlawful for any person taking razor clams to return any to the beach, regardless of size or condition. There is no size limit on razor clams.

THE FIRST 18 CLAMS DUG IS THE BAG LIMIT!

LOCATION OF
RAZOR CLAM BEACHES

N

DRIVING ON CLAM BEDS PROHIBITED

It is forbidden to drive on the razor clam beds at any season of the year because of potential damage to the clams. Drive only on the uppermost portion of the beach. The speed limit on the ocean beach is as posted on beach approaches. No parking or camping is permitted on beach approaches.

SCALE IN MILES
0 5 10 15 20 25 30 35

WASHINGTON STATE
DEPARTMENT OF FISHERIES

One of the best razor clam areas in the Northwest is along the Washington coast. At left is method of digging.

When the shells pop, drop them in cold water. Remove the gills and digestive tract with a knife or scissors, then "steak" the meat for frying.

The four major Washington beaches are Long Beach, Twin Harbors, Copalis, and Mocrocks. There is also some digging near Kalaloch and on some beaches along the Strait of Juan de Fuca.

In Oregon the most popular beaches are in Clatsop County, Tillamook Bay, Netarts,

Puget Sound islands are favorite spots for shellfish hunters

Nestucca Bay, Siletz Bay, Yaquina, Reeds-
port, Coos Bay, Bandon, Port Orford, and
Gold Beach.

The daily limit in Washington is the first
eighteen dug with no size limit. The season is open twenty-four hours a day from

March 1 to May 31; June 1 to September 15 from twelve midnight to twelve noon; and from September 16 to February 28 on Satdays, Sundays, and legal holidays.

Each person must dig his own clams and only hand shovels or cylindrical tubes are permitted. It is unlawful to return any clams dug to the beach. Driving on clam beds is forbidden also.

In Oregon similar regulations prevail, except the limit for bay clams is the first thirty-six dug and for razors the first twenty-four. The possession limit is two daily limits in seven days. The season is open all year except for the Clatsop beaches. Whale Cove in Lincoln County is closed to taking of shellfish because of an experimental program going on there.

A synopsis of shellfish regulations can be obtained free from most tackle and bait shops, and from game wardens and state police. The Washington version is also a handy informative guide to digging, cleaning, and preparing, as well as a guide to the best areas.

Also published by the Washington Department of Fisheries in Olympia is a new "Shellfish Cookbook," by Iola I. Berg. It's a first-rate manual on shellfish as well as a cookbook that contains many recipes not found anywhere else.

In addition to clams, the book contains information and recipes on oysters, crabs, shrimp, scallops, freshwater crawfish, mussels, sea cucumbers, skates, octopus, and abalone. This booklet is definitely an indispensable guide for anyone interested in shellfish.

This man is "gunning" a clam, not trying to keep from getting his feet wet

13.

North Pacific Shell Game

The North Pacific Rim is rich in shellfish in many varieties. The principal ones are:

Bent nose clam (*Macoma nasuta*)
Butter clam (*Saxidomus giganteus*)
Geoduck (*Panope generosa*)
Horse clam (*Schizothaerus nuttali*)
Mud or soft shell clam (*Mya arenaria*)
Piddock (*Zirfaea gabbi*)
Razor clam (*Siliqua patula*)
Rock or little neck clam (*Paphia staminea*)
Common cockle (*Cardium corbis*)
Pacific hardshell clam (*Paphia phillipinarum*)
Dungeness or Pacific crab (*Cancer magister*)
Coonstripe shrimp (*Pandalus danae*) also (*Pandalus goniurus*)
Pink shrimp (*Pandalus borealis*) (*Pandalus jordani*)
Red shrimp (*Pandalus hypsinotus*)
Sidestripe shrimp (*Pandalopsis dispar*)
Spot shrimp (*Pandalus platyurus*)
Eastern oyster (*Ostrea virginica*)
Native oyster (*Ostrea lurida*)
Pacific oyster (*Ostrea gigas*)
Washington oyster (*Ostrea gigas kumamoto*)
Common mussel (*Pytilis edulis*)
Common scallop (*Pecten hericius*)
Sea scallop (*Pecten caurinus*)
Rock scallop (*Hinnites giganteus*)
Squid (*Loligo opulescens*)
Red abalone (*Haliotis rufescens*)
Kamchatka abalone (*Haliotis kamschatkana*)
Octopus (*Polypus honkongensis*)
Alaska king crab

Most oysters are "farmed" on private tidelands in the Pacific Northwest, although in certain localities state and federal tidelands have been set aside for public use. Regulations vary, but the bag limit is usually around thirty to forty a day and may be taken by hand or manually operated devices, or on a daily subsistence basis. In many areas it is unlawful to return any oysters or shells to a different beach than the one of origin. This is to prevent the spread of any oyster drills. Most sportsmen and visitors simply buy the oysters they want from convenient commercial outlets.

Shrimp is a relatively new and unexploited fishery in the Northwest, and it is believed there are areas of immense undiscovered beds. Oddly enough, the "poaching" by Russian and Japanese fishing fleets off the Oregon and Washington coasts resulted in almost complete decimation of the hake, which in turn triggered a population explosion of shrimp upon which hake feed.

Crab fisherman beaching his craft after a trip

At present shrimp are most readily obtained from commercial sources, but one who has the time to make a study of the subject and to find productive shrimp holes (a navigation chart with soundings helps here), can just about start himself a new sport fishery.

Generally (there are always local exceptions) the shrimp season is from April to October, using a hand dip net or any hand-operated trap or ring. The bag limits, where applied, are usually around ten pounds in the shell.

The Dungeness crab is found from California to the Bering Sea. Usually there is no closed season, but the size and sex are restricted to males not less than about six inches long. Females and softshell crabs are usually verboten. The bag limits vary, but figure on about a half dozen. Crabs can only be taken in rings or pots, and spearing of shellfish is prohibited in most places.

Scallops are becoming increasingly popular and are also regulated by law as to bag limits and method of taking.

Squid have no seasonal limitations and usually may be taken only by hand methods, no spears. The same is true of the octopus, but the bag is limited, usually to two.

There is a bag limit on abalone (two in Washington, where the taking of red abalone is prohibited).

Clams are the most popular of all shellfish for sportsmen. The principal varieties taken are razors and geoducks, and in most places the season, bag limits, and method of taking are strictly regulated. Driving on clam beds is always prohibited. Most areas also require the bag limit to be counted as the first clams taken—no throwing back and trying for bigger ones. In some areas, such as the Clatsop beaches of Oregon, a ban on clamming is clamped down for a couple of months each summer to cut down on the wastage by people who dig and then discard small clams.

The hardshells such as razor, butter, little neck, and geoducks (pronounced (gooey-duck") are among the choice seafoods. The cockles, mud clams, and horse clams also have a good flavor but are tough and are best chopped or ground for chowder.

Butter clams are usually steamed after cleaning in a large steamer or kettle with about one inch of water in the bottom. After ten minutes or so of steaming, open the shells and serve hot with side dishes of melted butter and strained clam juice.

Tops are razor clams. They should be cleaned immediately and removed from the shell, the gills, dark area of the neck snipped off, digestive organs (all dark parts) removed, cleaned, and rinsed. They are then ready for cooking in various ways.

The geoduck should be washed and cleaned immediately, removed from the shell, and the neck or siphon clipped away from the body. All of the clam is edible but most discard the body. Blanch the neck in boiling water and skin. Then rinse in cold water and grind up or slice. Fry the slices quickly in butter or use in chowder. Overcooking toughens the meat.

Oysters are prepared by scrubbing under cold running water. Discard any open shells, because these are dead and not good to eat. Open shells with a strong, blunt knife or tool, prying apart at the hinge. Cut the muscle from the shell, retain the liquor if possible and strain for later use. Refrigerate until used. Oysters can also be steamed open. Do not overcook oysters either. In fact, they are best raw on the half shell.

Crabs are brought in alive and dropped into boiling salted water. Put them in upside down and the crab will fold its legs against its shell. The water must be at a rolling boil to kill the crab instantly. A fourth cup of salt to a quart of water is the usual ratio. Boil twenty minutes. Cool quickly in cold water. Lift the top shell from the rear and pull off, discarding the shell and yellow fat. Discard the gills also. Turn over and scrap out the belly fat and entrails, flushing the cavity with cold water.

Cracking and picking then get to the meat of the thing.

Shrimp, which are from one to three inches long are also cooked in boiling water, with the same proportion of salt. Only five to eight minutes are necessary for shrimp. Drain and cool, and peel off shells. Remove the dark sand vein. Eat as is with a sauce dip or with other dishes.

Scallops are usually in deep water, but in some places are found in pools at low tide. They should be shucked as soon as caught. Usually only the tender white meat is saved. Rinse and clean before cooking.

Mussels are found attached to rocks at low tide. They are bluish-black clusters, which look like barnacle-covered rocks. Wash and scrub the shells thoroughly in fresh water, scraping off the beard and barnacles with a sharp knife. Cover with cold salted water and soak for twenty minutes. Mussels also must be alive when cooked. You can tell if alive by the tightly closed shell or a shell that closes when touched. If eaten raw or on the half shell, first remove the hinges and pry open the shells. During the summer months they may be toxic. Also do not eat mussels taken from polluted water. Inquire locally.

Sea cucumbers are also edible and should be cleaned immediately before they soften up. The muscle is the edible part. Cut off both ends of the cucumber, split from end to end and shake out the internal organs. The muscle is the layer on the inside. Cut loose and strip it out with a sharp knife.

Surf dories are used by some alongshore crabbers

The meat will be anywhere from white to pink and will roll up into a finger-size portion to fry after blanching in boiling salted water. Roll in crumbs and fry slowly, or chop up and use in chowder.

Another edible species is the skate. These are plentiful in northern waters. The wing muscle is the only part used. This can be cut off from the cartilage. A white firm flesh much like scallops, it can be fried or used in chowder.

Small octopus are the best eating. Only the outer layer or mantle of the body and the tenacles are used. This is a tender piece of meat that does not have to be pounded usually. Blanch the meat and peel off any skin. The arms must be pounded to tenderize. Cut in pieces, the meat can be cooked in various ways, usually boiled and then browned.

Most abalone in northern waters are taken by skin divers. The muscle is the only part used and must be pounded before cooking. It has a clamlike flavor.

14.

Fish Poisoning

There is a great deal of misunderstanding and misinformation regarding human consumption of marine fishes and seafoods. This is particularly true these days of greatly increased numbers of tourists and "inlanders" heading for the seashore for fishing and recreation.

Fish poisoning in the Pacific Northwest is not as common as other areas such as Hawaii where as many as one hundred cases of poisoning from eating certain edible fishes are reported annually. The most dangerous species are usually found in tropical or semi-tropical waters—but not all of them.

Other Pacific waters do have toxic varieties, and also have some that are toxic only at certain times of the year, or merely as a result of eating another fish that is inedible.

The worst offenders, at one time or another, or "out of season," are:

barracuda	red snapper	butterfly fish
pompano	sea bass	clams, crabs
mackerel	perch	mussels, shellfish

During certain times of the year, mussels, clams, and other shellfish become toxic sometime during the period from May through September. The reason is they are feeding upon marine plants and animals that have a high concentration of poison during the summer months. There are local exceptions to everything, and simple inquiry is all that is necessary to establish the situation any time.

Shellfish poisoning is fatal in about 10 percent of the cases. Medicos say that if a patient survives the first twelve hours or more he will recover.

Symptoms of shellfish poisoning are numbness and tingling of lips, tongue, face, and extremities; nausea and vomiting progressing to respiratory paralysis dramatized by difficulty in breathing; possible convulsions. If fatal, death usually occurs from respiratory failure.

Treatment includes first removing as soon as possible the undigested shellfish by inducing vomiting. If a doctor or hospital is handy, a stomach pump and cathartics are first on the list.

The patient is usually treated for shock.

General safety precautions to prevent shellfish poison in the first place are to avoid eating them during the summer months; and make it a point to learn which seafoods can be dangerous and at what time of the year in what areas.

However, the old wives' tale about eating seafood only in months which have "R" in them is largely unfounded. In practice there are certain times of the year when certain seafood is scarce, or when the flesh is soft and watery, such as occurs with oysters, but the infamous "red tides" of poisonous microscopic organisms are rare in the North Pacific.

PART FOUR

Places to Go

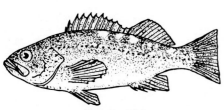
Bass Rockfish

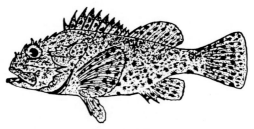
Scorpionfish

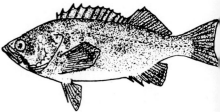
Blue Rockfish

I.

Northern California

Although an occasional salmon has been caught as far south as San Diego, one can call this a freak occurrence. Using the range of salmon and steelhead as a standard, for purposes of the sport fishermen, the "southern limit" of the Pacific Northwest can be considered Avila, California.

AVILA. Party boats available, as well as skiff rentals. Personal skiffs may be launched from pier for a fee. Salmon fishing is "occasional," usually in the spring. The late spring and summer offshore salmon area extends as far south as opposite San Luis Obispo Bay.

Marine species from here to Monterey Bay include sea bass, rockfish, lingcod, cabezon, barracuda, yellowtail, chilipepper.

Pier and bay fishing and skin diving include abalone, geoducks, razor and pismo clams, rockfish, jacksmelt, surfperch, starry flounder, black perch, California halibut, sharks, kelp greenling, and other species.

Skin diving, pier and skiff fishing along this coastline, are considered excellent, and they are extremely popular.

Offshore albacore come within ten miles of the coast here in August, September, and October.

MORRO BAY. Salmon fishing is occasional, as at Avila. Party boats and rental skiffs are available. Skin diving facilities.

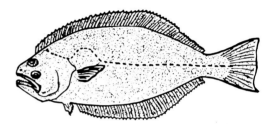

California Halibut

Cutthroat (Sea-run) Trout

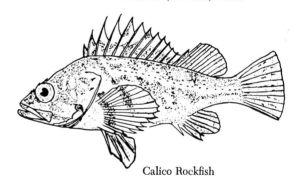

Calico Rockfish

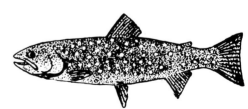

Dolly Varden Trout (Sea-run)

Dogfish Shark   Sablefish   Kelp Rockfish

MONTEREY. Party boats and rentals available and personal skiffs may be launched from pier at several places for a fee. There is also a free public launching ramp on shore. Salmon fishing is similar to Santa Cruz, best in spring and fair in summer and fall. Albacore can be taken offshore in late summer.

Monterey Bay area has more species of fish, and more fishermen, than any other section of the coast north of Point Conception.

Salmon range over the entire offshore and bay area, but no longer are they as plentiful as in the "old days." A good salmon area is off Pacific Grove.

Shore fishing includes surfperch, jacksmelt, silver perch, striped bass in summer, black perch occasionally, cabezon, kelp greenling, rockfish, although there is very little surf fishing practiced.

Other alongshore fishing includes gaper clams, abalone, night smelt in summer, pile perch, California halibut, white croakers, and pismo clams.

MOSS LANDING. Party boats and rental skiffs. Private skiffs can be launched through the surf in the protected harbor. Salmon fishing similar to Santa Cruz. Marine species same as Monterey Bay in general.

CAPITOLA. Rental skiffs. Private skiffs may be launched from pier for a fee. This place is a few miles east of Santa Cruz on Monterey Bay.

SANTA CRUZ. Party boats and rental skiffs. Private skiffs may be launched from pier for a fee. Salmon fishing best in spring and fair to good summer and fall. The mouth of the San Lorenzo River is a popular and heavily fished coho and steelhead spot.

Albacore fishing, salmon fishing, skin div-

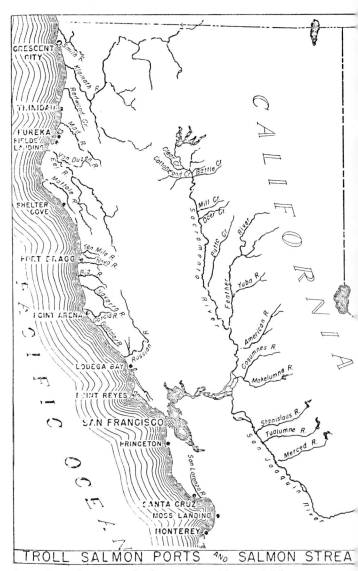

Map shows the principal salmon rivers and coastal fishing ports in California.

ing, and skiff fishing are the same as for the rest of Monterey Bay. A popular offshore bank is Portuguese Ledge, two hundred or three hundred feet deep, with yellowtail, widow, green-spotted, bocaccio, and chilipepper. Sand dabs, starry flounder, sablefish, and white sea bass are also plentiful in this area.

PRINCETON. From Santa Cruz to Halfmoon Bay, there are numerous surf and rock fishing spots. "Poke poling" alongshore for rockfish, striped sea perch, surf-perch, and white croakers is popular. The Nuevo Island area is a good one for abalone. Lingcod, cabezon, and California halibut also are popular.

Princeton has party boats and rental skiffs. Salmon fishing is fair to poor. Most fishing is for marine species.

POINT SAN PEDRO. This place has the only skiff rental and launching facility between Princeton and San Francisco Bay. Skiffs can be launched for a fee. Salmon is mainly chinook (kings) but some coho (silvers) are taken.

Offshore the tuna grounds are from 35 to 150 miles out and are fished in August, Sep-tember, and October. The Farallon Islands, off the Golden Gate, are fished by private boats, and by charters and party boats from San Francisco and Halfmoon Bay. Around the islands are yellowtail, rockfish, bocaccio, lingcod, blue rockfish, and vermilion rock-fish.

From Halfmoon Bay to the Golden Gate the bottom fishing includes rockfish and lingcod; skiff fishing for rockfish, lingcod, cabezon, crabs, flounder, sand dabs, striped bass. Skin diving is popular for red abalone and halibut.

Shore fishing is for rockfish, surfperch, kelp greenling, lingcod, flounder, white croaker, eels, sculpin, day- and night-run

Chinook salmon (left) and a striped bass

smelt, striped bass, California herring, and many other species.

Small feeder salmon are taken alongshore, just outside the surf in this area.

SAN FRANCISCO BAY. A major sport-fishing area, party boats and charters, operate out of numerous marinas and basins, including Sausalito, Berkeley, Gas House Cove, Fisherman's Wharf. Sport and bait shops can furnish complete up-to-date information on all types of fishing.

Party and charter boats operate all year around, weather permitting, and during the fishing seasons. The offshore skippers take parties of six to eight out as far as the Farallons. Reservations are generally necessary as this is the most popular fishing center in California, north of San Diego.

Most salmon are taken trolling with bait and lures, and heavy tackle. Tackle can be rented from the skipper. Because of the heavy wear and tear on gear in this type of fishing, it is recommended you don't use your own if you think anything of it.

The Sacramento River system is a major salmon, steelhead, and striped bass waterway. These species are present in the system almost all year around in varying numbers. The number of sport landings, marinas, and other establishments catering to the angler is beyond belief.

San Francisco Bay and San Pablo Bay are highly polluted and while they have large populations of bottom species and shellfish, almost all of them are inedible. I have caught striped bass in the San Pablo channel that had more oil in them than the crankcase on my Volkswagen.

Shore and surf fishing for striped bass is popular on both sides of the Golden Gate. The last time I fished there I almost had room enough to turn around, providing we all did it in unison.

On the north peninsula, military reservations take up most of the best spots, although there are some undeveloped state parklands reached from Marin City and Mill Valley.

MUIR BEACH. From Lime Point northward there is some excellent pier, rock, and surf fishing. It is rugged, however, and accessible in only a few places. Rock fishing for surfperch, cabezon, and kelp greenling is tops, and so is poke-poling at low tides.

Striped bass fishing is fair to good, on and off, around Fort Barry and Point Bonita.

Tennessee Cove is still closed to the public, but access may be obtained to the Fort Baker pier from the Provost Marshal, Presidio, at San Francisco. Public fishing is allowed in Fort Barry and Fort Cronkhite in the Rodeo Lagoon area.

Angler measures an abalone for size

Herring are taken from shore during the spawning period, December to February, in the Fort Baker area.

BOLINAS-STINSON BEACH. Access is extremely difficult from Marin County Overlook to Rocky Point. Bolinas Bay is being developed as a small craft harbor for boat moorage and launching. There is no breakwater yet and navigation is still hazardous.

Good shore fishing for surfperch and striped bass from the mouth of the bay to Stinson Beach. Rockfishing and poke-poling are good at Duxbury Point. Shellfishing is popular for gaper and Washington clams inside the bay, and littlenecks on the rocky tidewater pools from Duxbury Point to the mouth of the bay.

Shore fishing access is located at Agate Beach, north of Duxbury Point.

Skin diving for red abalone and trolling alongshore for salmon are carried on from April to December, with the spring chinooks in April-May, and the fall chinook from July to mid-October. The channel between the mainland and the Farallons is trolled heavily in season. There is also rockfishing offshore at Cordell Bank.

DRAKE'S BAY AREA. Salmon fishing from Duxbury Point to Drake's Bay, same as above. Access from land is via State Highway 1. Skin diving and shore fishing, clamming, surf casting, rockfishing all along this stretch, which is part of a proposed federal park, the Point Reyes National Seashore.

The principal fishing centers are Tomales Bay State Park, McClure Beach, Drake's Bay County Park, Point Reyes Lighthouse Station, Abbotts Lagoon, and Tomales Point, which is reached by boat from the east shore of Tomales Bay.

Gaper and Washington clams are excellent inside the Estero. There are some commercial oyster beds here. Surfperch are taken from the beach inside the bay and on the outer coast beach from Point Reyes to Abbotts Lagoon. The cliff area at Point Reyes is inaccessible.

There is an undeveloped bottom fishery which includes rockfish, lingcod, cabezon, greenling, and others.

From Point Reyes north along the beach the access is only by foot trails from Sir Francis Drake Boulevard. Most of this area is privately owned. March through June are the best surfperch months. There is a sea lion rookery at Point Reyes.

TOMALES BAY. The coho salmon fishing in the upper bay south of Inverness starts in October and is short-lived. There are some chinook salmon in the bay all year around the entrance, taken by shallow trolling with six- to ten-ounce weights. The chinooks are there feeding on the small fish. Local anglers take skiffs through the jaws into the ocean, which is extremely hazardous for strangers. There is a fast outgoing tide, and breakers often form at the entrance. There is a public launching ramp near Nick's Cove.

There is skiff launching at Miller Park. Surfperch and jacksmelt are taken winter and spring from small piers and skiffs inside the bay. Some steelhead are taken near Point Reyes Station and at Inverness. The season is open only from November to February.

Some striped bass show up around Inverness, and there are California halibut there most of the year. Larger halibut are taken in summer around the entrance.

DILLON BEACH-McCLURE BEACH. Party boats from Dillon Beach for bottom fishing off Tomales Point and Bird Rock, and for salmon trolling alongshore. Best salmon months, July-November. Skiff rentals and launching facilities are from Miller Park.

Rockfishing, poke-poling, and abalone picking are done from Dillon Beach north and on Tomales Point, the latter accessible by skiff only. Skiffs can be landed also at Avalis Beach from which trails lead to the beach areas.

Skin diving is popular at Tomales Point

for abalone and bottom fishes, for California halibut at the mouth of the bay. Best months for halibut, June-September. There is clamming inside Tomales Bay for gapers and Washington clams.

BODEGA BAY. At this point skiffs frequently operate offshore for salmon. They may be launched at a ramp in Doran Park on the east side of the bay, reached by a

A double catch of chinook salmon and striped bass

Clamming at Pismo Beach

paved road, with plenty of parking. Much lead is needed for salmon trolling. Bottom fishing is good.

Skin diving is popular. California halibut is taken off the bar as well as perch and starry flounder. It is in fact one of the most popular skin diving areas in the state for abalone, cabezon, rockfish, and lingcod. Perch is taken from piers and beaches. Some excellent smelt runs are found along the beach around the mouth of the Russian River.

Party boats operate all year for bottom fish and for salmon in season, weather permitting. There are no ocean skiff rentals at this writing.

Jetty and rock fishing is for jacksmelt, surfperch, flatfish, greenlings and other spe-

cies. Both the east and west jetties should now be open to the public.

Skin diving is from skiffs at the west jetty and reef, around Bodega Rock and toward Bodega Head. Surf netting for smelt is done at the Salmon Creek Beach and at several other points north to the Russian River. Gaper and Washington clams are dug inside Bodega Bay. Digging is now prohibited in the University of California biological reserve.

There is a Coast Guard station in Bodega Harbor.

RUSSIAN RIVER AREA. The Sonoma coast state beaches include Salmon Creek, Miwok, Coleman, Arched Rock, Carmet, Schoolhouse, Portuguese, Wrights, Shell, and Blind beaches.

The mouth of the Russian River is reached by State Highway 12 from Sebastopol via Duncans Mills, Bridgehaven, and Jenner. There is parking close by the jaws and jetty fishing. Some skiff rentals and launching sites are available, but the river mouth is dangerous.

Surf casting is for perch, redtail, occasional striped bass, and a few steelhead are picked up from the beach and jetty.

Surf netting is popular on both sides of the river mouth. Access to the south bank is from Goat Rock. There are public and private campgrounds close by. Russian Gulch Beach north of the river is private and access is by permission only. State Coast Highway 1 runs nearby.

About one hundred miles of the Russian River upstream are open to winter steelhead fishing. Most of the river is accessible, and is heavily fished because of its proximity to the San Francisco area.

The river flow is partly regulated by Coyote Dam. Good runs of steelhead enter from November through February. Late-spawning chinook salmon have been introduced in an effort to establish a run in early winter when the water is cold enough. Some coho are taken each year, mostly in the lower forty miles.

Many of the smaller streams and creeks from here north to the Oregon border have steelhead runs and a few coho salmon, as well as sea-run cutthroat. Local anglers

Party boat off Santa Cruz

An abalone catch from the San Mateo beaches

throat are found only from the Eel River north. Strangers should not plan on these streams unless they have some local friends and a lot of time.

One of these, the Gualala, years ago was a favorite hideout of mine.

FORT ROSS-SALT POINT. Feeder salmon are taken in this stretch most of the year, coho in October-November. Skiffs can be launched through the surf here in several places on calm flat days. There are no party boats in this section, but boats from southern ports come this far north. This area also has some of the best bottom fishing on the coast. It is an important skin diving area, and abalone are still plentiful in spite of the pressure. There is a good deal of rock and surf fishing where access is possible. Much of this is in private ownership, where fees are charged. The only public access from the Russian River to Gualala is at Fort Ross Historical State Park. This is ranch country, backed up by forested hills inland.

GUALALA. Most of this area is in private ownership, closed to the public, but several ranches have fee access. At Salt Point and Stewarts Point are beaches where small skiffs can be launched on flat days. Skin diving for abalone and bottom fish is good. Rock fishing includes greenlings cabezon, surfperch, and rockfish. There are no party boats here.

POINT ARENA. Some rental skiffs available and skiff launching for a fee. Salmon fishing best during July and August, both chinook and coho. Bottom fishing includes lingcod, rockfish, kelp greenling, and pier fishing includes perch, and smelt as well. Skin diving and abalone picking are popular. Best area from lighthouse station to Anchor Bay. Light skiffs that can be carried over the beach are launched at Anchor

have good sport in the fall and winter when the rains start, opening up the sandbars at the mouth so the fish can get in. The cut-

Bay. Surf netting is done at the mouths of Alder Creek and at Garcia River. Surf casting is also popular for redtails at Alder Creek.

The Navarro, Albion, Noyo, and Big Tenmile rivers are also located in this area.

FORT BRAGG. This Noyo Harbor section has party boats and skiffs, and private boats can be launched. Trolling with bait and lures is best for salmon. Both chinook and coho are taken close in alongshore. Fishing is good through the summer.

The tidewater fishery for coho runs from October to mid-December, alongshore from June to October. There is much skin diving and abalone picking.

The top fish in this area is the lingcod, with the rockfish, cabezon, and greenlings next. Surf fishing is for redtail and calico perch, and smelt. Perch fishing is all year. Both night and day smelts are taken.

The party boats are available at Noyo and sometimes Albion from April to October for both salmon trolling and bottom fishing. The chinook are the most plentiful. This area has some of the best close-in bottom fishing on the coast.

Skiff rentals are in Noyo and Albion. The coho move into the rivers in September-November where the skiffs operate. Best outside months are July and August.

Pier fishing is carried on at private docks inside the harbor for surfperch, jacksmelt, and herring all summer long.

The north jetty brings one kelp greenling and perch, and some rockfish and flatfish. Limited access is available for skin diving. Best places are near Westport and MacKerricher State Park; at Caspar, Russian Gulch State Park; Mendocino, Van Damme State Park; and at Albion.

From January through the summer surf netting is done at all the creek mouths from Jackass Creek to MacKerricher State Park. Best catches of night smelt from February to April and surf smelt from April through August.

SHELTER COVE. I once owned forty acres of timber in this area, which I bought for a song and doubled my money—and now wish I still had it. There was nothing here then. Now anglers launch skiffs and troll for salmon alongshore. The surf here is tricky for strangers, however. Some camp facilities are available. Garberville is the nearest town.

July and August are best for salmon. Bottom fish include lingcod, rockfish, cabezon, kelp greenling.

There is some surf netting at the mouth of Dead Man's Creek. Also some skin diving and rock fishing. The coastline is rugged here around Cape Mendocino and the coast highway does not go through. Access to places like Mattole River is difficult.

EEL RIVER LAGOON. Skiff fishing for salmon is best in September, chinook, October—November for coho. Crabbing is excellent, done from skiffs with crab ringnets. There is a lot of surf fishing along here, and off the jetties. The famed Eel River and its tributaries, such as the Van Duzen, dominate the news here.

Off the coast there are trolling for salmon, bottom fishing for flounder and turbots, rockfish, lingcod, greenling, and other species. Trolling in tidewater is popular for salmon, August to October. Pier and rock fishing is also popular all around the bay for perch and flounder.

From here on north, sea-run cutthroat are added to the anadromous bag, along with steelhead, and salmon, in most major streams.

The Eel River is most famous for steelhead but also has some salmon, especially in

A hefty catch of chinook and stripers from waters off the Golden Gate

tidewater. Upstream as far as the South Fork the river flows through a narrow valley, accessible at all points. U.S. Highway 101 parallels the South Fork for fifty miles. Most of the stream is accessible through a magnificent redwood forest. Fall fishing is often hampered by high water and mud.

Late August to October is best for trolling in tidewater. During the fall and winter chinook are caught upstream depending on water conditions. Coho fishing starts in October.

The famed "half-pounders"—small steelhead—are taken in late summer and early fall from the mouth of the Eel up to the mouth of the Van Duzen, with good spinner fishing for big steelhead in the lower river in the fall.

Clear water offers the best steelhead and salmon fishing regardless of time of year.

HUMBOLDT BAY. Skiffs and party boats available at Buhne Point, between Fields Landing and Eureka. There is fair to good salmon fishing during the summer at the entrance to the bay and just outside. Most are taken by trolling with sardines, herring, anchovies, close to the bottom, and by mooching.

Early season fish are mostly chinooks, in August and September both coho and chinook. Launching ramps are available.

The harbor entrance is fished only on the incoming tide, as in most West Coast bars. The outgoing tide creates extremely hazardous conditions, often breakers in the channel, at which time it is suicidal for small boats. Skiff and small-boat operators should avoid, at all cost, getting trapped outside the harbor on an outgoing tide. The outside ocean in this area is, frequently, extremely rough.

Supply points are located at numerous places around the bay. Local bait and tackle stores can give detailed information on fishing and other topics. The bay harbors a large skiff and party-boat industry during the summer and fall. Also the commercial fleet is based here. Bottom fishing is limited for lack of rocky areas.

Clam digging is best on the tidal stretches, shoals, along the sloughs, and on the South Bay Flats. Gapers and Washington clams, softshell, and littlenecks are abundant.

Spawning salmon fighting their way up the Trinity River

Jetty fishing is done at Buhne Point and on the Humboldt jetties. South Jetty road is impassable at times, during storms. Pier fishing is available at a number of private docks inside the bay.

The Elk and Mad rivers enter the ocean in this stretch also.

TRINIDAD HARBOR. Coho salmon is best in August-September. Surf netting for smelt is good at Luffenholtz Beach. Pier fishing, party boat and skiff fishing, and skin diving are popular sports. The coastline along here is characterized by sandy beaches and dunes, with numerous offshore sea stacks and rocks. This is redwood country, with numerous state parks and campgrounds in the area. U.S. 101 highway runs close to the ocean from here to Oregon. Launching ramps are located at Big Lagoon State Park and other points.

KLAMATH RIVER AREA. This is a top salmon fishing area, also famous for sea-run cuts and steelhead, fall and winter. Fishing is done mostly from skiffs, and at times the river and estuary are a solid mass of boats. Best months for chinook are August and September; for coho, September and October; for cutthroat, winter and early spring.

Surf netting is good at the mouth of the river, north at Wilson Creek Beach, and south to Gold Bluffs. Candlefish (smelt) spawn in the Klamath and can be netted from shore during the spring run. Sturgeon, flounder, and redtail are also plentiful.

Boats can be launched at Klamath Glen skiff site. The towns of Klamath, Camp Klamath, and Requa are principal centers.

The main run of chinook enters the Klamath from July through October, and fish are found in the upper river and tributaries well into winter. The spring run is small compared to the fall run.

The old ironhead, however, is the Klamath's most famous fish. Much of the river is accessible, and some of it runs through some really beautiful country. There is a relatively lightly fished winter steelhead run also, mostly in the upper river, with January and February the best months. Sea-run cuts are most plentiful in the lower river in fall and winter.

CRESCENT CITY. Party boats operate out of here and there is some good skiff trolling as well for salmon outside the harbor. Best fishing is during the summer. Skiffs can be launched from a public pier.

Bottom fishing is best from May to September. These include lingcod and black rockfish around the reefs toward Point Saint George. August to November is best for lingcod.

Pier fishing, skiff launching, and moorage are at Citizens Pier. Some good razor clam digging and surf netting on the south beach are available; also skin diving and shore fishing from the north breakwater to Point Saint George.

SMITH RIVER LAGOON. There is a large salmon skiff sport fishery here. Best months for chinook are September and to November; for coho, October-November. Cutthroat trout are taken from shore and boats in the fall and winter. Some steelhead are taken inside the lagoon. There are a number of skiff launching areas and bank fishing spots on Smith River. Surf casting is done from here to the Oregon border.

2.

Oregon

WINDCHUCK RIVER. Enters ocean almost on California border, crossed by U.S. 101 close to outlet. Cutthroat and rainbow trout spring and early summer. Sea-run cuts in fall. Coho and chinook salmon from October into December. Steelhead, December and January. Check regulations for local closures. Brookings is center for supplies, services, but campgrounds and motels are numerous in area.

BROOKINGS. Delightful little city on Chetco Bay at mouth of Chetco River. Complete services and supplies for vacationer and angler. Chetco Harbor is headquarters for sport and commercial offshore fishing fleet. Charter boats and rentals available. Chetco River is a top trout, salmon, and steelhead stream. Sea-run cuts (blueback or harvest trout) in late summer. River stocked with rainbows. Chinook and coho salmon, late fall, peaking in October-November. Steelhead, December-January. Some early salmon fishing from May on. Flounder, perch, rockfish, and some smelt in tidewater. Red abalone and rock scallops alongshore.

PISTOL RIVER. Small stream just south of Gold Beach. Sea-run cuts, rainbow, salmon and steelhead. December, January, and February for winter steelhead; coho and chinook best in October-November. A plunking show. Not adapted for boats. Local regulations. Supplies and services at Gold Beach and Brookings. Red abalone and rock scallops alongshore. Surf casting.

HUNTER CREEK. Just south of Rogue River. Sea-run cuts on flies late summer. Rainbows, spring and early summer. Excellent steelhead and salmon fishery, although small. Coho and chinook in November and December. Steelhead, December-January. Gold Beach and Wedderburn for supplies, accommodations.

GOLD BEACH. This city at the mouth of the famous Rogue River is headquarters for a relatively new offshore charter fishery during the late summer and fall salmon runs, and for bottom fishing just offshore at the Rogue Rocks. Jetty fishing for marine species, salmon, and steelhead on both the north and south jetties. Bay fishery during salmon runs features the "hog lines." Upriver, "salmon boards" are popular (floating planks tied to shore, on which an angler can walk out far enough to reach main channel).

The Rogue, one of the most famous fishing streams in the world, has a good fishery most of the year. It was one of Zane Grey's favorites (his cabin still stands at Winkle Bar), and he was one of the first to run the river from Grants Pass to the sea.

Road now reaches Agness on the south bank, but mailboat and passenger service still in operation. Fishing starts in March for salmon. April, May, and June are tops for the special Rogue strain of chinooks, which run to forty pounds and are better eating than even the Columbia's royal chinook. An early steelhead run also comes with the spring salmon. Guides and drift boats are plentiful along the lower river. Oceangoing charter boats make the offshore trips, beginning in June, weather permitting. The fall salmon runs, chinook and coho, start in late August and September and continue through November. Fly fishing for both salmon and steelhead is a time-honored Rogue sport, but most fish are caught on bait and hardware.

Winter steelheading starts in November, continues through February. Local regulations affecting trout, salmon, jack salmon, and steelhead are many and varied. Check locally.

The perch and other marine species also furnish a superb saltwater fishery, although locals seldom fish for them. The offshore salmon fishery is from June through September.

EUCHRE CREEK. One of at least two streams of this name on the Oregon coast. Nice trout fishing. Some chinook and coho salmon in fall on the high tides, late October, November. An increasing winter steelhead fishery is in prospect, also. Surf fishing all year. Port Orford and Gold Beach are nearest supply points.

HUMBUG MOUNTAIN. This beautiful headland, with its sheltered inland side, harbors an excellent campground, a little-known meandering creek, and some fine rock and surf fishing. Port Orford is closest.

PORT ORFORD. An old fishing and lumbering town on a shallow crescent bay

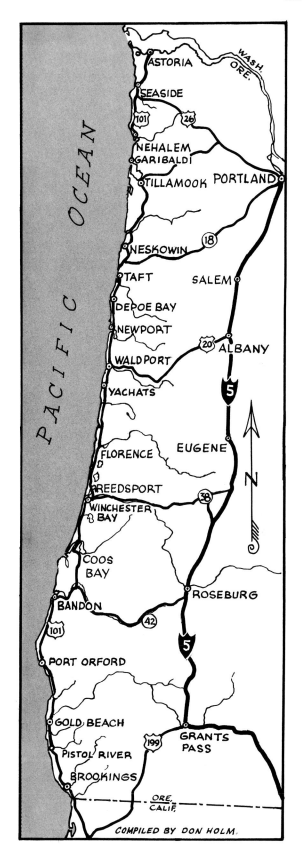

COMPILED BY DON HOLM.

exposed to southwest weather, but has limited small-boat facilities, and bases a number of commercial craft. No established charter business but surf and bottom fishing is virtually untouched. The town is also a center for local streams and lakes.

CAPE BLANCO. Bold promontory, with untouched surf and rock fishing for snapper, perch, flounder, and other marine species. Nearby Elk and Sixes rivers have small but superb sport fisheries. Little-known Sixes, just north of the cape, is one of the best streams on the coast, with top steelheading from November through January. There are also substantial late fall chinook and coho runs. The fall sea-run cutthroat are also excellent. Trout fishing is good but early.

Nearby Elk River is another top coastal stream, just south of the cape. Steelhead and salmon runs coincide with Sixes. October-November best for salmon, January-February for steelhead. Some trout fishing early.

Floras Creek or New River has surprisingly good, and almost unknown, sea-run cutthroat, steelhead, and salmon runs in the fall and early winter.

Bandon and Port Orford are nearby supply points. Local exception to regulations in effect.

BANDON-BY-THE-SEA. The Coquille

Typical unused surf and rock fishing stretch of Oregon coast

Coquille River mouth and jetties at Bandon-By-The-Sea

River, Bay, and Coquille Point provide an excellent sport fishery inside as well as alongshore and offshore. Chinook and coho salmon arrive in the fall, steelhead, late fall and winter. There is also a fall run of striped bass. A limited charter boat business has been built up here, inside and offshore. Many commercial boats are based in the harbor. Tidewater fishing includes snapper, perch, flounder, and other marine species, crabbing, jetty fishing, and surf casting. A pleasant, friendly community, Bandon is also noted for cheese, cranberries, and flowers.

The Coquille River is one of the largest freshwater drainages on the coast, and has almost every kind of freshwater fishing, including catfish, as well as the sea runs. Summer and fall are best for cutthroat in tidewater. Striped bass start in the summer and continue through fall. Steelhead begin in November, run through December. Sal-

Rugged but beautiful section of Oregon coast near Florence

mon runs start in summer, but don't become important until early fall.

Supplies, services, boat launching sites, and other facilities are numerous in the harbor and close by.

COOS BAY. A major West Coast shipping port, with several towns and cities located around the estuary and on the rivers which flow into it, the Coos Bay area is also a major sport and commercial fishing center. In the summer and fall, striped bass are found in the bay and in the Coos and Millicoma rivers, as well as the saltwater sloughs. Sturgeon are common in the bay and Coos River. Clams and eastern cockles are found in the sloughs and flats. There is an excellent spring shad run. Flounder, perch, and

crab are plentiful in the bay and around piers. There is a smelt run at various times. Chinook and coho salmon start running in early fall, lying in deep holes along the jetties and in the bay, and moving up the rivers with the tides. Cutthroat trout are found in the bay and rivers all year. There is a winter steelhead run.

A major offshore sport fishing and charter business centers around Charleston and its small boat harbor. Literally thousands of anglers make the offshore salmon run during the summer and early fall. There is also an increasing number of boats going out after albacore in the summer, which often are as close as ten miles.

From Cape Arago northward there is a

heavy bottom fishery for marine species such as lingcod, black and vermilion rockfish, greenling; and this is the northern limit of red abalone. The jetties are good spots for greenling, flounder, and perch. There is a major halibut ground around the whistle buoy just north of the jetty. Clams and gapers are found on the flats just inside the jaws. Crabbing is excellent during the season. The alongshore chinook season is from April to October, for coho, from mid-June to October.

TENMILE OUTLET. This connecting link between the Pacific Ocean and the chain of freshwater lakes just north of Coos Bay may one day become a major route of anadromous fishes such as salmon, steelhead, cutthroat, and possibly others. A comprehensive program of rehabilitation is now under way by the Oregon State Game Commission after poisoning the large population of trash fish in the lakes in 1968. Summer and fall are best for cutthroat, late fall for coho salmon and jacks, with November and December best on the coast. The all-year resort town of Lakeside provides all necessary services and accommodations. A number of excellent state parks and camping grounds are nearby. Extensive sand dunes and long beaches also provide recreational opportunities. The offshore fishery generally centers around nearby Winchester Bay.

WINCHESTER BAY. This estuary of the Umpqua and the Smith rivers, including the first-class county facility, Salmon Harbor, along with the offshore and alongshore sport and commercial fisheries, is a major West Coast mecca for sportsmen. The lower Umpqua and Smith have a summer striped bass and shad fishery from boats and bank, as well as chinook and coho salmon, sturgeon, and catfish, to say nothing of sea-run cutthroat and planted rainbows. There are also crabbing and clamming in the bay. The salmon fishing, bar and ocean, runs from June to October. The spring chinook run is from April through May; fall chinooks, September and October.

Inside the jetty are flounder, perch, and lingcod at the right on the bar. Bottom and jetty fishing includes lingcod, snapper, surfperch, and starry flounder; halibut, clams, crabs. Some tuna boats go out from here also. Salmon Harbor is a major charter boat center. Everything from salmon canneries to smoking and shipping is available, as are all services and accommodations, including many campgrounds and trailer parks.

Superb winter steelhead begins in October and continues through the winter, with a peak in January. There are many local exceptions to the regulations.

The Winchester Bay entrance is also one of the most dangerous on the West Coast.

A fog and windblown day along the south coast of Oregon

Licensed charter boats are safe, but amateurs and weekend sailors should exercise caution and good judgment. Newcomers should inquire first of the Harbormaster.

FLORENCE. The Siuslaw River and bay support a major sport fishery, but not one as well known as some of the other coastal centers. The jaws at the entrance can be dangerous but during the summer from June to October, there are more good days than bad ones and the offshore fishing is well worth it. The fishing inside the bay is also excellent from late summer right up through November, for both coho and chinook salmon. There is also an excellent jack salmon and sea-run cutthroat fishery in the bay and river up to the head of tidewater. An excellent small boat harbor and launch site are operated by the Port.

Clamming and crabbing are excellent here. Rock and bottom fishing in the bay includes perch, flounder, and sometimes lingcod. Gapers and softshell clams are plentiful on the flats.

Offshore bottom fishing includes skates, smelt, halibut, flounder, lingcod, rockfish, perch, greenling, and sculpin.

The sand dunes and beaches are extensive in this area also.

TENMILE CREEK.   A little-known but top-notch fishing stream located about twenty miles north of Florence. There is much cover and it supports a large population of trout, sea runs, and salmon. The blueback run is best early and late in the season. The fall coho run is excellent and is best in late October. The winter steelheading starts soon after this and peaks in

Yaquina Bay and Newport, Oregon

January. There are campgrounds and motels nearby, and major supplies in Yachats, Florence, and Waldport. Check local regulations.

CAPE PERPETUA. This is a relatively "new" area although Yachats was a pioneer summer home area. The small and brushy Yachats River has some good cutthroat and rainbow fishing. Some steelhead and coho fishing is to be had here in the fall—October and November for salmon, and December for steelhead. Rock and surf fishing here are popular and great sport. It is also a mecca for marine biologists and oceanographers, as well as naturalists and zoologists, for the ecology of the tidewaters and pools mingling with that of the Coast Range is unique. The new United States Forest Service visitors center on the cape features

lectures, color movies, and self-guided nature trails from the mountains to the sea.

WALDPORT. The Alsea River and bay comprise a major sport fishing area on the Oregon coast, but have nowhere near the pressure like that on other centers. The fishing is largely confined to the bay and tidewater river, however, as the bar is not navigable. This is also the site of one of the world's most unique salmon hatcheries—Lint Slough, a tidal creek where the Oregon State Game Commission has an experimental "super salmon" program going, in which coho salmon are bred and raised roughly to twice the usual size in half the normal time.

The bay and river have unusually late runs of salmon and steelhead, but the fall chinook, coho, cutthroat, and steelhead are superb. It's mostly a trolling show. The sea-

Salmon Harbor at Winchester Bay, which has since been enlarged

run cuts start in midsummer and continue to Labor Day. The chinook start showing in July and continue into September. Most of the jacks are caught in late summer and fall. The big fish show up in October and November.

Bay fishing also includes flounder, perch, with some crabbing and clamming.

All facilities and services are located conveniently with numerous camping and trailer sites available.

NEWPORT. Yaquina Bay and the river are a major West Coast center, and the site of the Oregon State University oceanography center, some private marineland attractions, an extensive charter and commercial fleet, one of the most picturesque waterfronts on the Pacific Coast, with every manner of fishing and marine recreation possible. Moreover, it is a major resort and retirement community.

Boats go out from here for the tuna waters, and also the offshore banks. Alongshore are extensive bottom fisheries of lingcod, black, orange, and china rockfish, halibut, flounder, perch, sculpin, and other marine species. In the bay are flounder, halibut, herring, top smelt, skates, perch, and green sturgeon, to say nothing of crabbing. You can catch herring from the docks, sometimes several at one time, using plain, brass hooks tied several on a line.

Yaquina Bay is a major crabbing area, with bait and traps obtainable locally. The clamming is also excellent, mostly butter and littlenecks, cockle, gapers, and softshell. There are some private oyster beds in the bay, and also some shrimp beds.

There is a nice sea-run cutthroat fishery from midsummer to October. The salmon are predominantly coho and jacks, with chinooks in the minority but running up to forty pounds. The salmon season starts in June and continues to fall. The Yaquina is not noted as a steelhead stream but eventually may be built into one through stocking programs.

The Newport beach area is also long famous for its agates and other rock-hound attractions.

DEPOE BAY. A small, cozy, haven from the restless sea, Depoe Bay is largely man-made and has no natural fishing river or estuary as such. The port takes up most of the space between the narrow entrance under the U.S. 101 bridge, and the basin. It is, however, a major sport and commercial fishing center, with a large fleet, some of which operates offshore in every month of the year. Bottom fishing for marine species, and alongshore salmon trolling and mooching, make up most of the activity; but with an increasing number of boats running out after albacore during the summer. Depoe Bay is also a resort settlement with all the usual facilities and accommodations, some of them rather plushy.

TAFT. Siletz Bay and river, with its tributaries, are easily one of the finest fishing and recreation centers on the Oregon coast, and one of the most convenient to visitors.

While the bar is dangerous and should not be attempted by amateurs—or even approached on the outgoing tide—there is excellent boat fishing inside the bay and in the tidewater river. Also, the bank and surf fishing here is the best on the Oregon coast. Bank casting with big salmon streamer flies for coho is especially good in the fall at the jaws. Clamming and crabbing are excellent in the bay. Bay bottom fishing for perch and flounder is also tops. Tomcod and greenling also come into the bay.

The Siletz is one of the finest steelhead and cutthroat streams in the state, and Drift Creek, for its size, is not far behind.

Sea-run cuts and salmon start coming in midsummer and continue through the fall. September and October are months when some really big chinook hogs are caught. Jack salmon fishing is also excellent, with a special bag limit on these. The offshore fishing here is done out of Depoe Bay. Taft and the surrounding area are a really fine family vacation and resort area with every kind of service and accommodation available in every price range. It is also convenient to the Lincoln City complex, and to freshwater Devils Lake, an all year around fishing water.

The winter steelhead and salmon runs in the Siletz River start in October-November. There are many local regulations on the up-per river because this is a principal stream in the Game Commission's steelhead program. There is also some outstanding steelhead fly fishing on this river. For its size it ranks close to the famous Rogue in quality as well as quantity. It has long been a favorite of the experts.

SALMON RIVER: This gentle, meandering tidewater stream, which enters the ocean beneath Cascade Head, is now largely bordered by private property, but enough public access remains to make it worthwhile. It is a bank fishing show, except in the lower reaches.

Some really fine fly fishing for planted rainbow and sea-run cutthroat can be found here, especially below the bridge at Slick

The snug little "dog hole" at Depoe Bay

The excellent small boat harbor at the mouth of the Chetco River at Brookings

Rock Creek. The fall and winter rains bring some surprisingly big steelhead and chinook salmon into this stream. Jack salmon are also plentiful. Rock fishing at the mouth for marine species is also productive. Lincoln City is the closest supply point.

NESKOWIN. This is an old-time resort area, with many beach homes, a golf course and bridle paths. Surf fishing is possible, but not practiced much. Neskowin Creek was once one of the finest steelhead and salmon streams in this section. It is now suffering from an overdose of commercial development.

It is stocked each year with trout, mostly cutthroat. When water gets high enough in the fall, there is a coho run. Some steelhead arrive in December and January. It is all bank fishing.

NESTUCCA BAY. This is a fabulous

sport fishing center, now off the main highway, but may soon be in the path of a new water-level route. The bay itself receives the water from the Nestucca and the Little Nestucca and their tributaries which head in the Coast range. The bay is too shallow for boat operations, although in pioneer days even oceangoing schooners came across the bar and tied up to a cannery at Porter Point on the south side. The bay has some excellent clamming and crabbing on the flats, however.

A long sandy spit, leading northward to Cape Kiwanda, separates the bay and lower Nestucca from the sea. Under the lee of Kiwanda is the home of the famous surf dories which have operated here for nearly a hundred years. These dories are handled by commercial and sport fishing guides, and by private owners from June through September alongshore for salmon, and occasionally far offshore for albacore.

River drift boats are used on the Nestuc-

ca. The river has an almost continuous series of salmon, steelhead, and cutthroat runs from May on through the summer and fall, and into December and January. The winter steelhead run in November and December is one of the best on the West Coast.

Facilities, supplies, services, and guides can be found in the settlement of Pacific City, which also has a state-owned landing strip; in Woods, Cloverdale, Hebo, and Beaver. Services include a salmon cannery, boat works, campgrounds, and accommodations of every kind, although none of the plush variety.

The bottom fishing includes flounder, some large halibut, sea bass, lingcod, greenlings, perch, and other varieties. Almost unknown, even to many local residents, is a run of chum salmon in the bay, which will under some circumstances take lures, and even flies.

SAND LAKE. A tidal basin connected with the ocean just north of Tierra del Mar

Nehalem Bay is an excellent fishing spot, but the bar is dangerous

and just south of Cape Lookout, is a little-known recreation and fishing spot, with some handy nearby camping and picnic sites. The "lake" is a unique aquatic basin which has a surprising variety of fishing. There are a steelhead run in February, a chum salmon run in November and December, a coho run in October, November, and December, sea-run cutthroats in July and August, as well as perch and flounder and crabs.

TILLAMOOK BAY. This is the second largest estuary in Oregon, and one of the largest on the West Coast. Although generally shallow and badly shoaled up, it supports a number of communities such as the city of Tillamook, Garibaldi, Barview, Bay City, and around on Cape Meares such popular resorts as Oceanside and Netarts.

The bay is fed by outstanding fishing streams such as the Tillamook, Trask, Kilchis, Wilson, and Miami, all of which have first-class runs of salmon, steelhead, and cutthroat.

In June the alongshore and offshore salmon fishing begins and continues into November, weather permitting. Many boats also go out from here for the albacore waters. Ports like Garibaldi are important commercial fishing as well as sport fishing centers.

The first salmon start coming into the bay in August, and bay fishing is good from then on into October. Some of the chinooks go as high as fifty pounds. The coho season runs from June through September. The winter steelhead season, which begins in October and runs into January, has been, in recent years, superb.

There is an important, but not so well-known sea-run cutthroat fishery in the rivers entering the bay, mostly in tidewater.

The bay is noted for its excellent crab-bing and clamming, carried on most of the year. Razor clams, gapers, softshell, little-neck, and butter clams are to be had.

Herring has been plentiful in the bay most of the year. Rock, jetty, and bottom fishing goes on almost all year around and includes perch, flounder, lingcod, rockfish, halibut, kelp greenling, rock bass, and others.

An extensive charter fleet operates out of Garibaldi. Campgrounds are numerous, especially around the north side.

NETARTS BAY. Nestled between Cape Lookout and Cape Meares, shallow Netarts Bay is one of the largest estuaries in the state but is virtually unnavigable because of its shoals. It is noted mainly for its clamming and crabbing and some bottom fishing. There is good camping at Lookout State Park and supplies can be had close by. Boats, crab pots, and bait can be obtained from several moorages. Some motels are located in the area. The bar is extremely dangerous and should be avoided.

NEHALEM Bay. This is a first-class sport fishing site, wherein terminate the Nehalem River and the North Fork Nehalem, both excellent salmon, steelhead and sea-run cutthroat streams. The first fall rains bring the salmon in, and the fishing in the bay gets hot first. The jacks come first, followed by the chinooks, and last the coho salmon. The steelhead begin to show up in the late fall. Spring and early summer are devoted to bottom fishing, clamming, and crabbing. The surf and jetty fishing is usually excellent, with flounders and perch the most abundant.

The bar is very dangerous and should not be attempted except under the most favorable conditions.

Several state parks, public boat launching ramps, and a number of moorages are located in the vicinity. Most services and supplies are available in Wheeler or in the town of Nehalem.

SEASIDE. This Coney Island type resort under the lee of Tillamook Head, is also a sport-fishing center. However the Necanicum River is one of the finest winter steelhead streams for its size on the north coast. The river is also heavily stocked with rainbow and cutthroat trout. Some coho show up in the late fall as well.

The Clatsop beaches from the mouth of the Necanicum north to the Columbia, are also famous for razor clams, the most important on the Oregon coast.

COLUMBIA RIVER. "Mother River" for the Pacific salmon, this majestic stream system drains an empire and supports an incredible fishery that ranges from smallmouth black bass to sturgeon, eel, and shad. The salt chuck extends upstream for thirty to forty miles, and the tides are measurable as far as a hundred miles inland, at Vancouver, Portland, and almost to Bonneville Dam.

The Columbia is the ancestral home of the "Royal Chinook," named thus because it was so highly prized by the royal families of Europe in the last century. It is also the home of the coho or silver salmon, the sockeye or blueback, of numerous races of sea-run steelhead, some of which go all the way up to the Continental Divide to spawn; of several species of native trout; whitefish, green and white sturgeon (some of which have been known to reach twelve feet in length and weigh 1,200 pounds); numerous miscellaneous species such as lampreys and squawfish; and several varieties which were introduced from the East such as shad, smallmouth and largemouth black bass, catfish, and other spiny rays. Even striped bass, which were introduced into the Sacramento from the East, have been known to appear in the Columbia.

A world shipping port, as well as a major West Coast sport fishing center, the Columbia Estuary is really a series of fishing centers. In addition to Astoria, there are Warrenton and Hammond on the Oregon side, and Chinook and Ilwaco on the Washington shore. The charter boat business here is the most highly developed in the Pacific Northwest, with literally hundreds of boats operating regularly during the season. There are marinas, small boat harbors, and all the attendant facilities capable of handling thousands of sport-fishing and pleasure boats. The huge commercial fishing fleet is based here, along with major fish-packing and processing plants. The Oregon State University marine biology and fisheries laboratory is located here.

The entrance to the Columbia can be described as one of the world's most treacherous stretches of water at times. It is extremely dangerous for the amateur or the foolhardy. It can also be mighty unpleasant for experienced skippers and oceangoing craft up to and including the largest passenger vessels. However, it is heavily patrolled and during the height of the salmon season there may be anywhere from 1,000 to 5,000 boats on the bar, just inside, or strung out outside up and down the coast, and out to the lightship.

On the other hand, one just doesn't know what salmon fishing is until he's experienced a trip out across the Columbia Bar.

The fishing area alongshore extends from Long Beach southward to Gearhart, and out to the Columbia Lightship. Bottom fishing for halibut, rockfish, lingcod, black cod, flounder, greenling, perch, redtail, and other marine species is available all year around, weather permitting.

Feeder salmon can be found off the mouth also much of the year.

The north and south jetties are popular fishing spots for bottom species, and once in a while a salmon is caught from the rocks as well.

Steelhead fishing runs from November to March in the lower tributaries such as Lewis and Clark River, Youngs River, Klaskanine, Big Creek, Grays River. In the main Columbia the steelhead run from July through September. Coho salmon enter the river in September, and the chinooks move up in a series of runs in the spring, summer, and fall, with the fall race being the major one. The offshore salmon season starts in June and continues through Labor Day.

August and September are the peak months for both coho and chinook over the bar.

There is a large run of cutthroat in the summer and fall, right up into December. Fishing for white and green sturgeon goes on all year around in the lower river.

Pier and bottom fishing in the estuary is excellent much of the year. Crabbing in the summer in Baker Bay and other locations is popular. On the ocean beaches, razor clam digging is also productive. Surf casting for redtail perch is excellent all along the Clatsop beaches.

A special breed of adventurous sport fishermen has been going offshore, sometimes as far as seventy-five miles each summer after albacore since the early 1930's.

3.

Washington Coast

CHINOOK (Columbia Estuary). Small village and popular sport-fishing center during salmon runs, located on north bank, just west of Astoria bridge approach. Boat launches, trailer and campgrounds, charter service, picnic grounds and other facilities. The channel along here is heavily fished for chinook and coho in August and September, and when the bar is too rough to go outside. Sea-run cutthroat and steelhead also are caught alongshore in summer and fall, and in nearby tributaries.

ILWACO (Baker Bay, Columbia Estuary). A major sport-fishing center, one of the finest small-boat harbors on the coast; a highly developed charter boat port with first-class professional facilities of all kinds. The harbor is well sheltered, and opens to the Columbia Bar through a short channel between Sand Island and Cape Disappointment.

Salmon and steelhead during regular season. From the jetties, lingcod, perch, redtail, black and yellowtail rockfish, greenlings; excellent crabbing in summer. Access to state parks and campgrounds, and to jetty area on the ocean side of the cape.

From June until Labor Day, this is a crowded, popular mecca for sport fishermen who come from every state and many foreign countries. For salmon seasons, see listings for Columbia Bar, Warrenton, Astoria, Hammond, Chinook, and offshore.

LONG BEACH PENINSULA. Little or no fishing on this sandy spit stretching north from Cape Disappointment to Leadbetter Point, but there are plentiful razor clams in season.

WILLAPA BAY. Entrance twenty-four miles north of Columbia River, a large shallow bay fed by a number of tributaries, famous for oyster beds, and lumbering. Fish, seafoods, logs, and lumber products are shipped from Raymond. The bay bar, three miles out, is dangerous and marked by shifting sands and tidal currents.

Green and white sturgeon are caught in the harbor in summer. In winter they migrate up the freshwater streams. Cutthroat and steelhead are found in the tributary rivers such as Palix, Nasselle, North Nemah, and Willapa. Chinook are caught inside the bay in summer. Perch and flounder are taken off the point on the north side, and Dungeness crab and hardshell clams are also found there.

Willapa Bay opens into the major salmon-fishing area alongshore, and offshore boats also leave from here. Pink or humpback salmon are taken alongshore in odd years. Chinook and coho fishing is excellent from April to October.

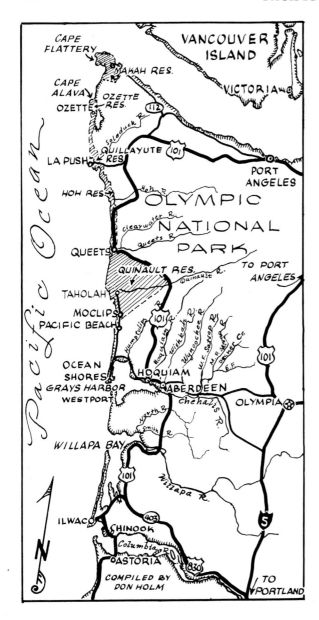

The ancient Quinault Indian dugout canoes are still used, but with modern outboard motors.

(Above) A descendant of the old North Pacific tribes practices his drum beating on Lake Quinault. (Below) A section of the raw Olympic Peninsula coastline.

Along the beach stretching northward are surfperch and razor clams. The jetties and rocks here and north to Grays Harbor are excellent spots for perch, lingcod, rockfish, kelp greenling, cabezon or bull cod, and starry flounder. The offshore bottom fishery includes halibut in spring and summer, several kinds of rockfish, true cod in fall, starry flounder, lingcod, sand sole, petrale, and jack mackerel.

In this section, extending north to Flattery, the coho salmon tend to be offshore in spring, closer in during the summer and fall season. The chinook are found offshore from April to late June, and close in from early July on.

WESTPORT (Grays Harbor). This settlement, just inside the south entrance, is a major sport-fishing center, and one of the best known salmon ports in the world. The salmon season here is one of the longest on the coast and the most productive next to the Columbia.

The bar here is extremely dangerous for amateurs; however, an extensive charter fleet operates from April to October, most boats making two trips a day.

There is some late summer and early fall trolling just inside the bay for chinooks and coho. Bottom fishing is also excellent in the harbor for starry flounder, Dungeness crab, and hardshell clams. Green and white sturgeon are taken in the outer tributary channels. Sea-run cuts and winter steelhead are found in the Johns and Chehalis rivers, and also in the Humptulips River which flows into the North Bay.

Grays Harbor also has several other major sport centers, including the cities of Aberdeen, Hoquiam, and Ocean Shores on the north peninsula.

The Olympic beaches extend north from here to Cape Flattery. Much of this is within Indian reservations, with one national park corridor, and access by car is limited to a few communities. This section of the coast is also a major clamming area, a popular summer recreation area, with some surf

The small boat harbor at Westport, Washington, just inside Grays Harbor

(Above) Grays Harbor, looking west. (Below) Willapa Bay

(Above) Bellingham Bay and breakwater. (Below) Port Angeles on the Strait of Juan de Fuca

Quinault River below the lake. This stretch of river is popular with steelheaders who run it with Indian guides and canoes

fishing and alongshore fishing with surf-boats. The major salmon fisheries operate out of shelters at the mouths of major streams.

MOCLIPS.   Near the mouth of the Moclips River, a steelhead stream, reached by State Highway 109 from Hoquiam, where clamming is also done.

TAHOLAH.   An Indian village near the mouth of the Quinault, which is the outlet of Lake Quinault. This is a salmon and steelhead stream, and is unique for its Indian guides who take you out in cedar dugout canoes equipped with modern outboard motors. The Quinault is one of the best known trophy steelhead rivers.

The shoreline here is one of steep white and yellow cliffs. The river is safe for small craft and outboards but facilities are limited.

QUEETS. The Queets River is the largest between Grays Harbor and Flattery.

The coast here is broken by steep cliffs but has broad low-water beaches with rocks and sea stacks offshore. The Indian settlement of Queets is reached by U.S. 101. From here the Olympic National Park ocean corridor extends north to Cape Alava.

LA PUSH. This is a major ocean fishing area and is north of Hoh Head which marks the mouth of the Hoh River, another famous peninsula steelhead and salmon stream. La Push itself is at the mouth of the Quillayute River and is protected by a jetty. There is a channel leading into a small-boat basin at the Indian village, but local knowledge is needed for navigation across the bar. Indian guides and boats are available, as well as other facilities.

The salmon fishing is done in the river and just offshore. Chinook and coho are taken in summer and fall. Bottom fishing includes rockfish, lingcod, halibut, perch, greenling, and flounder. Steelhead and cuts are taken in the lower river and tributaries, such as the Soleduck, Calawah, Sitkum, and Dickey.

CAPE ALAVA. Most westerly point on the coast of mainland United States, this place is reached only by road from the strait side of the peninsula and is on the Ozette Indian Reservation. Big Ozette Lake is also located here.

There is excellent rock and surf fishing along here, cutthroat and kokanee (land-locked sockeye salmon) in the lake, and sea-run cuts in nearby streams.

From Umatilla Reef just off the cape, northward to Cape Flattery, and around the cape into the Strait of Juan de Fuca, is a heavily fished major alongshore salmon region. Some halibut are also taken offshore in the vicinity of Flattery.

CAPE FLATTERY. Reached from Neah Bay through the Makah Reservation, this is an isolated area. Some surfboats are launched by Indians on Mukkaw Bay. Shore and rock fishing includes lingcod, rockfish, and greenling. The extensive salmon fishery offshore and alongshore brings commercial and sport boats by the thousand. Most of them operate out of Neah Bay and other strait ports. Salmon fishing is done mostly by trolling, feeder coho in summer, adult pinks (humpbacked), chinook, and coho in late summer and early fall.

This is open sea, big water, and subject to sudden and often violent storms—no place for amateur and foolhardy boat operators.

The Quinaults and other Indian tribes control much of the coastal strip of the Olympic Peninsula

4.

Strait of Juan de Fuca

The legendary Strait of Anián (meaning a secret passage to some fabulous Asiatic province) from the Atlantic (which was then known more commonly as the Western Sea), was long the goal of adventurers. It was even listed in Richard Hakluyt's famed *Divers Voyages.* Finally it became the Strait of Juan de Fuca in honor of an entirely mythical voyage of an imaginative self-promoting Greek named Juan de Fuca, who related a tale to Michael Lok in Venice in 1596 of having sailed through North America by way of the long-lost strait.

The strait which now bears Juan de Fuca's name was probably first explored by Captain John Meares, a freebooting English trader, in June, 1789. At little Neah Bay, just inside the Strait from Cape Flattery, the Spaniards in 1791 actually built a permanent settlement—the first one ever established by white Europeans on the Northwest coast of what is now the United States. Neah Bay is today a busy harbor on the Makah Indian Reservation and a major sport-fishing center.

The strait, which is the entrance to Puget Sound and the Inland Passage, is a busy rugged waterway exposed to the open Pacific, and not a place for the amateur and the foolhardy (although you find a lot of both there during the summer).

During the summer months this area from Tatoosh just off the tip of Flattery, and inland to Port Townsend, north to the San Juans, and back out along the southern tip of Vancouver Island, draws sport fishermen by the thousands from all over the Northwest, from every state, for the salmon runs.

It is worked by the commercial fleet, of course, which also operates off Swiftsure Bank, west coast of Vancouver Island, and along the coastline. Some sports also operate offshore in that area, but most work around Flattery and southward to Mukkaw Bay, and return. For the latter, Neah Bay is the home port. But the shoreline along the United States side of the strait is also heavily fished not only from Neah Bay, but from a number of other sport centers.

One reason for the unusually good fishing in the strait is the nature of the bottom. The soundings show an irregular underwater terrain, broken by ledges and banks, with a deep submarine valley one hundred fathoms deep and two to four miles wide extending thirty-seven miles out from the entrance.

Tidal currents are strong through here, and the entrance is subject to strong winds and much fog in summer. There is usually a heavy swell extending inland as far as Port Angeles and Port Townsend.

In summer prevailing northwesterly winds increase in the evenings to ten knots usually. During the "non-summer" months, the entrance is as a rule subject to exceptionally severe weather, with heavy seas breaking and strong currents. The heaviest rains occur during December and March, but the rainfall is considered heavy even in summer.

The entrance, and for fifty miles inland to Race Rocks, is about twelve miles wide, then opens to sixteen miles for another thirty miles to Whidbey Island. The water is deep near to shore which brings the salmon runs in close.

Here is where the salmon runs are first encountered each season by sport fishermen. Here also some of the really big chinook "hogs" and some hefty coho also are taken as they move into the Puget Sound and interisland areas. The early runs of the big chinook start in May and continue into September. During the summer there are peaks of various races such as spring, summer, and early fall chinook. Coho fishing reaches a peak in September and October, especially in the vicinity of Clallam Bay and Sekiu. The winter fishing is carried on mostly around Port Angeles and inland because

of weather and seas. Local experts, however, tell me that the finest blackmouth fishing is had during the winter months out of Neah Bay and Sekiu.

As mentioned, the troll and mooching fishery is carried on close to shore, and out around the cape. This area is also excellent for rockfish and halibut. Inside the strait the channel abounds in halibut, lingcod, cabezon, kelp greenling, and rock—fish the ledges and shelves. Feeder salmon are found in the strait all year around. Alongshore there are rockfish, lingcod, halibut, greenlings, and shellfish.

Off the mouths of streams emptying into the strait there is excellent steelhead and cutthroat trout fishing. These include the Sekiu, Pysht, Hoko, Elwha, Dungeness, Lyre, and other streams.

NEAH BAY. This bustling Indian village and harbor have all facilities, including charter boats, available. The bay is closest to "outside" fishing. It is reached by highway from Sappho or Port Angeles. Between here and Sekiu, farther inside the strait, there are numerous small coves and beaches where boats can be launched or casting done from the rocks and beach. The highway runs close to the strait most of the way.

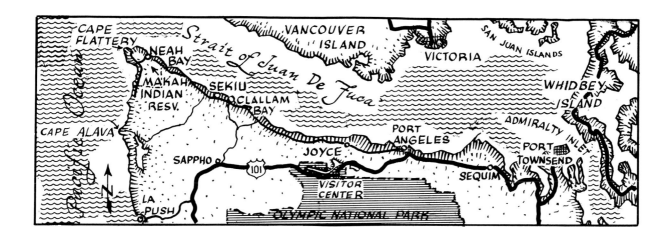

SEKIU-CLALLAM BAY. This is a major sport fishing center, not only for the saltwater fishing but for steelhead and cutthroat fishing in the peninsula streams. Pink or humpbacked salmon and coho are taken in this vicinity in late summer and early fall, chinook from May to mid-September. Bottom fishing for marine species is also excellent along here. All facilities, including lodgings and boat launchings, are available here.

PYSHT. This is a smaller but important sports fishing center in the shelter of Pillar Point, with the same general fishing as Sekiu and other strait areas.

PORT CRESCENT. This is a popular beach area on a loop road off the highway from Joyce. There is excellent bottom fishing for lingcod, halibut, rockfish, and greenling, as well as salmon fishing. Between here and Port Angeles, Freshwater Bay is a

A 15-pound "blackmouth" caught off Sekiu. Note snow on hills.

popular skin-diving area as well, and the winter fishing for bottom species such as lingcod, rockfish, cabezon, and octopus is excellent. Skin divers of the Washington Department of Fisheries have discovered recently vast beds of geoducks and other shellfish in deep water which have never been exploited either commercially or for sport.

PORT ANGELES. The most important city on the Olympic Peninsula, this of course is a major sport and outfitting center, and with all manner of lodgings and facilities and transportation available. There is excellent fishing also in the adjacent area and even inside the harbor.

Feeder chinooks are found close in all year, and the adult fish mostly in summer. Coho and humpbacks are caught in summer and fall, in the area around Ediz Hook. Alongshore and from rocks and jetties, bottom fishing includes lingcod, halibut, rockfish, and greenling. Skin diving in winter for lingcod, rockfish, cabezon, and octopus is popular and productive. Steelhead and cutthroat fishing is excellent in local streams such as Morse Creek and Dungeness River. The steelhead are mostly winter fish with a few summer runs. The Dungeness also has some Dolly Varden trout as well as cutthroat.

DUNGENESS BAY. This area is somewhat off the beaten track, but is a popular and productive spot for steelheaders and sea-run trout fishermen, as well as alongshore salmon anglers, bottom fishermen, clammers and crabbers. Most of the salmon fishing is done around and just off the point. Crabs are caught inside the cove with dip nets both winter and summer. There are several local settlements in the immediate area such as Old Town, Jamestown, and Dungeness.

The harbor at old Port Townsend, the innermost end of the Strait of Juan de Fuca

SEQUIM. (Pronounced "Squim.") A major sport fishing center, between U.S. 101 and the waterfront. It is the outfitting point for Sequim Bay and the entire area between Dungeness and Port Discovery. There are many individual fishing facilities scattered alongshore in the area, and several camp-grounds and parks. This immediate locality has what amounts to a meteorological phenomenon—the weather here is often delightful when only a few miles away it is miserable. Feeder chinooks are found in the bay and in Port Discovery all year, with adult coho mostly in the fall. Offshore at Dallas

Bank, near Protection Island, there is a good halibut and bottom fishing bank.

PORT TOWNSEND. This historic old town on the tip of Quimper Peninsula (named for an eighteenth-century explorer-trader) is a major sport center, as well as a quaint and colorful waterfront community. Subject to economic ups and downs over the years, it will probably emerge in its true destiny as a recreational center.

Shallow Discovery Bay, as already pointed out, is a salmon fishing area, and is close by the offshore banks around Protection Island. Local communities and facilities are found all around the heavily wooded peninsula, reached by the loop road off U.S. 101.

Just off Point Wilson halibut are caught in April and May, with bottom fish, including four species of rockfish, starry flounder, English sole, rock sole, sand dabs, sablefish (black cod), kelp greenling, and two kinds of perch, to be had in the channel between the peninsula and Whidbey Island.

Salmon are caught all around the peninsula and in the channel. Alongshore in the harbor of Port Townsend they have some excellent sea-run cutthroat fishing between Point Hudson and Kala Point. In the spring halibut are found around Admiralty Head on Whidbey.

The tideflats in the area and around Indian and Marrowstone islands are shellfishing grounds.

Whidbey Island can be reached by ferry from Port Townsend and other points.

5.

Puget Sound

Narrow, tidal Hood Canal forms the eastern shore of the Olympic Peninsula from Port Ludlow and Port Gamble on the north to Potlatch and Hoodsport on the south. U. S. 101 runs along the west shore of the canal connecting with Shelton, Olympia, and the Interstate 5 Freeway. The islands and inlets and peninsulas that make up much of Puget Sound are connected by ferries to the mainland in key places. Systems of state and county roads connect with most of the little snug harbors and ports of the island country. There is salmon and trout fishing, as well as bottom fishing for marine species, clamming and crabbing almost everywhere. While some of the islands are still largely undeveloped, the booming Pugetopolis, fed by the industries of Seattle, Tacoma, Everett, and Olympia, has created a real-estate broker's paradise as people spread out trying to find elbowroom and to get away from each other. As a result, most of the island and mainland waterfront areas are locked up in private ownership, which often includes the tideflats in front of the property. Access for sport fishermen is mainly from resort communities and villages on the waterfront, and from a few major centers.

Most of the mainland waterfront and all of the islands are densely wooded, with a shoreline that varies from tidal basins and rocky beaches to steep sheer cliffs that drop abruptly into the water.

The tidal currents are strong and in some places dangerous, as they swirl in among the islands and out again. The best salmon and trout fishing (sea-run cutthroat mostly) is in these tidal swirls and rips, and it was here that the modern technique of "mooching" was developed.

Common to the lower Puget Sound island are skin diving and bottom fishing for lingcod, rockfish, sand dabs, English sole, perch, flounder, and many others. Feeder salmon are taken almost all year around. The so-called "blackmouth" fishing in winter in several parts of the sound is nothing more than feeder chinook fishing. Adult chinooks are taken in summer and early fall. Adult coho, and in some places pink or humpback (in odd years), are taken in late summer and fall. There are winter runs of steelhead in most of the Olympic Peninsula streams tributary to the sound with such musical Indian names as Dosewallips, Duckabush, Hamma Hamma, Skokomish; and on the mainland side in the Seattle-Tacoma-Everett areas as the Nisqually, Duwamish, Snoqualmie, Skykomish, Stillaguamish, and Skagit.

Lake Washington, "behind" Seattle, is

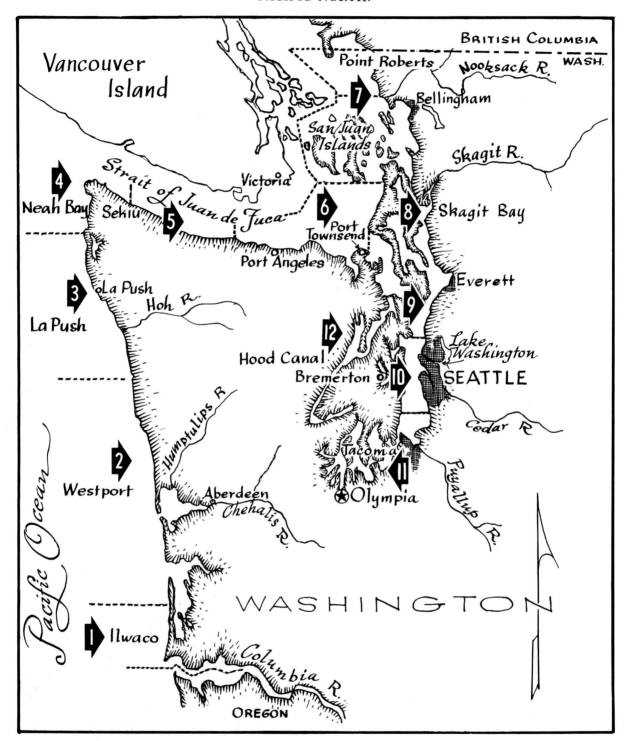

Numbered arrows on map indicate key saltwater fishing areas of Washington state

badly polluted but contains cutthroat, rainbow, perch, bass, some salmon, and kokanee.

There is a limited winter steelhead fishery in Shilshole Bay and the connecting waterway to Lake Union and Lake Washington.

In Elliott Bay, just off Seattle, are found

winter chinooks (blackmouths), coho, and chinooks in late summer and fall. Shilshole Bay and vicinity have winter and spring feeder chinooks, fall coho, and late summer and fall chinook (August-September).

Winter and spring chinook are found in the Port Madison and Point Jefferson areas. Feeder salmon are found all year around Bainbridge Island. In the Bremerton area waters, feeder salmon, as well as sea-run cutthroat are taken—the latter by trolling close to shore under the lee of cliffs in summer.

At the lower end of Hood Canal, steelhead and sea runs are taken around the mouth of the Skokomish River, feeder chinook in winter and spring in alongshore areas, coho in October and November, and chinook in late summer and fall. Some big coho are taken in October and November in Hood Canal and opposite the mouth of the Lilliwaup River.

The waters around Vashon Island are noted also for sea-run cutthroat.

Pick any waterfront town on the map of the Puget Sound country and one will pick a major saltwater sport-fishing center. Generally, however, the ones on the west side are small and numerous and the ones on the east side are overwhelmed by the big metropolitan industrial complexes. The best way is to pick a bay, an island, or an area one wants to fish; go there and let it happen to you. Personally, I can't get excited about fishing in sight of city office buildings, and around docks crowded with ocean vessels and busy tugboats. Give me the out-of-the-way places reached only by ferry or by boat.

Northward from Seattle, along the mainland shore, the odd-year humpies are found in the channel of Possession Sound and off Edmonds and across to Point No Point. The same area has many of the marine bottom species, feeder and adult salmon in season. Cutthroat are caught trolling close in to high-bank shore all through this area and as far north as the San Juans.

Mukilteo, Port Gardner off Everett itself, and the mouths of the Snohomish and other rivers are traditional spots. Farther north in the channel of Port Susan cutthroat and Dolly Varden are taken alongshore and off Camano Island. The mouth of the Stillaguamish and the tidewater river is a famous humpback, coho, chinook, winter and summer steelhead, and cutthroat water.

The channel between Camano and Whidbey Island, and close alongshore on both sides, is a highly productive salmon and cutthroat water. Holmes Harbor, on the east shore of Whidbey, is a famous salmon and

Looking down into a dangerous tidal channel along Whidbey Island.

cutthroat spot as well as an excellent bottom fishing area. Oak Harbor, on Whidbey, and the adjacent area is top water.

Northward, Skagit Bay is another cutthroat and Dolly Varden area; and of course the Skagit River is one of the world's best steelhead streams. Hope Island, between Whidbey and Tosi Point, is famous for its big Hope Island "hogs"—some of the largest chinook ever taken came from this area. This opens to Deception Pass, a narrow slit through Whidbey, through which the tidal currents boil ferociously at times. Going through the pass to the other side of Whidbey, one comes to important salmon waters of Rosario Strait. The narrow channel along Guemes Island leads back into Padilla Bay, noted for winter chinook, then north into Bellingham Bay. Some of the finest winter chinook fishing is along the east side of Lummi Island, and in the channel leading to Lummi Bay. On the west side of Lummi, reached by ferry from Gooseberry Point, is the ancient site of the Indian reef net fishery and is a productive spring and summer chinook water, and also for odd-year humpbacked. All the fish moving through here are bound for the Fraser River.

The San Juan group, located between the mainland here and Vancouver Island, is composed mainly of Orcas, Lopez, San Juan, and hundreds of lesser islands, including such privately owned ones as Blakely. It is a boatman's and a fisherman's and a vacationer's paradise. In recent years elbowroom-seekers have been flocking to the San Juans trying to escape the evils of urbanization. Moreover, on weekends there is a heavy influx by private airplane and yacht from Seattle and other metro areas. The result is some of the charm and a great deal of the solitude and elbowroom is fast

Deception Pass, a picturesque waterway, but subject to strong tidal currents.

disappearing. The San Juans still beat whatever is in second place as a retreat.

Not the least of the San Juan's attractions is its remarkable climate. Storms can rage all around the islands, while the island group itself enjoys banana-belt weather. Apparently this is another local phenomenon created by the prevailing winds and currents.

Around the islands marine bottom species such as rockcod, true cod, lingcod, halibut, rockfish, and numerous other species are abundant. The general salmon season is summer for chinook in most areas, coho in late spring through summer in the entire area, and another run from midsummer through fall in some waters. The summer chinook fishing is poor around the northern islands in the group, although there are many feeder coho in the area.

The channels along the west side of the San Juan group are in the main path of salmon going to the Fraser, with coho predominant around Waldron in summer, and the big winter chinook of December, January, and February off the tip of San Juan, Stuart and in Haro Strait.

The San Juans can be reached by airplane, by private boat, and by ferry from several points on the United States mainland and on Vancouver Island.

Two other points of departure for sport fishermen on the United States side are Blaine, the border town on the mainland, and Point Roberts, the isolated little United States community reached only through Canada or by boat, on the tip of a peninsula hanging down from the Fraser River delta.

Snug harbor for this sailing yacht in the San Juans, is in the cove off the end of the aircraft runway on Blakely Island

6.

Vancouver Island

Famous Campbell River, where the long narrow Campbell Lakes enter the Strait of Georgia, has attracted the great and obscure to its fabulous fishing for nearly one hundred years. This is the home of the Tyee Club where only a salmon of thirty pounds or more is counted a salmon; and it is still as popular as it was when Zane Grey made his pilgrimages to it.

A good paved highway now leads from Victoria, the capital of British Columbia, on the southern tip of the island to Kelsey Bay, north of Campbell River. From Kelsey Bay there is ferry service to the Upper Coast ports on the mainland.

Ferry service to Vancouver Island is available from mainland United States and Canadian ports at several locations connecting with this island road system. There is a main road from Parksville and Qualicum Beach across the island to the west coast port of Alberni at the sea head of Alberni Inlet. From Duncan, north of Victoria, a road leads to Cowichan Lake. With the exception of two or three short pieces of highway between isolated points, the island is mountainous and densely wooded, with most of the population and built-up areas along the east shore between Victoria and Campbell River. This section is also the most popular resort and sport-fishing area.

Along the southern coastline, adjoining the Strait of Juan de Fuca, it is possible to reach places like Rocky Point, Sooke, River Jordan, and even Point Renfrew by road.

Elsewhere, travel is difficult and facilities and accommodations are still primitive. One must have his own transportation, preferably boat, in order to reach some of the superb fishing areas that are unexploited by sportsmen as yet. There is an interisland boat service along the west coast of the island, and around the northern coastline, and charter float plane service is also available from Victoria, Nanaimo, Courtenay, and other places.

A secondary road leads from Port Alberni, a crowded busy little fishing and lumbering city, around the lakes and through the mountains to Ucluelet and Tofino on the ocean side. Scheduled ferry service touches the principal stops around the island.

A graveled road from Campbell River crosses through Strathcona Provincial Park to Gold River on Muchalat Sound. Englewood, Port Hardy, and Port Alice are also connected by a graveled road.

The fjords and inlets and island chains along the west coast and the banks offshore are popular and productive commercial fishing grounds. Clayoquot, Nootka Sound, Es-

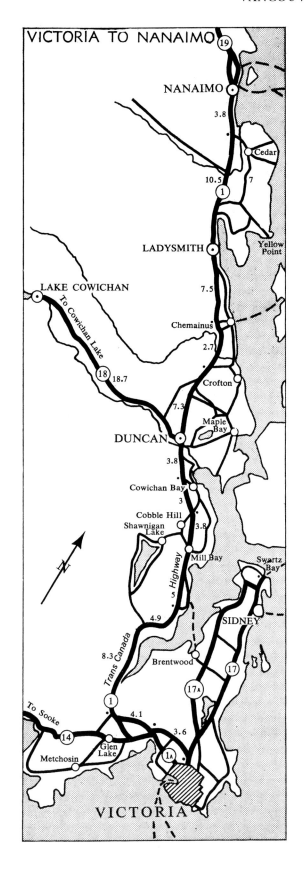

VICTORIA TO NANAIMO

NANAIMO

3.8

Cedar

10.5   7

LADYSMITH

LAKE COWICHAN   7.5

To Cowichan Lake

Chemainus

2.7

18   18.7

Crofton

7.3

Maple Bay

DUNCAN

3.8

Cowichan Bay

3

Cobble Hill

Shawnigan Lake   3.8

Highway

Mill Bay   Swartz Bay

5

4.9   SIDNEY

Trans Canada   8.3

Brentwood

17

1

17A

To Sooke   4.1

3.6

14   Glen Lake

Metchosin   1A

VICTORIA

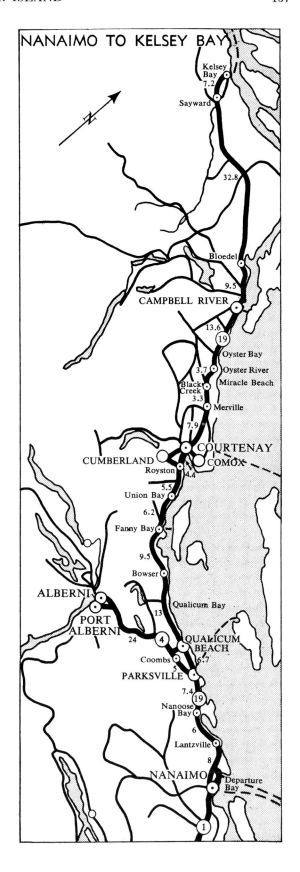

NANAIMO TO KELSEY BAY

N

Kelsey Bay   7.2

Sayward

32.8

Bloedel

9.5

CAMPBELL RIVER

13.6

19   Oyster Bay

3.7   Oyster River
Black   Miracle Beach
Creek   3.3   Merville

7.9

CUMBERLAND   COURTENAY
Royston   COMOX
4.4
5.5
Union Bay
6.2
Fanny Bay
9.5
Bowser
ALBERNI   Qualicum Bay
PORT   13
ALBERNI   QUALICUM
24   4   BEACH
Coombs   6.7
5
PARKSVILLE
7.4
Nanoose   19
Bay
6
Lantzville
8
NANAIMO   Departure Bay
1

peranza Inlet, Kyuquot Sound, Quatsino Sound, and Barkley Sound are all steeped in romance and history of the eighteenth century explorer-trader era, and are fascinating places to explore as well as fish. All can now be easily reached.

7.

British Columbia Marine Parks

Many of these marine parks are accessible only by boat and include:

Beaumont. At Bedwell Harbour on South Pender Island.

Newcastle Island. A 760-acre island in Nanaimo Harbour.

Montague Harbor. On the west coast of Galiano Island, 30 miles north of Victoria.

Pirates Cove. Southeast coast of De Courcy Island, which is 10 miles north of Nanaimo.

Plumper Cove. On the northwest coast of Keats Island which is in Howe Sound.

Princess Louisa. At the head of Princess Louisa Inlet, 90 miles north of Vancouver.

Rebecca Spit. On the east coast of Quadra Island about 140 miles north of Victoria.

Sidney Spit. On the north end of Sidney Island about 20 miles north of Victoria.

Smugglers Cove. At the north end of Welcome Passage, 12 miles north of Sechelt.

Tent Island. Off the south tip of Kuper Island, 3 miles east of Chemainus, Vancouver Island.

Additional ones are being added.

8.

Fishing British Columbia Waters

Steelhead. Found in most streams along the mainland and on Vancouver Island. Along the south coast, the Fraser and its tributary, the Thompson, are two of the best steelhead streams from September until May. The Nahatlatch has a good run in April and May.

The Bella Coola River is excellent from November to April. The Brem and Dean are two famous steelhead rivers but hard to reach. The Squamish and Powell rivers also are good.

In the Prince Rupert area, the Skeena River system includes the Kispiox, Morice, Telkwa, Copper and Bulkley. The record thirty-six-pound steelhead was taken from the Kispiox in October, 1954. This part can also be reached by road highway from Prince George.

The Vedder is by far the best steelhead river in the lower mainland area, with a run from December to April. The Chehalis, Coquitlam, and Alouette also have good runs from December to March. The Capilano, and the Semour near Vancouver, have runs from December to March and in June and July.

The Queen Charlotte Islands have superb steelhead fishing in the Copper, Tiell, and Yakoun rivers.

On Vancouver Island there is excellent steelheading on both coasts. On the west the best streams are: Ash River near Alberni, with summer and winter runs from June to October and December to March; Stamp River from July to September and December to March. On the east shore the best streams are the Cowichan, Nanaimo, Little Qualicum, and Puntledge rivers from December to April; Campbell River from December to March, plus a small summer run.

At the north end of the island, the Nimpkish River has an excellent run from November to March.

Generally, the finest steelhead fishing is during the late fall and winter months when the rivers are high. A few streams have summer runs, however.

Coastal Cutthroat. This fine anadromous trout is found in all waters open to the sea along the entire coast of the mainland and most of the islands. The sea-runs enter the streams in late November and continue through to May. They reach a size of about four pounds maximum. These trout also readily take flies, even in saltwater. There is no closed season on this fish.

Along the upper coast the best spots are the Bella Coola, Brem, and Dean rivers, as well as many more that are yet unknown to the fishing public.

In the Queen Charlotte Islands all the rivers are excellent cutthroat waters, and the fish are of the highest quality. Cutthroat, fresh out of saltwater, are the best eating fish that swim.

Vancouver Island streams on both coasts have varying runs of cuts, and most of the lakes which are connected to the salt chuck by rivers also have large populations of resident fish. Best lakes are the Cowichan, Great Central, Sproat, Buttle, Campbell, and Nimpkish.

Along the lower mainland, streams like the Nocomeki, Campbell, and Serpentine rivers in January and February are good. From Hope to the coast, bar fishermen on the Fraser find the best cut fishing from August to late fall.

Chinook salmon. All the waters of the British Columbia coastline are filled with the five species of salmon. The present world record on sport tackle is ninety-two pounds caught in the Skeena River near Terrace. The chinook is found all year around in all coastal waters.

A boat is almost a necessity for salmon fishing. Trolling with bucktail flies streamers for coho, and with spinners and bait is the accepted method. Strip casting is also popular.

Chinooks are also known as "tyee" (for over thirty pounds), spring, king, and black-mouth. In these waters the principal food is herring and needlefish.

The peak of the chinook fishing is in July, August, and September, although the salmon are present all year around.

On Vancouver Island the most popular places are Port Alberni, Campbell River, Cowichan, and Comox. However, all coastal waters are productive.

Along the mainland, the chain of islands, channels, and inlets are all prime chinook fishing grounds.

Around the Gulf Islands, where a moderate climate is found most of the year and a lower rainfall, the fishing is excellent, with the late summer and fall the best.

Jack salmon. The jacks of all species are found entering the spawning rivers ahead of the adult run in June and July usually.

Coho salmon. These are found with the chinooks in all coastal waters, with the best fishing from May through September. However, August and September are the best months.

The Queen Charlotte Islands are especially good coho waters, with the Copper River and bay on Moresby Island probably one of the best coho grounds in the world. The Tiell and Yakoun rivers also have excellent runs. These are hard to reach, but offer superb sport.

9.

Queen Charlotte Islands

This little-known group of British Columbia islands is about sixty miles off the mainland, across Dixon Entrance, Hecate Strait, and Queen Charlotte Strait. The three main islands are Kungit, Moresby, and Graham.

Reached only by boat, water taxi, or ferry, and by air on scheduled feeder line and charter service, these islands are virgin fishing grounds for the sportsman, although well known to northern yachtsmen and commercial fishermen.

The fishing is superb in the salt chuck around the islands, and most species of freshwater game fish are found in the main rivers—Copper, Deena, Yakoun, and Tiell.

The visitor is on his own in most areas of the group. There are hotels at Sandspit, Queen Charlotte City, and Masset. There is a road from Masset at the ferry landing on the northeast coast of Graham Island to Sandspit at the south end of the island. This touches Port Clements, Tiell, Queen Charlotte, Skidegate, Sandspit, across the bay on Moresby Island, also has a short road to Aliford Bay.

The rest of the group is primitive for all practical purposes, with numerous coves, inlets, and bays around the coastline where an occasional cluster of fishing boats and gasoline floats is found.

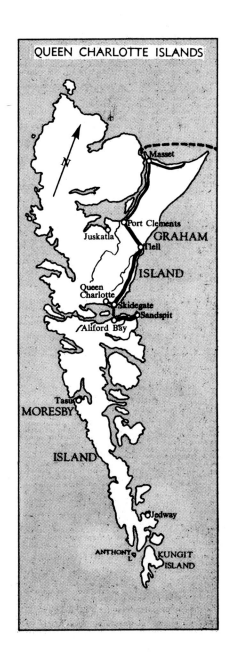

10.

South Coast British Columbia

This mainland section of British Columbia includes the city of Vancouver, a major metropolitan center of the West Coast, located on the lower estuary of the Fraser River.

Fishing areas, boat and charter services, moorages and other facilities number in the hundreds. In addition, there is a ferry service to Vancouver Island fishing areas. A modern highway leads northeastward up Howe Sound and into the primitive coastal mountains.

A ferry across Howe Sound lands at Langdale and connects with a highway along the coast to Earl Cove and Prince of Wales Reach; and from there a ferry crosses to another section of coastal Highway 101 which leads to the mill city of Powell River, and finally ends a few miles north at Lund. The coastline here is marked by numerous inlets, fjords, connecting coastal lakes—all bordering on the Strait of Georgia. There are also numerous islands in the strait, some of them quite large, such as Texada.

North of Lund there are no roads on the mainland, and the Inland Passage becomes a series of islands with narrow channels between them. Some are dangerous for strangers to navigate because of tide rips and extreme currents, underwater reefs, and floating logs.

The mainland is veined with long narrow saltwater fjords, leading in some cases for a hundred miles back into the coastal mountains, and are headed by glaciers. There are numerous fishing and Indian villages, fuel barges and landings, fish scows, moorages on islands, and an occasional airstrip or seaplane moorage.

Charter service for sportsmen is available at Vancouver to fish these rugged waters. Otherwise, the visitor must have his own marine transportation.

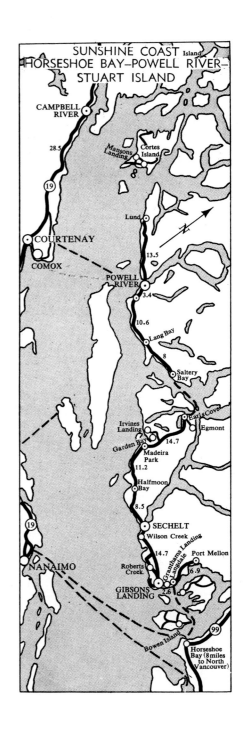

II.

Upper Coast British Columbia

Some of the finest saltwater sport fishing in the world can be found along the mainland north coast of British Columbia. The area is not readily accessible, however, reached only by private boat, float plane, charter service, or by ferry to regularly scheduled stops from which local charter service or rental boats might be had by the sportsman.

From south to north, the best-known places are Butte Inlet, Jackson Bay, Port Neville, Cracroft, Minstrel Island, Mamalilaculla, Simoon Sound, Thompson Sound, Tribune Channel, Alert Bay, Malcolm Island, Kingcome Inlet, Sullivan Bay, Allison Harbour, Seymour Inlet, Belize Inlet, Smith Sound, Fitzhugh Sound, Calvert Island, Rivers Inlet, Burke Channel, Bella Coola, Ocean Falls, Dean Channel, Bella Bella, Princess Royal Island, Douglas Channel, Kitimat, Grenville Channel, Pitt and Banks islands, and Skeena River.

Prince Rupert, which is the principal seaport of this section, is the terminus of the overland highway from the interior and also of the Canadian National Railway. A side road leads by land to Kitimat.

This is the terminus of an overnight auto ferry service from Vancouver Island and from southeast Alaska. There is regularly scheduled interisland boat service, air

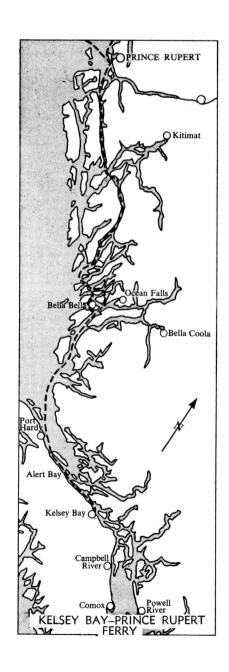

KELSEY BAY–PRINCE RUPERT FERRY

service, and charter service. Summer cruise ships also call here and at other coastal ports.

The last Canadian fjord before reaching Alaska is Portland Canal, a long narrow inlet that winds back into the mountains to Hyder and Stewart, which are surrounded by glaciers and peaks. Portland Canal is the international boundary. Hyder and Stewart are jumping-off points for big-game expeditions into the interior and are the terminus of a roadway under construction to connect with the Alaska Highway.

The Skeena Mountains and Stikine Plateau in the interior are among the most primitive areas left on the continent.

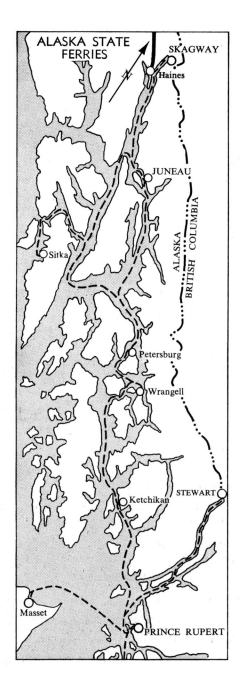

12.

Alaska Waters

Alaska, largest of the United States, ranges from the southeast tip at Dixon Entrance to Point Barrow at 71°23′ N. 156°28′ W. The state extends westward to Cape Wrangell at 52°55′ N. and 172°26′ E. on Attu Island (note the longitude is *east* of the International Date Line). The southernmost point is Cape Muzon on the historic parallel of 54°40′ (remember "Fifty-four forty or fight?"), between the United States and Canada, on the north side of Dixon Entrance, 480 nautical miles northwest of Cape Flattery.

The United States purchased Alaska from Russia in 1867 for $7,200,000, or about two cents an acre. For half a century Alaska was a wild region which might have been described as "no law north of 54-40." What passed for law and government was administered by visiting jurists from San Francisco, some of whom were only interested in exploiting the resources for their own profit. In 1912 Alaska became a territory, and on January 3, 1959, Alaska officially became the forty-ninth state. In 1960 the population was 226,157, which compares to a population of about sixty thousand when I first arrived in the territory in 1938.

Southeast Alaska, or the Panhandle, is the coastal strip, including the islands, from Dixon Entrance to Cape Spencer, about 250 nautical miles with a tidal shoreline of 11,085 miles. The coastal strip is about thirty miles wide and the island chain which makes up the Inland Passage, about eighty miles wide. The islands are mountainous and broken, covered with dense growths of spruce, hemlock, and cedar. The mainland mountains rise abruptly and are higher, usually snow-covered, and a traveler frequently sees blue glaciers in narrow defiles hanging down out of low gray clouds. In summer the snowline is at about 2,000 to 3,000 feet on the mainland. The island mountains are too low to carry snow through the summer.

The sea bottom is characterized by deep water, absence of shoals, numerous submerged and exposed rocks and reefs. There are innumerable coves, inlets, and bays in which boats may find shelter, but charts and pilot books should be consulted for local conditions and the nature of the bottom. There are many unmarked ledges around the islands, numerous fish-trap installations and other hazards to navigation. Kelp grows on rocky bottoms and should always be considered a sign of danger.

The principal communities in Southeast Alaska are Ketchikan, Juneau (state capital), Petersburg, Sitka, Skagway, Wrangell, Pelican, Haines, Douglas, and Craig.

In the days before radar, ships navigated

Dr. Dean Watt of Midwest Research Institute, gathering clams on an uninhabited island about 12 miles from Ketchikan

through the Inland Passage in heavy fog by means of sound. The length of time taken for a blast on the horn to echo off the cliffs and mountains was measured and the distance estimated from the elapsed time. In narrow channels a ship was kept to mid-channel by navigating so that the echoes returning from both sides arrived at the same instant. On my first trip to Alaska aboard the S.S. *Alaska*, the entire distance from Ketchikan to Juneau was through a dense fog navigated by means of the above sound system.

The average daily tide is from ten to seventeen feet, with the greatest ranges inside the Inland Passage. The prevailing current sets northward, with an average velocity of 1.5 knots. Velocities of four to six knots and more are not uncommon in the narrow channels of the Inland Passage, and their strength and direction do not always coincide with the published tide tables.

The weather of Southeast Alaska is dominated by winds from the Pacific Ocean which has been warmed by the Japan Current. The islands have a marine climate; the mainland coast strip generally has a continental climate, becoming more so farther inland. The climate generally is marked by high humidity, fog, heavy cloud cover, small temperature range, and rain. From my own experience, I would judge the best weather to be in late June, July, August, and early September, with July the most summery. From late fall to early spring, the pressure gradients are steep because of the intensity of the semi-permanent Aleutian low which lies between the Siberian high and the Pacific high.

The Gulf of Alaska and the Aleutian area

are the birthplaces of storms which move down across the continental United States and Canada. There is extensive cyclonic activity—an almost continuous procession of cyclones and anticyclones.

The prevailing winds in Southeast Alaska often reach gale force, with the gulf serving as a catch basin for storms. Among the island chain the winds vary greatly in intensity and direction because they follow the land contour. It is interesting to note that there are winds which reach sixty to seventy miles an hour at some portion of the exposed coastline every month of the year.

The Kispiox River, British Columbia, is famed for its trophy size steelhead such as this

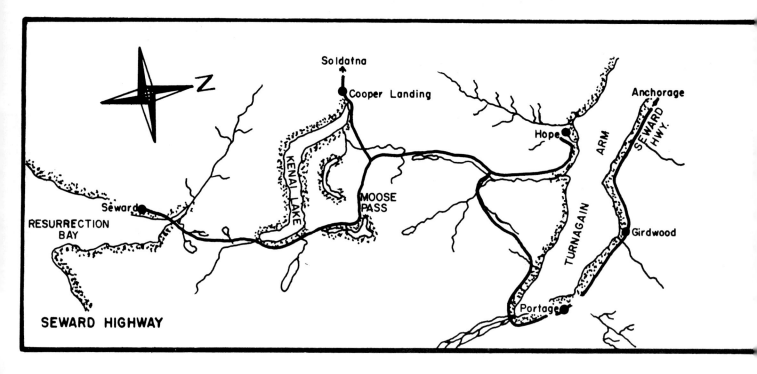

The Seward Highway (above) connects many excellent saltwater fishing spots in the Anchorage-Seward area. The Cordova area (below) between the Gulf and the glacier, has many good fishing spots.

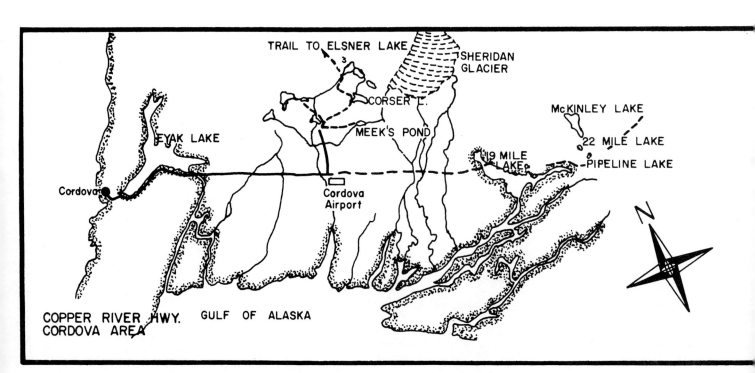

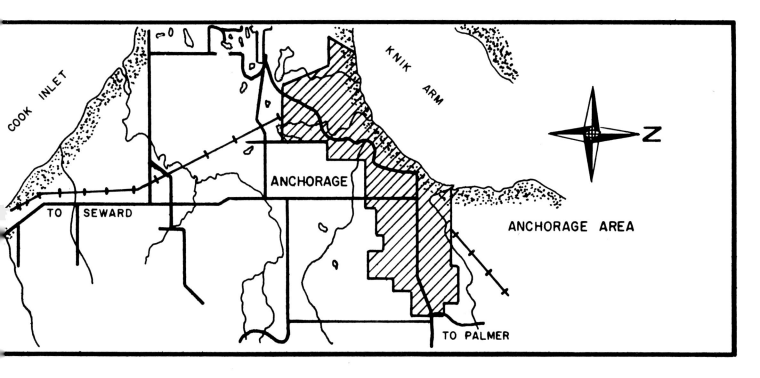

Anchorage (above) is more important as a jumping-off point for anglers and hunters, but also has some fine fishing within commuting distance of the city. The Palmer-Matanuska district (below) is accessible over a road network.

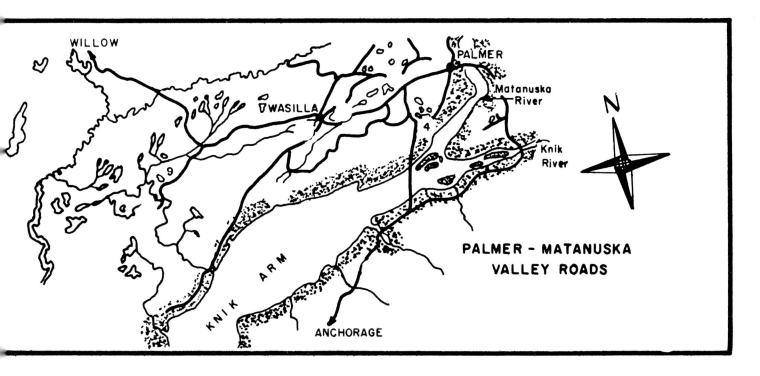

Downslope winds known as "williwaws," originating from the cold air mass over the interior, often reach incredible velocity, and in heavily populated areas such as Juneau, can cause considerable damage. Sometimes they are accompanied by blinding snowstorms. In Juneau a strong wind known as a "taku" (from Taku Glacier) is a local phenomenon.

Generally the winds are from the southeast quadrant during the winter, bringing most of the "weather." The east to northeast winds during this period bring snow, but the southwest and northwest winds bring clearing weather accompanied by high barometric pressure. In summer, local conditions influence the direction and velocity of winds, which frequently blow strongly along northwest-southwest channels. Nights are frequently calm, with the wind rising at sunrise, increasing to midafternoon, then moderating at sunset.

Winter gales continue for many days, usually from the southeast. Temperatures are mild in winter and the summers are cool, with the sun always at a lower angle in the sky than visitors from the south are accustomed to. Photographers will note that exposure meter readings are frequently misleading. Summer mean temperatures are in the fifties. Most snowstorms come in January, during which time the average temperature is about 30° F. In summer highs of 70° and extremes to 90° are not uncommon. Normal precipitation ranges from sixty inches over the mainland mountain ranges to one hundred inches a year over the maritime zone. Alaska's heaviest rainfall is at Little Port Walter where for an average of 269 days a year there is precipitation which adds up to 221 inches a year.

Light fog prevails over the maritime zone most of the year, with a heavy fog drifting against the coast on fifteen to twenty-five days a year, mostly in summer. Summer fog arrives about midnight and stays until noon. In winter fog is less frequent but lasts longer, up to ten days. Southeast Alaska is cloudy most of the year with the most cloudiness from September through December.

Icebergs and growlers are encountered in all months of the year, broken off glaciers. This ice is usually covered with mud and rock and sometimes appears as rocks awash. All ports, however, are ice-free all year, although floating slush ice is not uncommon.

A record halibut caught near Ketchikan weighing 405 pounds and estimated to be 40 years old.

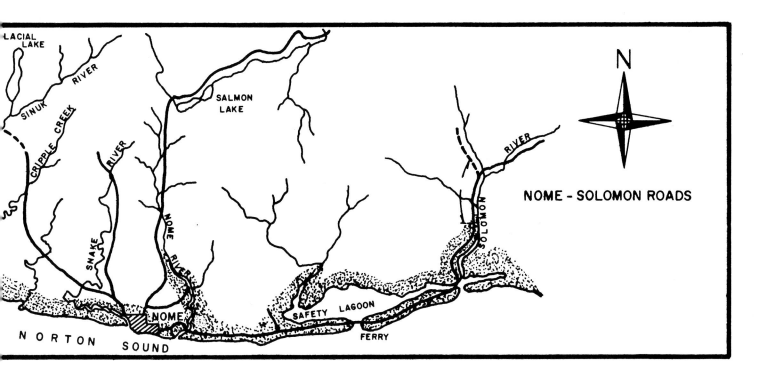

The little-known Nome area (above) is also a first class sports fishing region and is surprisingly accessible. The Kotzebue area (below) is more remote and is the gateway to the Brooks Range. Fishing camps and guides are available.

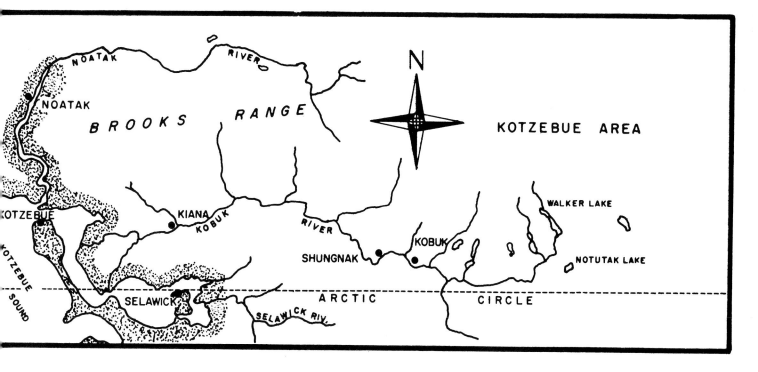

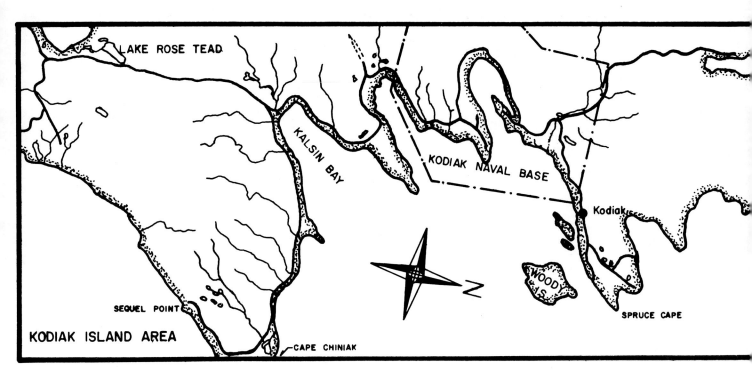

Good fishing is taken for granted in the Kodiak area (above), which is also one of the leading commercial fishing ports of the world. Bristol Bay (below) is famed as a sockeye gillnetting area, but also has some top sport fishing.

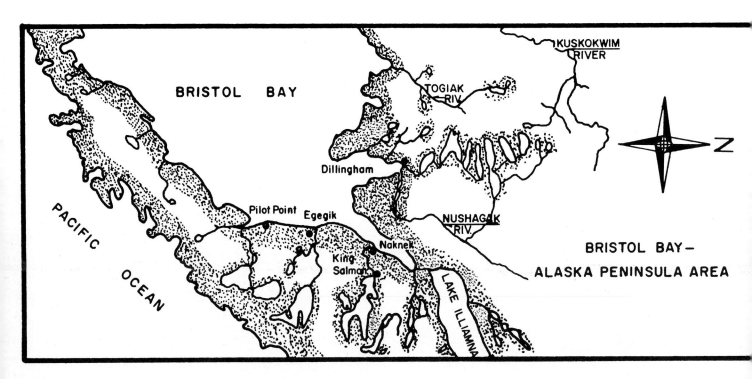

A wanderlust journey in pre-World War II days, brought this adventurer into Alaskan waters.

From Cape Spencer to the Beaufort Sea, the Pacific and Arctic coastline of Alaska totals 5,520 nautical miles, and the tidal shoreline is an incredible 18,377 nautical miles. This includes the Gulf of Alaska, the Alaska Peninsula, the Aleutian Islands, the mainland coast of the Bering Sea, Chukchi Sea, and the Beaufort Sea.

From Saint Elias to Cook Inlet, the coastline is generally rocky, the water deep, with rugged islands and mountains close up to saltwater. The main ports are Cordova, Valdez, and Whittier in Prince William Sound, and Seward in Resurrection Bay. In Cook Inlet the shores are strewn with boulders, the tides are extreme. The principal port here is Anchorage, Alaska's largest city.

Westward and through the islands off the Alaska Peninsula, the coastline is rocky. The principal harbor is Kodiak on Kodiak Island and Sand Point in the Shumagin Islands, King Cove and False Pass.

The Aleutians are rugged and mountainous, with few good sheltered anchorages. The main ones are Unalaska and Kuluk Bay.

The Bering is a shallow sea with extensive sand and mud flats alongshore and in the bays and inlets, with few rock formations. The main ports are Naknek in Kvichak Bay, Dillingham on Nushagak Bay, Bethel on Kuskowim River, and Nome on Norton Sound. Most of the anchorages are subject to violent squalls. Kelp grows on all rocky bottoms, with live kelp a sure sign of depth less than ten fathoms.

Tide rips and swirls are common all along Alaska's tidal coasts, sometimes of frightening velocity, and these can be a danger to navigation for vessels of any size.

The earthquake of March 27, 1964, had a tremendous effect on the Prince William Sound, Cook Inlet, and Kodiak areas, making great changes in the ocean bottom,

A nice chinook salmon caught on sport tackle near Juneau

which still render chart soundings unreliable. In some places the land rose and in others sank more than thirty feet. The coast of Alaska from Attu to Cape Spencer is occasionally subject to seismic sea waves which cause widespread damage to waterfront areas and shipping. An effective warning system is now manned for the entire North Pacific area. However, one of the world's most active seismic regions parallels the south side of the Aleutian chain and the Alaska Peninsula, and another active belt parallels Southeast Alaska and British Columbia, so earthquakes are frequent and often local in nature.

In these areas one should take immediate note of any earth shock or any unexplained sudden advance or withdrawal of the sea within an hour or so after a quake is felt. This is nature's warning of a tidal wave.

The weather to westward covers two distinct climatic zones—the dominant marine zone of southeastern and the southwestern coasts, including the Aleutians and north to the Bering Sea; and the Arctic zone from the Bering Strait around the hump of Alaska to the Arctic coast of Canada.

Most of the south and southwest coasts are dominated by maritime weather with small temperature ranges, high fog frequency, cloudiness, and lots of precipitation. Around on the Arctic coast the coastal plain is low rolling tundra with many lakes and ponds. The Brooks Range is a barrier which results in a narrow limit of temperature variation, light precipitation, and colder air.

The whole of the Alaska region is one big weather factory, which takes "getting used to" for most people, but is by no means in-

tolerable for these dynamic extremes of weather even have a compelling attraction for many people.

The Gulf of Alaska, the Aleutians, and the Bering, of course, are subject to strong winds most of the year, with velocities of up to sixty knots almost every month of the year at some stations.

The unsheltered Bristol Bay and west central section of the Alaska coastline have frequent strong winds, with the average velocity for the year of thirty knots, with winds of sixty knots common.

Over the Arctic coast between Icy Cape and Point Barrow in summer the predominant winds are from the northeast quadrant.

The south coast of Alaska is cool in summer with mild temperatures in winter. July and August are the best months, with January the coldest. On rivers or protected bays the temperatures at times drop to minus 30°.

The Aleutians are generally relatively mild with February being the coldest month, near freezing, and August the warmest, averaging 50°.

Along the Arctic coast the mean annual temperature is from 10° to 20°, with extremes ranging from a high of 85° to a low of minus 59°.

The precipitation ranges from a maximum of one hundred inches a year on the south coast to the dry Arctic coast. All the Aleutian and Gulf of Alaska ports are ice-free all year, except at the upper end of Cook Inlet. North of Unimak Pass, the ports are icebound to one degree or another for varying lengths of time each winter.

13.

Southeast Alaska

Sometimes called Alaska's "soft underbelly" and even its "banana belt," the Southeast hangs like a loose appendix from the main bulk of the largest state, snuggled closer to British Columbia than the rest of Alaska.

Part of the old First District of the territorial days, the state capital is still located in Juneau, a small city up at the head of Gastineau Channel, under the lee of Mount Juneau and walled off by Douglas Island. First settled by two prospectors named Harris and Juneau, it is the site of the old Treadwell mine on the island, and the Alaska-Juneau or "AJ" mine which in the late 1930's was the largest of its kind in the world.

Approximately five hundred miles long from Dixon Entrance to Yakutat Bay and seventy-five miles across, the island waterways from Ketchikan to Skagway and Cross Sound are more properly known as "Southeast Alaska," at least to the inhabitants. When you leave the protection of the Inland Passage at Cross Sound, round Cape Spencer on the run to Yakutat, you're getting into the Gulf of Alaska and an extremely different environment.

But the island waterway region, that includes also the mainland strip between the salt chuck and the Canadian boundary, is a contiguous, timbered and mountain empire, with glaciers and mud flats, and river deltas, misty waterfalls, rain forests, heavy overcast skies, dense fogs, narrow passes through which tidal races bore, Indian villages, canneries, logging camps, fleets of trolling vessels and purse seiners, and a climate that does not vary too much the year around.

Transportation is solely by airplane—bush planes on floats, amphibious craft, and transports that stop only at two major ports, Annette Island and Juneau—and by boat. The wooded islands are inhabited by Sitka deer, black bear and the huge brownies, and game of all kinds. Thousands of fresh-water lakes are found on the islands, most of them good fishing. The waterways around the islands, of course, are among the best fishing in the world. And most of the land is still in public ownership.

Principal towns and cities are Ketchikan in the south, reached by Alaska state ferries, steamship, private boat, and by air transport to Annette Island and by shuttle service from there to downtown Ketchikan; Wrangell, a little farther north, located at the delta of the Stikine River, an isolated little town supported by lumbering; Petersburg on Kupreanof Island, a historic fishing center; Juneau, up at the other end of Stephens Passage; Sitka, the historic old Russian capital, out on the ocean side of

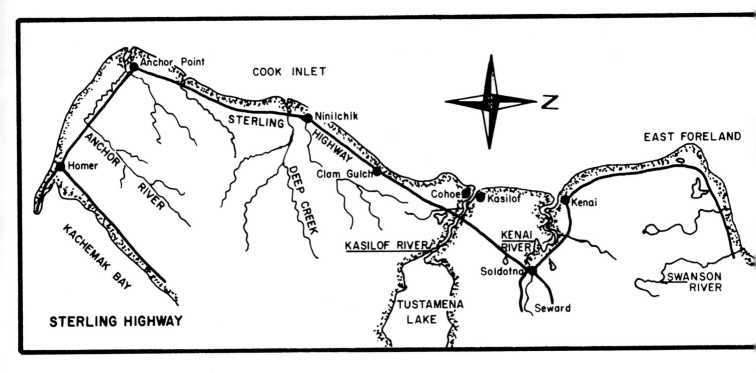

Many good fishing spots are now accessible by road (above) in the Seward-Homer area. Ketchikan anglers (below) must go by boat or float plane.

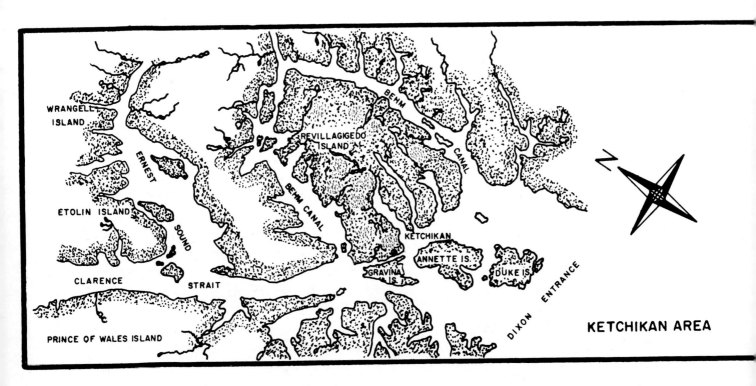

Baranof Island; and Skagway, the famed jumping-off point for the Klondike at the foot of Chilkoot Pass.

All of this is an entity called Alexander Archipelago, and a fascinating, beautiful region with more than nine thousand miles of coastline.

In addition to the above named towns, there are a number of other sport-fishing centers in more remote areas, on the outer islands, such as Hydaburg, Craig, and Klawock on Prince of Wales Island; Port Alexander, Chicagof, Hoonah, Tenakee, Chatham; Hawk Inlet, Excursion Inlet, and many even more remote and obscure.

Guides and services can be obtained, however, in all of the major towns, and charters arranged to go anywhere.

Latest studies by the Alaska Department of Fish and Game in Southeast Alaska show the principal sport catch to be chinook and coho salmon, with some chum and humpbacked; a rather minor steelhead catch compared to other West Coast areas; and a popular and well-developed sport in sea-run cutthroat and Dolly Varden. The principal ground species caught by sportsmen are lingcod, Pacific halibut, Pacific cod, and various types of rockfish. Halibut is the most common species taken of all, next

Juneau harbor and the "AJ" mine in pre-World War II days

to salmon. Bottom or groundfishes are most often taken as incidental catches while fishing for salmon. The same is true of cutthroat and Dolly Varden to some extent; and therefore, they are most often caught on heavy salmon gear rather than light tackle more suited to them.

Most of the cities have organized salmon derbies running most of the summer, from approximately May through August, and extensive sport-fishing fleets. Many commercial boats are also sport-rigged for charter service in these derbies. The sport fishery in the Sitka area begins in mid-June and extends through August. In other areas the season is approximately the same.

Southeast Alaska has some excellent shellfish including several kinds of clams, Dungeness crab, and shrimp. As mentioned before there are hundreds of freshwater lakes on the islands containing kokanee, Arctic grayling (*Thumallus articus*), rainbow trout, cutthroat, and steelhead.

There are, in addition to the lakes, many excellent, although short, coastal rivers and creeks that need fishing.

Juneau harbor, with the Coast Guard cutter, *Haida*, and the Douglas Bridge in background, circa 1940

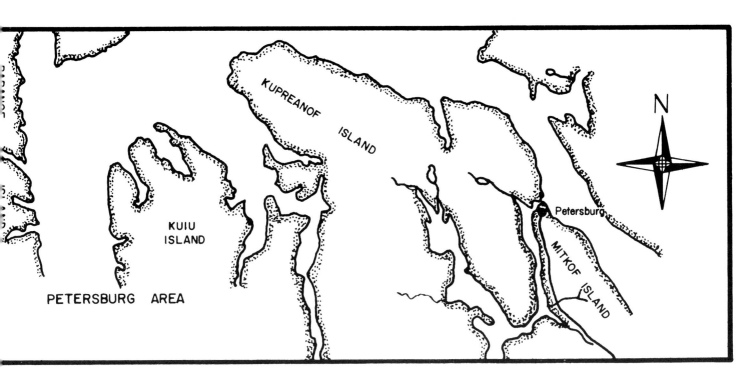

The Petersburg area has many fine sport-fishing opportunities (above) but a boat or float plane is needed. Wrangell (below) offers good sport in the salt chuck as well as in the Stikine River.

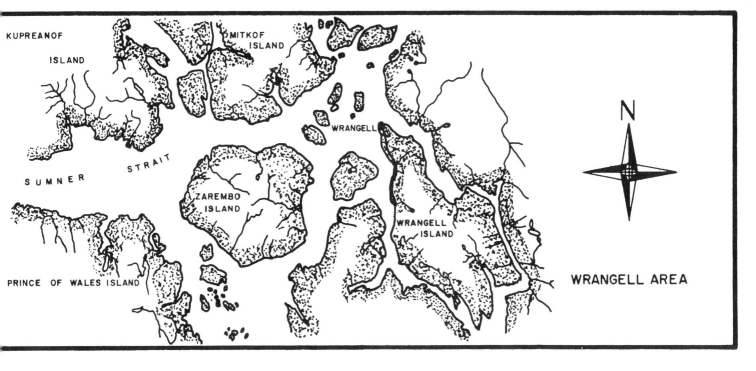

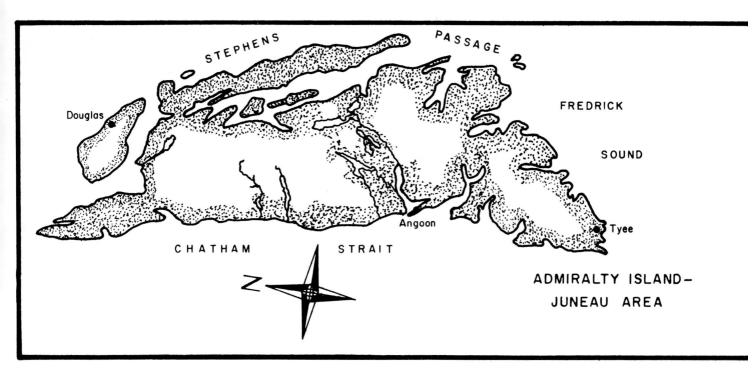

Admiralty Island (above) can be reached from Juneau by boat or float plane. A number of camps are maintained on the island. Baranof Island (below) includes the Sitka area, and remote camps reached by boat or plane.

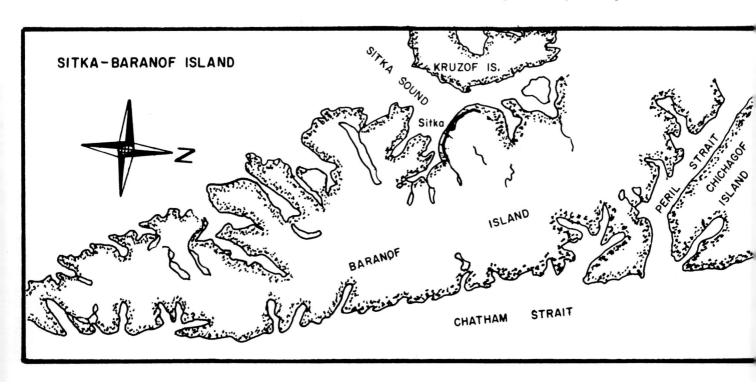

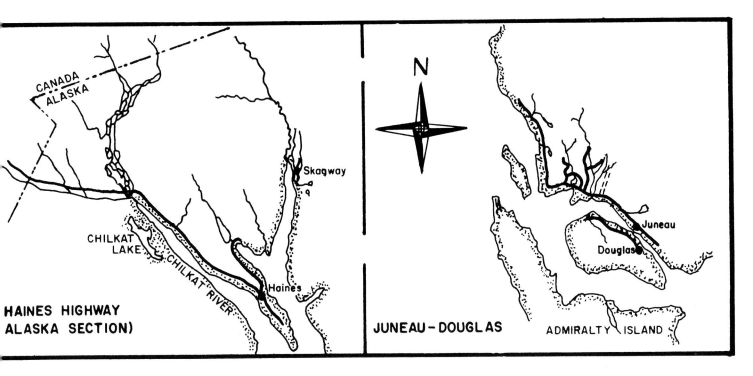

The Haines Highway furnishes access to the Skagway area, while Juneau has a local system of roads (above). Remote Yakutat (below) offers superb fishing but requires a bit of a safari to enjoy.

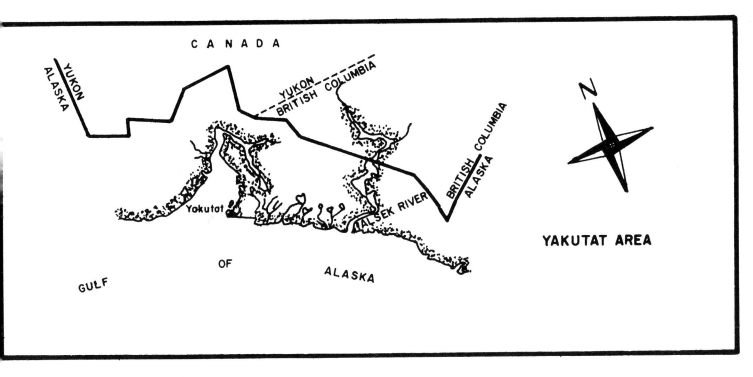

The chinook salmon season starts about May 1 and tapers off in August. The coho move in among the islands about August and continue through September.

Ketchikan Area. Commercial facilities, guides, rentals, and accommodations for hunting and fishing are readily available in the city of Ketchikan. Charter boats and airplanes operate out of here as well.

There are literally hundreds of miles of waterways and coastline for sportsmen, as well as many small lakes on the islands and on the mainland.

Principal species are rainbow trout, cutthroat trout, Dolly Varden, kokanee, steelhead, coho salmon, brook trout, humpback salmon, sockeye salmon, chum salmon, chinook salmon, rockfish, halibut, lingcod.

Guides are recommended for this area. Transportation is all by boat or air.

Ketchikan was once one of the world's top fishing areas, but nowadays commercial fishing is on the decline and lumbering has taken over.

Wrangell Area. This is an excellent sport-fishing area, as well as a cruising and hunting region which includes the mainland and the Stikine River, Zarembo Island, Prince of Wales Island, Wrangell Island, Mitkof Island. Kupreanof Island, and Sumner Strait.

The town of Wrangell is the principal supply point. Boat and air service is regular and available to other Alaska points. Charter boat and plane service are available. So are cabins and boats on the inland waters.

The Stikine River is a top sport stream, and there are several lakes within reach.

Chinook and coho salmon fishing is superb, the chinooks in the spring and the coho in the summer and fall. The fishing on the salt chuck is all from skiffs and boats.

Species include steelhead, cutthroat trout, Dolly Varden, coho salmon, humpback salmon, chum salmon, whitefish, sturgeon (in the Stikine), halibut, groundfish, rockfish and ground fish of all kinds.

Petersburg Area. This is an old but topnotch sport fishing area, based out of Peters-

Salmon being brailed into a cannery tender in Alaskan waters

burg on Wrangell Narrows. There are many miles of channels and island shoreline to explore and fish. There are also several good rivers and lakes. Air and boat service to other Alaska points is available at Petersburg.

Charter boats and aircraft available, as well as all commercial facilities, including boat and cabin rentals. The fall fishing is generally best, but there is something to catch most of the year.

Species include cutthroat, Dolly Varden, steelhead, rainbow trout, coho salmon, chinook salmon, sockeye salmon, halibut, rockfish, chum salmon, clams and crab.

Adjacent spots include Kupreanof Island, Mitkof Island, Baranof Island, Kuiu Island.

Admiralty Island. This is a popular spot, close to Juneau, located on Chatham Strait and Stephens Passage. It is only a few minutes from Juneau by air. Public cabins and one or two lodges with facilities are located on the island, which has many fine lakes and streams, as well as saltwater fishing. Boats are available at the lakes. There are some public camp shelters as well.

Boat transportation is also available from Juneau, fifteen miles away, where guides and other accommodations and supplies can be had.

Admiralty is also the home of the famed Admiralty brown bear, a huge ferocious relative of the Kodiak. On Pack Creek there is an observatory where the bears may be watched and photographed during the salmon runs.

Fishing includes rainbow trout, steelhead, cutthroat, Dolly Varden, coho salmon, and kokanee. Halibut, groundfish, and other runs of salmon are located in the surrounding waters. Schools of whales are frequently seen in the passages. The tideflats

in the bays and coves have some excellent clams. Fishing is from May to September.

Sitka-Baranof Island. This area, on the ocean side of the archipelago, has some superb freshwater and saltwater fishing. This includes a number of good lakes on the island. One excellent lake is located in the city of Sitka.

Boat rentals, guide service, air charters, tackle, and supplies are all available at Sitka, the historic capital of old Russian Alaska. Some of the lakes and creeks can be reached by road or trail from town.

Species include cutthroat, brook trout, Dolly Varden, rainbow trout, steelhead, chinook salmon, coho salmon, chum salmon, lingcod, halibut, grayling, humpback salmon, rockfish, clams, crabs.

There is a good run of sea-run Dolly Varden in the Nakwasina River. Sea-run cutthroat fishing is best in the fall.

Air and boat service is available from Sitka to other Alaskan points and the mainland.

Juneau-Douglas. The area around these towns, on Gastineau Channel, has a number of excellent lakes, creeks, and rivers, as well as saltwater fishery. There is a road from Douglas to the north end of the island; from Juneau one can drive several mouths southward, and north to Eagle Creek, Auke Bay, Tee Harbor, and Mendenhall Glacier.

Species include Dolly Varden, cutthroat trout, chinook salmon, coho salmon, whitefish, kokanee, chum salmon, brook trout, grayling, humpback salmon, rockfish, lingcod, halibut, crabs, and clams.

Fishing is from May through September. Party boats, charter boats, guide services, supplies, city-type accommodations, and complete commercial facilities for man, boat, or plane are available. There are campgrounds and lodges as well.

There is a salmon derby all summer long.

Skagway-Haines. This area at the head of Lynn Canal and at the foot of historic Chilkoot Pass is also the terminus of the Haines Highway which connects with the Alaska Highway. Chilkat River, Chilkat Lake, and the salt chuck are all excellent fishing, as are the small lakes and rivers.

There are pull-outs for cars, shore fishing spots. Boat rentals, guide services, and charter air service are available. There are a number of trails in the area, too.

Species include Dolly Varden, cutthroat trout, kokanee, whitefish, chum salmon, chinook salmon, coho salmon, rainbow trout.

14.

Alaska Westward

Yakutat Area. Nestled beneath the huge Malaspina Glacier, with 13,760-foot Mount Cook in the background, Yakutat Bay and the surrounding area are among the best hunting and fishing regions in Alaska, but not within commuting distance of anywhere.

Yakutat, just inside Ocean Cape, has an airport. Tongass National Forest, covers much of the area.

Transportation is by boat, skiff, or air. Guides and accommodations are available in Yakutat.

The bay, Situk River, Italio River, Lost River, and Ankau Creek provide most of the fishing. Spring and fall are the best times, and are truly superb.

Cordova Area. The coastline to Cordova is largely marked by ice fields and is totally exposed to the rages of the Gulf of Alaska. Once, while crossing from Yakutat to Cordova on the S.S. *Aleutian,* we ran into a "mild" blow and for several hours were throwing our propeller out of the water on every swell.

Cordova is a new, small city, largely rebuilt after fire, earthquake, and tidal waves demolished much of it. It has an airport and very few roads. Transportation is by boat or air. Many lakes and rivers in the area provide excellent fishing, but the fresh-water species are small, mostly Dolly Varden and cutthroat. In saltwater and tidal reaches of tributaries, coho and sockeye salmon are plentiful. The state of the bottom fishing offshore is not fully known, following the lifting and falling of the ocean floor after the earthquake.

There is a road from Cordova to Alaganik on the estuary of the Copper River. Boat and air service is available to Valdez, a larger town at the southern terminus of the Richardson Highway from Fairbanks, at the upper end of Prince William Sound.

Most of the coastline around the sound is in the Chugach National Forest.

The Glenn Highway from Palmer and Anchorage connects to the Richardson Highway just north of Valdez.

Valdez Area. More readily accessible than Cordova or Yakutat, the Valdez area has complete facilities for ocean, bay, and river fishing, accommodations, guide service, and charter air and boat rentals.

The sound is a superb bottom-fishing area for red snapper, halibut, crabs, and most varieties of groundfish.

The inland lakes, creeks, and rivers have Dolly Varden, rainbow, grayling, whitefish, lake trout, burbot, and other species. Tidal rivers and the salt chuck have excellent coho, chinook, humpback, and chum salmon.

Across the sound from Valdez are Anchorage, Alaska's largest city, and Seward, as well as a number of other towns and villages. The surrounding country is primitive wilderness and big game country.

Palmer-Matanuska Area. Located at the head of Knik Arm, north of Anchorage, this populous area at the mouth of the Matanuska River has excellent fishing and is accessible by car as well as boat and plane.

Freshwater species are rainbow, Dolly Varden, burbot; in the salt chuck, coho, and some groundfish.

Anchorage. This crowded metropolitan area on Cook Inlet is more a departure point, and outfitting point for hunting and fishing expeditions. There are a number of lakes and small streams in the vicinity, however, with trout. In saltwater there are humpback salmon, coho salmon, and ground species. There is a road to Seward, to Palmer, and to outpost towns like Homer and Nikishka on Cook Inlet.

The rugged Kenai Peninsula, of course, is a famous big game hunting region, and is surrounded by waters of the gulf that are practically untouched by the sportsman.

Seward Area. Seward, Resurrection Bay, and Turnagain Arm, all connected by road, have camping and parking facilities for visitors by car. In addition, air charter and boat rentals are available.

There are spring, summer, and fall fisheries. Supplies, maps, information, and accommodations are available locally. Many camps are located in the surrounding wilderness to which regular charter air service is available.

Freshwater species are Dolly Varden, grayling, rainbow, Arctic char, lake trout; in the salt chuck, smelt, chinook salmon, coho salmon, humpback salmon, and most of the groundfishes, clams and crabs.

Kenai-Soldotna-Homer. A road connects these Cook Inlet points with Anchorage and Seward. There are numerous campgrounds, parking areas, boat rentals, and commercial facilities. There is year around fishing in some places, but the spring, summer, and fall are best.

Species are rainbow, Dolly Varden, steelhead, halibut, razor clams, coho salmon, king salmon, humpbacked salmon, groundfish, among others.

Bristol Bay-Alaska Peninsula. You're really getting into Alaska's "outback" here, but there is frequent commercial and charter air service to many points such as Naknek, King Salmon, Pilot Point, Togiak River, Lake Illiamna, Nushagak River, Kuskokwim River and Bristol Bay spots.

Supplies and accommodations are available at Aniak, as are boats. Air charters from Dillingham and King Salmon. There is a road from Dillingham to Aleknagik village in summer and fall. There are some fishing camps at various places and fishing is generally excellent. Prior arrangements are necessary. One should be in fair physical condition, go prepared and well equipped, and have some emergency or survival equipment, including a suitable firearm.

There are in this area, whitefish, rainbow, Dolly Varden, grayling, Arctic char, king salmon, humpbacked salmon, coho salmon, sockeye salmon, northern pike, and sheefish.

Kodiak Island. Kodiak is the principal town. Much of the island is in National Forest lands and National Wildlife Refuge. There is considerable cattle raising on ranches as well.

There are many small lakes and streams on the island, with rainbow trout, Dolly Varden, grayling, and other species. Around the island in saltwater are chinook salmon, coho salmon, humpbacked salmon, sockeye salmon, chum salmon, halibut, rockfish, king crab, razor clams, greenling, and ground species of all kinds.

Kodiak, sportsmen might note, is presently the top fish producing spot in the world.

The weather is rugged, as are the waters surrounding the island. Scheduled air and boat service from the mainland is frequent and regular. Charter services, accommodations, and other facilities are all available at Kodiak town.

Kotzebue-Kobuk. This remote area astraddle the Arctic Circle on the Bering seacoast, is faraway, rugged, and rough, but a surprising number of sportsmen visit it. The fishing is practically all fly-in. Some river boats are available for charter. Commercial services are available. Guides are a must. Arrangements should be made in advance.

Commercial flights arrive from Fairbanks frequently. Both float and wheeled charter planes are available.

Principal settlements are Kotzebue, Selawick, Noatak. The Brooks Range reaches down to the sea here, and out of the mountains flow the Noatak River, the Kobuk River, the Selawick River, and other streams. There are a number of small fishing lakes in the area.

Species are sheefish, grayling, northern pike, Arctic char, lake trout, burbot, whitefish, chum salmon, Dolly Varden.

Char fishing is superb in the fall. Some really large lake trout come from this area. Late fall fishing is also excellent.

This is Arctic country. Dress and prepare accordingly.

Nome Area. South across the Seward Peninsula on Norton Sound is Nome, famed for its gold rush history. The modern

Salmon drying on a rack along the lower Yukon River

tourist boom, oil and mining explorations in the region, have created a new prosperity. There are quite a few miles of roads leading from Nome to outlying places, military installations, Eskimo villages, and various government facilities.

Transportation to Nome from the "outside" and other Alaskan cities is all by air. At Nome are complete commercial facilities, charter services, accommodations, guides, and rental cars. There are many readily accessible lakes and rivers in the area. Visitors will also see numerous reindeer herds.

Fresh and saltwater fishing includes humpback salmon, sockeye salmon, chum salmon, chinook salmon, halibut, flounder, black cod, Dolly Varden, coho salmon, grayling, whitefish, northern pike.

There are a number of Eskimo summer fishing camps with facilities for sportsmen.

Visiting a village on the Yukon River near Circle in 1940. Sport fishing at that time was virtually unknown in this area.

PART FIVE

The North Pacific Fishes

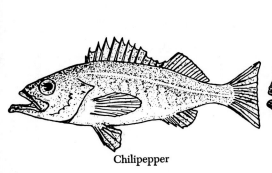

Chilipepper

China Rockfish

Sockeye Salmon

I.

Demersals, Pelagics, Anadromous

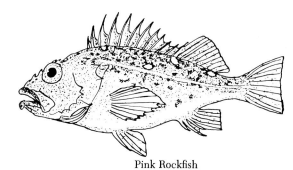

Pink Rockfish

The marine game and food fishes which occupy the interest of man can be grouped into three divisions, based primarily upon their behavior: the *pelagic*, the *demersal*, and the *anadromous*.

Pelagic means "oceanic" or "of the open sea." The pelagic species found in the North Pacific include the offshore, blue water tuna, herring, pilchard, anchovy, mackerel, and many others.

Demersal means "bottom dwellers" and includes halibut, flounder, lingcod, cod, perch, rockfish, sea bass, sculpins, and others. In fact, in other areas, such as along the New England coast, the bottom dwellers are known as "groundfish."

Anadromous means "to run up" or "to ascend from the sea to breed," and, of course, in the North Pacific the best-known anadromous fishes are the five kinds of Pacific salmon native to the North American continent (plus the one species in Asia), the steelhead trout, Dolly Varden, and cutthroat trout.

Not so well known is the fact that some sea-run brown trout are known to be in Oregon waters, although few if any have been caught and identified as such.

Other anadromous fishes are the shad and striped bass, but these I have arbitrarily classified as exotics since they were not orig-

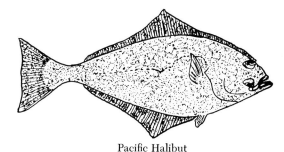

Pacific Halibut

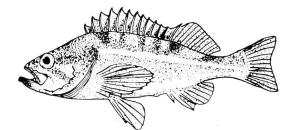

Redstripe Rockfish

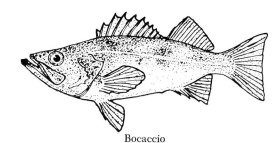

Bocaccio

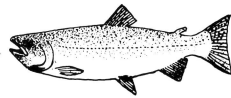

Pacific Cod

Slender Sole

Coho Salmon

inally native to the North Pacific. Another arbitrary classification of mine is the prehistorics—namely the green and white sturgeon.

For all practical purposes, I have ignored species such as the lamprey, so common in the Columbia and other systems, the sheefish of the lower Yukon, and the Pacific swordfish which has been caught as far north as Oregon.

2.

Demersals

The *demersals* or groundfish have been around longer, perhaps, than the more glamorous species, but this group of some two hundred species of which at least a dozen or two are game fish, is the least known and the least fished of any of the others.

In fact, the bottom fishery in the North Pacific is almost entirely unexploited by sportsmen, and even when something like a lingcod or halibut is caught while salmon fishing, more than likely it is discarded as a "scrap fish." It is unbelievable, but true, that even the superb striped bass is considered by some a scrap fish, which proves that there is almost no limit to man's bigotry and boneheadedness.

Most of these species live, feed, and breed on or near sandy bottoms, rocky underwater reefs, or in or around weeds and kelp. Many of them are found in great numbers even inside small bays and estuaries. A complete list and description of them is found elsewhere in this book.

Fishing for them is a wonderful sport, suitable for the skilled and unskilled, the young, the old, the aged and infirm. They can be caught from piers, docks, wharfs, rocks, barges, beaches, boats, jetties, skiffs, and from offshore party boats, practically anywhere along the continental shelf, at al-

Flounder

Cod

Ocean Perch

most any time of the year and in most places no license is required nor is there a bag limit.

They can also be caught on almost any kind of tackle, and any kind of bait—although the experienced anglers, as will be seen, have developed some standard techniques and equipment for this sport.

Washington fisheries biologist Frank Haw with a rockfish caught under the Tacoma Narrows Bridge

3.

Sturgeon

Of the twenty-five species of sturgeon in the world, and the seven in the United States, most are similar in classification to the green and white sturgeon of the North Pacific. These prehistoric relics, which comb the tidewater and brackish estuaries like self-propelled vacuum cleaners, are prized by both commercial and sport fishermen. The green sturgeon is the least desired, while the white variety is also found throughout the Columbia and Snake drainages. Most sport fishermen take sturgeon for smoking, while the commercial fishermen also market the roe for caviar.

In the olden days, sturgeon measuring twenty feet and weighing nearly a ton were taken. Today the big fellows are practically extinct and the game laws forbid taking sturgeon less than thirty-six inches long or more than seventy-two inches long (this measure varies from state to state). Sturgeon do not mature until fifteen years old, and are said to live to be more than one hundred.

Upriver from the mouth of the Columbia, on historic Sauvie Island, according to the legend of Squire Omar C. Spencer, a huge sturgeon came ashore periodically and stripped the fruit from nearby apple trees.

Since the white sturgeon, *Acipenser trans-*montanus, is North America's largest freshwater species, and one was caught once near Sauvie that weighed 1,285 pounds, who would dare gainsay the good Squire?

Sturgeon are slow starters, with a growth rate that takes about fifteen years to reach fifty pounds. Three sturgeon tagged in the lower Columbia were found to have grown in seven years only from three to four feet in length.

They spawn only once every four to seven years, and females with eggs are seldom taken. When they do spawn, however, they produce a large number of eggs—about 5,000 per pound of fish. A 50-pounder could have 250,000 eggs. In the Sacramento system, it has been discovered that only once every ten years is there a successful spawning in which not more than 2 percent of the mature fish actually spawn.

The history of the sturgeon fishery is another sad one. They were more often regarded as trash fish of no commercial value and, indeed, a predator of desirable fishes. They were often destroyed in whole schools. They are easily taken, usually on hooks baited with rancid or rotted meat or other fish, on the bottom. Probably no other fishery is so dramatically affected by overfishing. The result is noticeable almost immediately in the management of the species.

Artificial propagation of sturgeon has almost never been successful, and, in most places where it has been tried, has been abandoned. For one thing, even with a mass rearing program of young fish, these would have to be fed and protected for many years before they could fend for themselves.

The most valuable are the old, large fish, and a sustained yield depends upon a strict enforcement of the size limit regulations. An existing sturgeon population has been described as "a savings account in that it takes a large accumulation to yield enough interest to live on." (J. E. Lasater, Senior Biologist, Washington Department of Fisheries).

A sturgeon fishery can replace only very slowly those taken. An area of low yield will improve very little even with a twenty-year closure.

The range of the sturgeon is from California to Alaska. Principal diet includes, dead or alive, lampreys, suckers, carp, squawfish, clams, mussels, snails, insects, fingerlings of all kinds, and vegetable matter.

4.

Shad

A member of the herring family, the American shad is one of the exotics which have been introduced to the North Pacific. It, like the striped bass, has never been fully appreciated as a game fish—although a large commercial fishery developed in both the Sacramento and Columbia. Ironically, for many years the Columbia supplied the gourmet markets of the East where pollution and overfishing virtually destroyed the native shad runs.

The shad ranges from three to seven pounds in size. When hooked it is one of the gamest fish that swims. It has a very tender mouth and easily pulls loose unless played carefully. The commercial fishermen catch them in gillnets.

The shad were first introduced in the Sacramento River from the Atlantic coast, and from this and subsequent plantings in the Columbia, the Pacific's population of this fine fish grew. The range of the American shad is now the entire coast of North America north of Mexico.

Counts at the Bonneville Dam fish ladders increased from less than three thousand in 1943 to more than a half million in 1962, and the numbers seem to increase each year. They are now even found above the Ice Harbor Dam on the lower Snake. The shad enter the Columbia from mid-

May to the end of August. June and July are the best sport fishing months. They are caught on small spinners or "pippins" and large white wet flies.

Youngs Bay near Astoria is a good shad bank in late spring and summer. Fishing from sandbars in the Columbia is productive, also from "hog lines" at the mouth of tributaries and below the Oregon City Falls on the Willamette. The Sandy River is a popular shad stream. So is the Washougal near Camas. Bonneville Dam has a superb shad fishery, especially in the old locks at Cascade Locks.

Smoked shad is a delicacy. They are excellent when baked, but bony. The roe is a light pale pink and is known as the poor man's caviar. Shad roe does not taste of fish at all, and is delicious when fried with bacon.

Shad

5.

Smelt

Smelt, which might be grouped with the anadromous fishes, also furnish a popular sport and commercial fishery in California, Oregon, Washington mainly, although they are found along the entire coastline.

The adult Columbia River smelt or eulachon (in Alaska the natives always cooked everything in "hooligan" oil, besides using this rich oil for lamps, pemmican, and even hair slick) spawn in fresh water but go to sea to mature. Very little is known of its habits. The Columbia commercial dip nettery alone accounts for about 6 million pounds a year. The sport fishery is also popular and provides almost a ritual for devotees each spring when the smelt return. Sportsmen net them with longhandled dip nets, often wading up to the armpits in ice-cold water in a mass frenzy that matches that of the spawning hordes of fish.

The surf smelt along the coast also provides a profitable commercial fishery and a popular sport. These smelt spawn on the beaches during certain mysterious periods from April to October, and only during the afternoon tides just after high water. The spawning cycle is carefully timed so that the waves bring a group of fish in to spawn on the sand, which must be completed before the next wave comes in and takes them back to sea.

"Grunion hunting" is considered by wary newcomers to the West Coast in the same category as snipe hunting, however, it simply means catching surf smelt at night on the beaches as they are spawning.

6.

Sea-Run Trouts

The seagoin' trout of the North Pacific include the prolific cutthroat, Dolly Varden, the fabulous steelhead or sea-run rainbow, and to a lesser extent—in fact, almost unknown—a so far unsuccessful introduction of brown trout.

All these trouts are found along the continental shelf close inshore where the forage is, inside bays and estuaries and in the tidewater reaches of streams. The cutthroat and Dolly Varden are also numerous in the protected Puget Sound islands, along the British Columbia coast, and the Southeast Alaska island chain. They are found most frequently close to shore in along cliffs and deep drop-offs, in tidal rips, and backwaters. They all seek the gravel beds of freshwater streams for spawning, moving out to sea again as fingerlings to eat. They all spawn more than once, if they survive the natural hazards, and seem to move in and out of the salt chuck frequently, motivated more by food than biological impulses. They are often caught while salmon fishing, but few sportsman go after them deliberately with light tackle.

The steelhead (*Salmo gairdnerii*) is more like a salmon than a trout. It is, in fact, a member of the family *salmonidae*, to which the Atlantic salmon (*Salmo salar*), and the Pacific salmon of the genus *Oncorhynchus*

all belong. The steelhead is considered a sport fish or game fish almost everywhere but in Oregon, where fish packing politics has kept it classified as a food fish, therefore fair game for the commercial netters.

The steelhead differs from the Pacific salmon in many ways, mainly by the squarish tail, compared to the notched tail of salmon, by coloring and by the color of the flesh, which is a delicate pink rather than a deep pink or red. There are many other technical differences, of course, but it is unnecessary to go into them for our purposes.

The steelhead has been found in almost every stream and river from Southern California to the Bering Sea.

No one knows whether or not the freshwater or domestic rainbow went to sea and became a steelhead, or vice versa. It is believed, however, that the popular and prolific rainbow, which has been successfully transplanted almost to every part of the world and includes such huge races as the Kamloops and the New Zealand monsters, originated from the stock found in the McCloud River, a tributary of the upper Sacramento.

Steelhead spend their time in the ocean growing big and tough along the continental shelf, moving into the freshwater streams in a series of "runs" beginning in the spring and continuing through summer and fall. They are usually classed as two general races—the summer run and the winter run.

They reach a maximum size of about thirty pounds, but usually average about six to ten pounds. The famous "half pounders" of the northern California rivers are simply immature fish which haven't been given a chance to grow up.

In their spawning runs, steelhead used to swim all the way to the Continental Divide in Yellowstone Park. Now they are barred by dams and other obstructions. For example, in the Snake and Clearwater, except for the lower reaches, the steelhead is now extinct, blocked by huge dams from upstream migration.

The steelhead is a superb game fish for the fly fisherman, but most are caught on heavy salmon gear. Large numbers are taken by commercial fishermen in their salmon nets, since the net has not yet been invented which can tell the difference between the species.

It is not considered sporting to kill a "dark" steelhead, as this is a spawner. However, many anglers are either too excited or don't know the difference between a bright fish and a spawner. Since only an average of two or three out of five steelhead hooked on sport gear are beached or netted, it does take a lot of sportsmanship to release a spawner unharmed.

A lot of breathless pap has been published in the big colorful sport magazines about the "lunker" steelhead of the twenty- and thirty-pound class that seemingly are landed with little effort in the streams of the Pacific Northwest. I hate to disillusion anyone, but the chance of taking a steelhead in the trophy class is about 1 in 5,000. Most fish taken weigh in at from 6 to 12 pounds—which is a fair trout in any man's memory book.

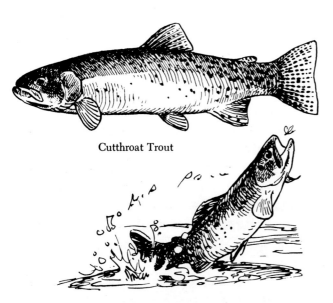

Cutthroat Trout

Cutthroat Trout

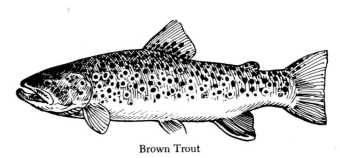

Brown Trout

7.

Species Oncorhynchus

Before talking about salmon, I'm going to make one thing clear right now: when I'm talking about "chinook" salmon, I mean old *Oncorhynchus tshawytscha*, in some areas called the king, or tyee, or a dozen other things. When I say "coho" I mean *O. kisutch*, known to man as silver or silversides. Regardless of what the local variations of these two most popular sport salmon, these are the names I used all through this volume.

Lewis A. McArthur, author of the classic *Oregon Geographic Names*, once wrote that as far as he was concerned there were only four kinds of salmon: fresh, kippered, smoked, and canned.

Scientists, packers, and sportsman, however, would not accept this oversimplification. They have succeeded in hanging upon the five species that inhabit the eastern rim of the North Pacific an incredible variety of names and nicknames.

The Pacific salmon were first discovered and described by Russian biologists in the mid-1700's, which accounts for the odd-sounding, nomenclature; these descriptions were generally adopted by others. In fact, it was Krascheninikov who described them almost simultaneously with George Steller, the naturalist with Vitus Bering, in 1731, and the Russian vernacular was used. In 1792 Walbaum adopted these vernacular names in a scientific nomenclature for the genus.

The nomenclature is seldom used, while the common names have evolved through whim, local custom, commercial grading and marketing, and many for unknown reasons. The five species are listed here by their scientific name, followed by the most prevalent common name, then in parentheses by the other names attached to it.

Oncorhynchus tshawytscha—C h i n o o k (king, spring, tyee, quinnat, Royal Chinook, Columbia River Red, etc.)

O. kisutch—Coho (silver, silverside, medium red, etc.)

O. gorbuscha—H u m p b a c k e d (pink, humpy, etc.)

O. keta—Chum (keta, calico, dog, etc.)

O. nerka—Sockeye (red, blueback, quinault, redfish, etc.)

O. masu—Masu (found from southern Japan to the island of Sakhalin, an extremely important food fish in Asia.)

In addition there is the "jack" salmon, an immature fish of any species which makes the spawning run but does not spawn, of course. These often make up as much as 80 percent of a run, and unless harvested would be a total waste.

Also, there is the kokanee, which is a race

of sockeye salmon that is landlocked in fresh water and seldom gets larger than twelve inches in length. Otherwise it behaves the same as the sockeye. The kokanee is also called the redsides and the silver trout. It is an excellent sport fish, furnishes forage for the massive kamloops trout in waters where they have been introduced, and smoked is one of the most delectable morsels ever invented. If you don't· believe me, stop in at Sandpoint, Idaho, some time and if you can find someone silly enough to sell or give away any smoked kokanee, you'll know what I mean.

The *coho*, in recent years, has turned out to be the Cinderella story of the biological world. Probably everyone knows the story of the amazing introduction of this species into Lake Michigan, which created not only a new sport and commercial fishery, but a new way of life for the Great Lakes region.

Following this successful experiment with a fish everyone thought could not survive in landlocked fresh water (highly polluted water at that), the coho is now being introduced into other strange and exotic places, far from its native home in the North Pacific.

Not only that, but now the *chinook* is undergoing the same experiments, in the Great Lakes, as well as many other places. Rex D. Forrester, a New Zealand guide and game specialist, told me that the chinook has long been a success in New Zealand waters, where it is landlocked, but goes through the same biological cycle as our Pacific variety, and is known there as the "quinnat"—a name borrowed from the Chinook lingo.

The range of the Pacific salmon, of course, is from about Morro Bay to the Bering, and then around to the Asia coast, native to all the streams and still found in most. The great chinook or king, however, is found nowhere in such numbers or qual-

A "red" or sockeye salmon

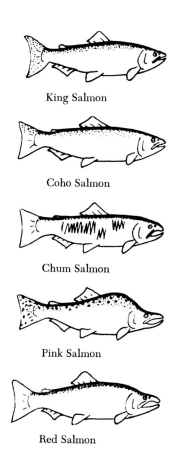

King Salmon

Coho Salmon

Chum Salmon

Pink Salmon

Red Salmon

ity as in the Columbia River system, which can be said to be the mother of this species.

It is interesting to note that in 1945, at LaJolla, California, a strange fish was speared in the ocean by Ramiro Comas, one of the group of divers who called themselves the "Manta Rays," at the west end of the La Jolla Caves. At the suggestion of Curtis Zahn, an outdoor writer who happened to be on the scene, Ramiro took his catch to the nearby Scripps Institution of Oceanography. There it was identified as *O. gorbuscha*, the pink or humpbacked salmon, a species that seldom gets south of the Oregon border.

The species also has been reported in Asian waters, far south of its breeding streams. Other catches have been reported by skin divers off the Coronado Islands.

Chinook salmon have been caught off San Pedro, coho off Baja California, steelhead off San Diego and even Baja California, where a "trucha" was tentatively identified as *Salmo nelsoni*, which proved to be, simply old *Salmo gairdnerii*.

The salmon are most generally found along the continental shelf, within ten miles of shore, but some have been taken illegally east of the 180° meridian by longline Japanese fishing fleets.

The various species of salmon can be recognized at various stages in their life cycles, by size, coloration, behavior, and method of feeding. But a general layman's description is as follows.

8.

Salmon Nomenclature

Chinook. Largest of the salmons, it has a deep, thick body with a small head. The back is a deep olive green and the sides and belly are silvery. The back, dorsal fin and caudal fin are marked with a varying number of round black spots. The sides of the head have a metallic luster. The chinook has an average weight of 22 pounds, but some go as high as 80 pounds, and one caught in a trap in 1939 near Petersburg, Alaska, weighed 126½ pounds.

The flesh is of a deep salmon red, but may vary to a lighter shade. The most important race of chinook is that of the Columbia River, which supplies two-thirds of the world's canned pack.

The chinook, as well as all the other species, when it enters fresh water on its spawning run, rapidly loses its bright silvery sheen and its "sea lice," turning progressively darker, until it is a sickly reddish brown after it spawns. At the same time, its lower jaw hooks outward and upward in a vicious curl until it almost seems like it is trying to bite off its own snout. It dies after spawning and its carcass supplies food to the fishlife of the stream.

Coho. Called "medium red" by packers because it is slightly lighter in shade than the chinook, this popular sport fish is the second largest of the Pacific salmons, aver-

aging nine pounds, going up to about thirty pounds maximum. It resembles the chinook, but the spots are fainter and fewer in number, and smaller in size. The inside of a chinook salmon's mouth has a black lining, whereas the coho and steelhead do not. In Puget Sound the immature feeder chinooks caught during the winter sports season are called "blackmouths."

The chinook and coho are also the two most important sport species and readily take all kinds of sport lures.

Sockeye. The "red" is a small fish, averaging 6½ pounds, going up to 12 pounds. The Columbia, Fraser, and Bristol Bay streams have tremendous runs of sockeye. It is so far unimportant as a sport fish, but an exceedingly valuable commercial fish.

The flesh is deep orange red, while the oil is red. The texture is firm and the fish makes an attractive and delicious "pack"— usually called a "fancy pack."

It is sometimes called the "blueback"— not to be confused with the cutthroat trout which is also called a "blueback" or "harvest trout." The body is slender with the small head roundly pointed. The back of the head and body are a clear bright blue above the rest of the body which has silvery spots.

Humpbacked. The "pink" is the smallest and most abundant of the salmons and furnishes more than 40 percent of the world's supply of canned salmon. It averages four pounds and rarely goes past eight pounds.

It is slender and delicately shaped, with a small sharp head and large tail. The color is light olive green, and the body has numerous black spots, especially on the tail. The flesh is light colored, delicate flavored, and high in food value. It is a delicious fresh-caught and eaten fish.

As a sport fish, it is surpassed only by the coho and chinook. It readily takes a lure or fly and, for my money, puts up rather more of a fuss than even the fightin' coho. In fact, if the humpbacked grew to the size of a chinook, it would kick the slats out of most small boats when landed.

It is a "two-year fish"—spawning either on the odd or even year, depending upon the location, and for that reason never grows large.

Chum. The chum or keta is also called the "white salmon," and is the least important. It averages about eight pounds, going to a maximum sixteen. It is when first seen along the coast, a dirty silver, sprinkled with small black specks, and looks "unkempt." The fins are dusky and the sides show faint bars. As the cycle progresses the male turns brick red or black and the jaws become greatly distorted.

The flesh ranges from light pink to yellowish white. The texture is firm and the oil light yellow. Because of its "off color," it brings a lower price, but is high in food value and excellent eating.

The chum will also take sport gear and even flies under the right conditions, but is practically unknown to most sportsmen.

The "grisle" is a young, usually first-year fish that participates in the spawning run. Actually this applies to the Atlantic salmon, which does not necessarily die after spawning (like the steelhead), but the term is used widely on Vancouver Island to describe a "jack." Another special name on Vancouver Island, particularly at the famous Campbell River, is "tyee" which really means a chinook salmon of thirty pounds or over.

9.

Pacific Salmon History

The adult of all species of Pacific salmon spawn in fresh water, the parents depositing the eggs in "nests" dug in the gravel of the stream bed where they themselves were born. The eggs are fertilized and covered to a depth of several inches.

The new-hatched fry have a yolk sac on the abdomen filled with nutritives to sustain them in their early stages. These young or larval salmon live in the nest for about thirty days, absorbing the sac's food. Then they wriggle up into the waters of the stream to find food for themselves.

The length of time spent in this varies widely, but presently the young salmon migrate toward the ocean again, where they stay for a year or more, feeding on the fruitful harvest of the sea, growing rapidly. When they reach physical maturity, the same biological urge starts them toward the stream of their birth to spawn and complete the cycle.

No species of Pacific salmon spawns more than once, although the closely related Atlantic salmon and the steelhead frequently do. All Pacific salmon die shortly after spawning; this is not necessarily true of Atlantic salmon and steelhead—although the mortality rate of the latter is frightfully high.

A Pacific salmon will lay from 2,000 eggs per female for humpbacks, to 5,000 eggs per chinook. During the early stages, all salmon feed on plankton. The sockeye, chum, and humpbacked eat mostly plankton, and the large copepods and shrimp throughout most of their life; whereas, the chinook and coho ravish the schools of candlefish, herring, and other forage fish while in the ocean. They also eat insects, and other minute life.

In fresh water, it was long thought that salmon did not feed. However, salmon with food fish in their stomachs, including smaller salmon, have been caught far up in fresh water. Twenty years ago people laughed at anyone who fished with fresh herring in the Willamette River. Today, it is these bait fishermen who catch the most and the biggest salmon.

Whether the salmon bite and eat these fresh-bait offerings because they are hungry, or because they are mad, is purely academic as far as the sports angler is concerned.

Of those salmon which reach the sea as smolts, a surprisingly high percentage return to spawn. Moreover, if fingerlings are transplanted from one river to another, they return as adults to the stream in which they were planted, and not to the one from which the eggs came. Eggs from Alaska have been shipped to the Columbia River where they were hatched, reared and liberated. At age eighteen months the young migrated to the sea, remained there two to three years, and then returned to the Columbia.

The age of a salmon is generally counted as the number of calendar years which have elapsed since the parents spawned, or the years elapsed from one generation to another. Age is measured in years, not months. A run of salmon which enters a river in June of a year, may have offspring emerge from the gravel in April or May the next year. These fingerlings go to sea and return June of the following year to spawn. They would actually be only about fifteen or sixteen months old, but would be referred to as "two-year fish," although they had only been in the ocean a year.

All species of salmon and trout in saltwater have a silvery appearance, and after they enter fresh water and begin to ripen sexually, the coloring changes distinctively. The chinook of both sexes become brownish-black, with dark colors on the side of the head. The coho males turn bright red sometimes, while the females are more bronze colored. The steelhead remains somewhat silvery, but with wide rosy bands, and bright blotches on gill covers.

The humpbacked males get red and more or less blotched. The dorsal hump becomes more pronounced and the jaws become elongated and hooked. The female humpy is olive green on the sides with dusky stripes.

The males of the chum also become distorted and the color varies from black to brick red, with mottled stripes or bars.

The sockeye turns brilliant red, with a dirty white on the belly. The females become dark red with green and yellow blotches.

Sea-run cutthroat vary widely in coloring, but keep an olive green shade on the sides with a darker green on the back and silver below. The sides of the head turn pinkish, and the lower fins orange.

In behavior, the salmon tend to roll in shallow water, while the steelhead leaps out, sometimes a couple of feet with fins folded and reenters the water in a straight dive.

The sexes differ in that the males have a sort of razorback appearance with a pronounced hooked snout, slimmer body. The females are more roundish, and sluggish.

10.

Range of Pacific Salmon

COHO SALMON.   These marvelous fish are found from Monterey Bay to Kotzebue Sound in the Bering Sea, and around in Asiatic waters to Japan. The largest populations are located in the streams of Oregon, Washington, British Columbia, and Southeast Alaska.

The coho has now been successfully transplanted into many exotic waters around the world, including the freshwater Great Lakes, and just maybe will become another miracle fish like the rainbow trout.

The coho spends about three months in hatching, and after emerging another month absorbing the food sac. Then they wriggle up out of gravel and are on their own. They usually emerge in the spring months, feeding on aquatic insects and gradually moving downstream to the ocean. They usually remain in these streams until the following spring when they reach four to six inches.

Once in the sea they feed voraciously and grow fast, during the one year they stay there. Their weight rapidly reaches as much as thirty pounds, with an average around ten to twelve.

The adult coho start the spawning run in the fall of each year, and the run lasts through December, depending upon the locality.

HUMPBACK SALMON.   The pinks are found from the Columbia (and some range even farther south), to the Bering and then over to the Siberian coast to North Korea. The most productive waters are Puget Sound, Fraser River, Southeast and central Alaska, and central Siberia. Southeast Alaska produces more than all the other areas combined.

The spawned eggs are deposited in gravel in the summer and fall. The young hatch the following spring, and the fry emerge from the gravel as soon as the yolk sac is absorbed. They migrate immediately to salt water. The humpback stays only one year in the ocean and then returns to spawn. Most mature humpies are only two years old. The streams which have an annual run, thus have two different races—the "odd year" and the "even year" fish.

This species reaches an average 18 inches in length and four pounds in weight, with some going up to 10 pounds.

The time of the run varies from place to place, but generally is earlier the farther north. In Puget Sound and British Columbia, most of them are taken from mid-August to mid-September, in Alaska from mid-June to mid-July.

Puget Sound waters are generally odd-year fish; Alaska has even-year runs. In Siberia, the heavy runs are in even-numbered years, but in the southern Tartar Strait area, the runs are in the odd-numbered years.

CHUM SALMON. These are found from southern Oregon to the Bering Sea, and in the eastern Arctic to the Lena River, then along the Siberian coast to the Tumen River in Korea, and northern Honshu Island, Japan.

The chum deposit the eggs in the summer and fall months, and the young hatch the following spring. As soon as the sac is absorbed they wriggle out and migrate to the ocean, where they spend from eighteen months to four years.

Some chum mature in two years, but most are three to five years old. They average twenty-five inches in length and nine pounds weight. Some huge ones up to forty pounds are sometimes caught.

The spawning runs extend from spring to late fall depending on the location, but most are during the fall months. In Puget Sound the chums show up in late September, and peak in early November. In Alaska the runs begin in midsummer and extend to fall. In Siberia a summer run is moving in June and July, with a fall run in September, October, and November.

CHINOOK SALMON. This species ranges from Monterey Bay, and even farther south, to the Yukon River, and from the Bering Strait to the southern Siberian coast. Some exotic runs have been established on South Island, New Zealand. The greatest chinook waters in the world, however, are in order of importance: the Columbia, Puget Sound, British Columbia, and the Sacramento-San Joaquin system.

The life cycle of the chinook varies widely. Some races spend only a few days in fresh water before starting for the sea; others wait until they are in the second year.

Some may not even go to sea until the third year. Once in the ocean, the chinook remains there for from one to four years. Some mature at two years, others reach seven years before they start the spawning run. The average is three to five years.

Chinook also vary widely in size, from precocious males of sixteen inches to huge "pigs" like the one taken in a trap at Petersburg of 126½ pounds. The average is about twenty-two or twenty-three pounds.

Chinook spawning runs also vary widely from early spring until late fall. The late summer and fall runs are the most numerous and most prized by sport and commercial fishermen alike.

SOCKEYE SALMON. "Reds" range from the Columbia River to the Yukon and from the Bering Strait to Japan, using almost all of the rivers in this circuit. Bristol Bay, Alaska, was long the greatest sockeye center in the world, but in recent years overfishing and poaching by Japanese fleets have seriously depleted this ground.

Sockeye hatch out in the spring of the year following the summer and fall spawning period. The young reds spend from a few months to four years in fresh water, preferably a lake. The landlocked variety which never go to sea are identical except for size, but are known as kokanee, silver trout, little red fish, or yanks.

The reds migrate to the ocean in the spring and stay there up to four years. At maturity they are from three to eight years old, including the incubation time.

They reach a maximum of thirty inches in length, and up to twelve pounds in weight, with the average about six pounds.

The run varies from place to place, with the first fish appearing in May and other runs coming as late as October. Each run peaks during a three- to four-week period.

II.

Salmon at the Marketplace

The flesh of salmon is rich in proteins, fats, and vitamins—a superb food. Because of its color and firmness, as well as oil, it is highly desirable for canning.

The Northwest Indians, for centuries before white man came, carried on a highly complex system of trade and barter in salmon, which was commonly preserved by drying and pounding into baskets weighing about one hundred pounds each. Indians today, in asserting their rights to the salmon resource, go back to the ancient times when fishing spots were as prized as mining claims today. All the early treaties tried to preserve these rights by guaranteeing the Indians forever the privilege of fishing for subsistence in their "usual and accustomed places in the traditional ways, but did not take into account future conservation requirements."

Modern tribesmen, who are often sharp businessmen, along with their lawyers, have increasingly used these treaties as excuses for fishing commercially out of season, and often as an issue to attract television cameras.

Lewis and Clark described this original commerce during their epic journey. From their description, it is possible to estimate that the Indian fishery amounted to as much as fifteen million pounds annually.

Of course, in those days the runs were so prolific that salmon often were solid bank to bank. The present level of the runs in the Columbia has been estimated to be now less than 10 percent, and probably less than 5 percent, of what they were before the coming of civilization.

The first record of the commercial salmon exploitation was in the early 1830's when Nathaniel Wyeth attempted to found a packing business on Sauvie Island, across the Columbia from the Hudson's Bay Company's fort, to salt salmon which would be shipped to the rest of the world via the Sandwich Islands, bringing in return trade goods for commerce with the Indians and early pioneers.

In the post-Civil War era when the railroads pushed to the Pacific Coast, and refrigerated cars were developed, a transcontinental trade in mild-cured salmon developed, to replace the heavy salt-cured product. Only the big, fat, red chinook salmon were used for this. Better refrigeration facilities also made possible a brisk trade in shipping fresh salmon to the big cities of the Midwest and East, and eventually of shipping frozen salmon to the East and even to Europe.

The flamboyant Frenchman, the Marquis de Mores, who was a contemporary of Teddy Roosevelt in the Bad Lands of North Dakota, in the cattle-raising business, also attempted a scheme to ship fresh salmon from Portland to New York in refrigerated cars. It was a good idea, but like many of his, was a little too advanced for his time.

The real profits in the commercial salmon industry, did not begin to roll in until three New Englanders began the new-fangled process of vacuum canning of salmon on the Sacramento River during the gold rush days. From there, they moved to the Columbia, then northward until they reached Alaska.

At one time there were more than thirty canneries on the lower Columbia alone. The fish packing created a prosperous boom that lasted almost fifty years.

The present status of the salmon in the Columbia is pretty much beclouded by conflicting statistics of self-seeking lobbyists, special interests, and political hacks. Lost sight of is the fact that the peak of the salmon resource (not the actual number of fish packed), was reached *before 1890*. The resource has been dwindling ever since, in spite of all that science can do.

Some inkling, however, of what the value of this fragile resource could be if given a chance was dramatically demonstrated in the Fraser River, where the sockeye run was restored after being extinct for many years, blocked by a massive slide in the upper canyon.

Once restored, this sockeye run (unimportant to sportsmen, but valuable to commercial netters) supported a fifty-million-dollar canning industry. One spawning bed in the upper river, with a stream area of only 350 acres, is estimated to produce about three million dollars in sockeye salmon for the packing industry.

In Michigan where the fabulous coho resource was begun with 800,000 eyed eggs from Oregon's salmon hatcheries, the value of the annual runs now is incalculable, but must reach well past one hundred million dollars.

On Battle Creek, a tributary of the Sacramento River contains some extensive spawning grounds for salmon and steelhead that is valued at $345,160 *an acre* based upon its returns.

12.

Super Salmon Coming

Because salmon are so valuable as a food resource, to say nothing of a recreational resource valued at millions if not billions, man and his science have been challenged. Since, for the time being, it seems unlikely that anything or anyone has the political muscle to bring about removal, by dynamite or nuclear blast, of some of the five-hundred-odd dams in the Columbia watershed, for instance, nor even do much about the pollution (at this writing there is no known instance of a municipality or an industry being successfully prosecuted and punished for violation of anti-pollution laws, for obvious reason), another approach has been attempted.

This is the attempt to develop "super fish" by biological and genetic means.

Take the Lint Slough experiment on coho salmon, conducted under the direction of Dr. John Rayner, chief of research for the Oregon Game Commission.

Lint Slough, a small tidal basin fed by a freshwater creek, an arm of Alsea Bay near Waldport, is the site. Here the Game Commission has built a system of dikes and dams which can be regulated at will to provide an optimum environment for salmon fry during the early period of growth.

It is "fish farming" pure and simple.

It may be the answer to the old question —why do salmon have to climb over dams and swim to the top of the Rockies to spawn?

Why not raise salmon where they are protected from hazards such as pollution, dams, predators like birds, otter, bear, and man; where disease can be controlled; where drought, logging, destruction of spawning beds can't occur; and where growth can be controlled and even increased tremendously?

At Lint Slough the key to this is controlling the salinity of the water, and to take advantage of the much greater nutrient content of cold upwelled ocean water.

The biologists here control Lint Slough's environmental rearing ponds with a system of canals and regulatory dams—one dam controlling the fresh water intake from the creek, the other at the ocean end controlling the seawater brought in by the tides.

In the wild state, the coho salmon deposit eggs in October, November, and December. When the eggs hatch the young have egg sacs clinging to them which sustain them with food for the first thirty to sixty days as they wriggle up out of the gravel. As they begin feeding on their own, they work their way downstream to the ocean, entering in May at about five or six inches in length.

A year and a half later they return as adult spawners, averaging ten pounds or so.

In Lint Slough, Dr. Rayner's lads have cut the year and a half to five months for the coho's growth cycle from egg to ocean fish.

Hatchery-raised fish were used first, fingerlings about two months old. Released in Lint Slough they were first exposed to mildly brackish water, about ten to fifteen parts salt to a thousand parts water. The salinity was then increased until it was thirty parts salt, about the same percentage as the ocean.

The fish grew amazingly fast, to five inch smolt size in sixty days, which normally would take them more than a year. When they reached this size, the gates were opened and they went out to sea to grow up. Eighteen months later the survivors returned to Lint Slough fully grown. In the first experiments about 2 percent returned, compared to about 1 percent in the natural process, and the size of the returning coho was much larger than the average wild fish.

The biologists even caught some and ate them—purely for scientific reasons—and reported them to be, as all coho should be, delicious.

This bountiful ocean, along the continental shelf, upwells phosphates, nitrates, algae-producing nutrients of all kinds, which can be found in few places in the world.

Temperature, too, is a factor and at Lint

Comparison of "natural" salmon fingerlings (top four) with the bottom three "super salmon," raised at Lint Slough show the difference in growth for the same period.

Slough this is controlled artificially by use of the sun for warming and the ocean for cooling.

"Actually," said Dr. Rayner, "this is a cold mathematical summary of the factors involved in the salmon's cycle—egg taking, upwelling, water temperature, and season. They are all timed to come out right."

"Right" is when the coho's biological clock says it's time to go to the ocean. In this case it is May, and that's when the experimental "season" is timed for.

Another experimental "farm" is now in

A coho salmon with a marked left maxillary

operation near Cape Meares, on a tidal basin of Tillamook Bay, using chinook salmon. Early results indicate this, too, may be successful in producing super salmon.

The key to rapid growth, however, Dr. Rayner says, is temperature and wind. The wind must blow just right off the coast to bring the upwelling, and the water temperature must rise higher than normal in order to speed up the metabolism and increase the feeding rate.

Fish and food grow at a more rapid rate in warmer than normal water. So do disease-producing organisms.

This disease factor has arisen in recent years to strike at otherwise successful programs to restore or to increase salmon production. At a hatchery near Wenatchee, disease wiped out entire runs that had been produced artificially.

Up on the Fraser River, once blocked by a landslide and its sockeye runs destroyed, channels were built around the slide and the runs restored with dramatic success. Then, in 1963, a disease called columnaris struck, wiping out a major portion of the run that year—about 800,000 fish died without even spawning.

In February, 1969, an outbreak of "Sacramento River Chinook Disease" killed about 800,000 young salmon at the Feather River Hatchery near Oroville. This disease, a virus, causes severe kidney damage and produces hemorrhaging in the muscles of the fish. There is no known cure.

This is only one of many such incidents which tend to warn us that tampering with nature is still risky business, and in spite of scientific breakthroughs, actually very little is yet known about the biology of a salmon and what triggers its metabolism.

Ivan Bloch, son of the late composer Adolph Bloch, who is a well-known industrial consultant in the Pacific Northwest, has long warned of a new danger to anadromous fish runs, especially in the Columbia —thermal pollution from nuclear reactor power stations, which conservationists first embraced as an answer to the dam builders.

In an article in *Outdoor Life*, November, 1968, coauthored by Ben East, he asserted that nuclear power development presents the greatest single threat to fisheries and the environment the Northwest has to face.

His warning, in this case, was directed at the inevitable warming up of the river which would surely result from the cooling systems of nuclear power plants.

This is in addition to the threat from radioactive and pesticide pollution, both of which are almost at the point of no return now in the Columbia system. For example, the radioactive count of river water just below Hanford is measured at *two thousand times* that of normal water.

13.

Conservation and Outlook

The commercial fisheries have accumulated an image of wanton despoilers of our natural resources in recent years, a reputation that is not entirely deserved. It is not generally known, but it was the commercial salmon industry which created the first scientific propagation and restocking programs, and to dismiss this as something simply motivated by their own self-interest is merely begging the question. George M. Radich, Sr., of Astoria, an old friend who came to America from Yugoslavia with his family when just a lad and settled in the cannery village of Cliffton on the north side of the Columbia, has collected much research on the subject.

The first hatchery in the Columbia system was a "salmon breeding station," established on the Clackamas River near Portland in 1877 (the same year that Rudyard Kipling fished the Clackamas, incidentally, and then wrote, "I have lived!"). It was financed and operated by the Oregon and Washington Fish Propagation Company until the federal government took over in 1888.

In the period 1897-98, the Astoria Progressive Association maintained a steelhead hatchery on the Sandy River (the "Quicksand River" of the Lewis and Clark *Journals*), which produced one million fry the first year.

By the turn of the century at least three other salmon hatcheries had been established in Oregon, including a federal hatchery on the Sandy, a state hatchery on the Siuslaw, near Mapleton, and a private hatchery by R. D. Hume, of the famous Hume family canning enterprises, on the lower Rogue River.

The first ten years of the twentieth century were marked by a rapid expansion of hatcheries in Oregon (and in other states as well.) The Bonneville Central Hatchery was founded in 1909. By 1910 the Department of Fisheries (the commercial agency) had built hatcheries on the Snake, Wallowa, McKenzie, Tillamook, Yaquina, Alsea, Siuslaw, Umpqua, South Coos, and Coquille.

It is not true, however, that the coming of the big dams on the Columbia (and there are at this writing approximately 550 in the Columbia watershed) was the sole cause of the decline in the anadromous fish runs. Records show that the runs declined rapidly—as a result of overfishing, mainly—after 1889, long before the first concrete blockades were built. And they have been declining steadily ever since. Where and when the end will come, no one knows—and many don't want to think about it.

Finally, since only the chinook and coho salmon are of serious importance to sports

Chart shows what happened to, and who caught, a sample run of Washougal River hatchery coho during 1964 (the 1961 brood year). The Washougal is a principal tributary on the Washington side of the lower Columbia.

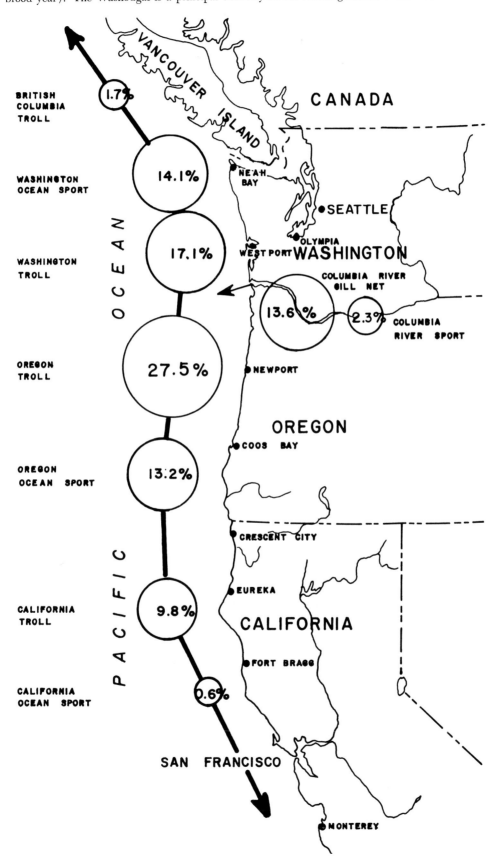

Range of chinook salmon from the Sacramento system, as indicated by returns from tagged fish

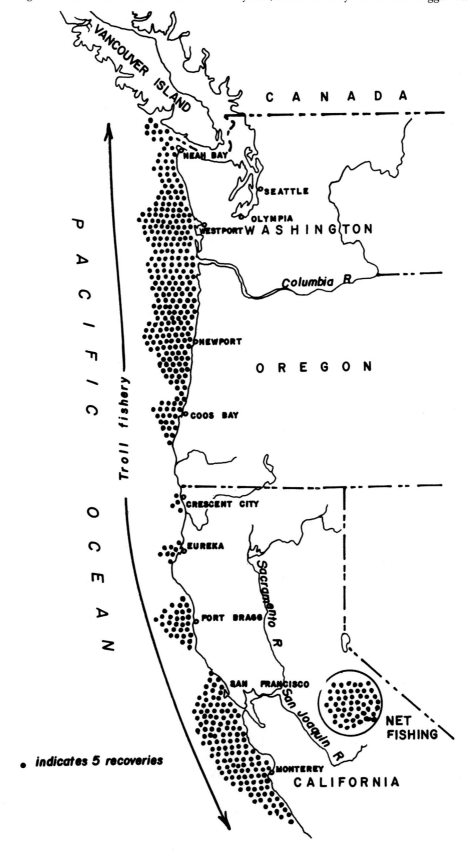

fishing at present, if the sockeye, chum, and to some extent the humpies were not harvested, they would be a total waste.

It is also ironic that American and Canadian agencies have invested millions of dollars in programs to study, protect, and increase the North Pacific salmon and halibut—to say nothing of the millions invested in these fisheries by industries—only to find the Russians and the Japanese working them over, sometimes right under the noses of the American and Canadian fishermen who are prohibited by conservation laws.

The history of the U.S. State Department's policy in the North Pacific fisheries has long been puzzling, often appearing to favor poaching by Japan and other nations in violation of existing treaties and against good conservation practices, and against the best interests of citizens of the United States and Canada.

I once interviewed a State Department official on the subject, and he not only defended Japan's poaching on American fisheries, but did so rather arrogantly, I thought. He was, incidently, married to the daughter of a wealthy Japanese family.

The story line these apologists usually give is that Japan and some of the other nations are supposed to be "have-not" nations. For this reason they should be allowed to deplete the resources of the ocean as they wish, completely unrestricted.

Truth is, some of these so-called have-nots are not really so have-not in the first place—and most of them have already been almost buried under American taxpayer dollars heaped upon them by Washington eggheads.

Anyone who believes Japan and Russia must poach on American fisheries to feed their own people should drop in at the neighborhood supermarket where they will find Japanese and even Russian seafoods taken from this side of the oceans and sold back to us at a profit.

As pointed out by Don Page, marine and labor writer for the Seattle *Post Intelligencer*, the United States finds itself sending its own representatives hat in hand to Tokyo and Moscow "to attend conferences on the management of our own fisheries on this side of the oceans; and to indulge in legalistic debates with them on why we should be allowed to keep and maintain our own fisheries."

As pointed out, these conferences, indeed, are completely dominated by the great commercial fishing cartels controlled by Japanese financial interests, and no particular humanitarian considerations are involved.

I once found myself entering into a banquet table argument on this subject with a representative of the U.S. Bureau of Commercial fisheries from Washington, and, when I finally asked him how many United States and Canadian fishermen were operating off the Russian and Japanese coast on *their fisheries,* he declined to answer my question.

Much has been said about Equador, Chile, and Peru seizing American and other commercial boats as far as two hundred miles off the coast of South America. Little has been said about why. Along that coastal shelf the upwelling in the Humboldt Current is what creates their tremendous fisheries. These fisheries are maintained and patrolled by the countries bordering this coastline. These countries consider these fisheries their responsibility, and since they extend beyond an arbitrary line such as three miles or twelve miles or whatever, they consider that their responsibility and supervision also extend beyond.

The record of ruthless exploitation and depletion of the fisheries of the world on the high seas by all maritime nations is a sorry one indeed, and there is no end in sight.

As long as fisheries are considered "international" there are not likely to be any real conservation methods practiced by anyone. It is simply dog eat dog, and let's get ours before someone else does.

PART SIX

North Pacific Grab Bag

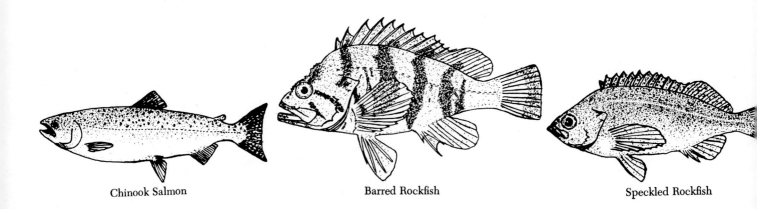

Chinook Salmon

Barred Rockfish

Speckled Rockfish

I.

There's Always Been a Dory

In all of maritime history there are few craft so universally used, which have had so much impact on boat designing, and which have been so seaworthy, easy to construct, so modest and inexpensive as the so-called dory. In it is surely embodied that classic fundamental of design that says function is the wellspring of beauty.

Thus the design itself may be as old as man's efforts to overcome his environment. The dory type has probably always been with us.

The earliest known origins, however, are found among the first colonists to reach North America, who settled along the New England coast and the Saint Lawrence River. There a plank canoe, pointed at both ends, was developed and known as the "plat." This evolved to "bateau," which means simply a boat. The bateau in turn developed into two types—a lumberman's craft and a fisherman's dory with the traditional lengthwise planking over floor timbers made part of the frames or ribs.

The word dory probably comes from "doree," found in early records of sailing and fishing in Massachusetts in the early 1700's.[1] The doree or dory was first used

_____
[1] "The Dory," Occasional Papers No. 7 (Halifax, Canada: The Marine History Department, Nova Scotia Museum).

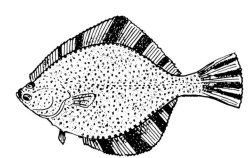

Starry Flounder

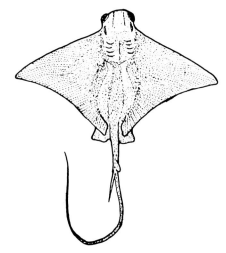

Bat Ray

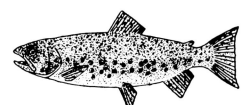

Brown Trout (Sea-run)

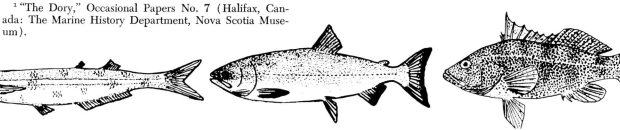

Grunion   Chum (or Dog) Salmon   Spotted Bass

alongshore. When the Gloucester fishing schooners began exploiting the Grand Banks in the early and middle 1800's, the "Banks dory" came into being, first merely as an adaptation of the old alongshore craft. It was modified only to make it lighter, stronger, and adapted for hoisting and lowering in a rough sea, and to nesting on a small deck. Then, as now, the Banks dory was built simply, and was amazingly seaworthy even when loaded with fishing gear and bait, and could be rowed easily—although it characteristically was tender in an unloaded condition.

By 1870 the dory had been standardized into 12-, 13-, 14-, 15-, and 16-foot lengths along the bottom, with the rake of the bow and stern adding another four feet. The 12-, 13-, and 15-footers were the ones used in Banks fishing. These are the classic models depicted so dramatically and colorfully in the Winslow Homer paintings and in *Captains Courageous*.

The larger dories were used for coastwise fishing off the beach and the 14-foot model became the universal dinghy and lifeboat for working vessels. The traditional buff-colored dory is still found aboard many commercial vessels.

By 1880 the dory was being mass produced. Refinements such as a hole in the forward thwart for a mast was common. Usually a small loose-footed lug sail was used, sometimes a jib was hoisted. The Gloucester dory I owned in Alaska was so fitted and made a tolerable sailing craft, although it also had a motor well in the stern. Incidentally, it was authentic even to the buff-colored paint. When sailing, steering was done with an oar through a sculling notch in the transom. The one I owned, however, also had a rudder fitted with pintles and gudgeons and could be unshipped when not in use.

In the middle and late 1800's sailing dories of all sizes across the Atlantic became a popular "sport," or at least a fad. Some were even rowed entirely across. There have been similar voyages in recent times as well. The passages of these tiny craft,

A typical modern square-stern dory under construction. Note extreme sheer, the motor well in stern, and simple plywood construction.

Starting the construction of a square-stern dory, showing the frames and method of construction. This is a 23-footer.

most of which made it, averaged about thirty to forty days—comparable to even the biggest sailing vessels.

Most followers of the sea know about the classic voyage of Captain Joshua Slocum in the sloop *Spray* alone around the world in the early 1890's. Not many know that Slocum made an earlier long voyage of 5,510 miles with his wife and two children from Brazil to the United States in the homemade 35-foot *Liberdade,* a modified dory design.

The dory, of course, found its way into all oceans and in large numbers on the West Coast of North America which became the last stronghold of the old sailing ships with San Francisco as the home port. The first whalers to the North Pacific and the Bering Sea brought dories with them. The early fishing schooners to the new cod banks off

Siberia used dories in the traditional Banks method. Later cod fishing fleets to the Bering Sea and Gulf of Alaska carried the Banks dory along. The halibut fleet used them, and most boats and ships in Alaska when I arrived there in 1938 carried one or more buff-painted dories nested neatly on deck.

These were the type built first by the settlers along the Northwest coast and particularly around the Nestucca River in Oregon. Local conditions, as usually is the case, resulted in some minor modifications, which mostly tended to make a bigger boat with more room for a cargo of fish. No major changes in design occurred, however, until the development of the square-stern surf dory about 1960. This was primarily to make it possible to use more power in getting through the heavy seas that often are found off Kiwanda, but also resulted in the happy discovery that the increase in maximum speed from ten miles an hour to more than thirty made them safer and more maneuverable in rough water. The square sterns are now brought into the beach under power, and almost surfing, whereas in the old slow double-enders the motor had to be unshipped beyond the breakers, and rowed in by hand—which often resulted in disaster when breaking combers crashed down on top of the slow boats.

Zack Taylor, boating editor of *Sports Afield*, described his first experience with the Kiwanda square stern as follows:

You bring the boat down to the beach and stand in the undertow holding its bow. Finally you see a calm coming. You push the bow into the deep water and shove off, climbing aboard the stern. A yank, and the engine roars. You gun it to 15 mph, throwing the small, choppy inshore waves aside as if they were nothing.

Ohmygosh! A wave top rises 150 feet ahead of you. No time to turn around. Only one thing to do. *Give it to her!* The boat roars at the wave. The wave climbs higher and higher and roars at the boat. The two collide just as the top starts to curl. The boat rushes up the wave, busts a hole through the curling break, and flies into the air on the other side of the comber.

You cut the power and flex your knees. *Boom!* The boat lands. (It may have leaped out of water its own length.) You gun it immediately as another set is coming, but you're well beyond the break now. You're fishing![2]

Today, surf dories are launched at many places along the Northwest coast, following Kiwanda's example, and indeed this has become almost an entirely new and thrilling sport for amateurs and landlubbers.

----

[2] *Sports Afield*, August, 1966, p. 68.

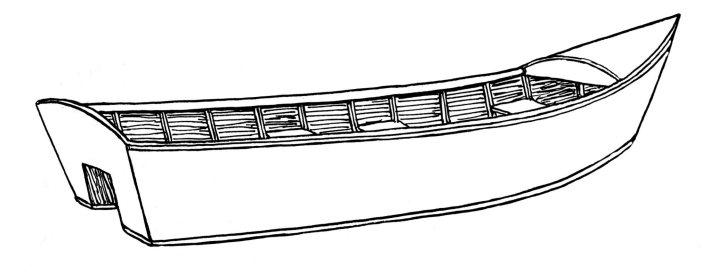

Sketch of the classic square-stern dory indicates its evolution from the old Banks dory. Prominent is the motor well in stern, for motors up to 55 horsepower.

The practice, of course, is inherently dangerous for the inexperienced and persons of poor judgment. The technique for small boat handling in the surf has been worked out by United Nations international aid agencies to a few simple rules.

For landing through the surf the key is to maintain the movement of the boat in such a way that the center of gravity is slightly behind the wave crest as it breaks. This will start the craft surfing or surfboarding. The operator should be careful not to get the CG ahead of the crest, or the wave will overrun the boat with the almost certain possibility of swamping or broaching.

Going out through breakers is a matter of waiting with the motor ready, picking up speed as the breaker passes underneath and picks up the boat. The CG should then be slightly past the breaking crest and the boat forced through and over with power. Failure to make it over can mean swamping under tons of green water, broaching, or even pitchpoling.

A North Pacific salmon trolling dory, designed for launching through the surf. The craft is trailerable and easily managed on land or sea.

2.

Weather, Safety and Boat Handling

The North Pacific coast has been described as having the roughest seas and weather to be found anywhere in the world. Rachel L. Carson, in *The Sea Around Us,* wrote of an incident at the lighthouse on Tillamook Rock off the Oregon coast where, during a storm, a rock weighing 135 pounds was thrown high above the lightkeeper's house, itself one hundred feet above the sea. A popular winter pastime in Oregon and Washington is to drive to the coast for a week during storms to watch the waves lashing against the rocky bulwarks, sending the surf crashing against cliffs, and spouts spewing up through holes a hundred feet into the air.

The North Pacific and its shoreline are subject to extremes of wind and weather at times, and each summer the toll of fatalities among hapless and careless swimmers and boaters becomes a sobering statistic. One of the most dangerous practices is that of camping or sleeping on the beach in summer, as well as beachcombing among the immense piles of driftwood and logs in some sections. "Sleeper waves"—huge, fast-breaking swells that occasionally rip along a shoreline, not from seaward, but *parallel* to the beach—can pick up a fifty-foot log like a matchstick and hurl it up on a bank. Anyone caught in one of these sleepers is almost certain to get hurt, if not killed. They often occur when the sea is otherwise quite "flat" during periods of good weather. For this reason, anyone beachcombing, surf fishing, or even walking along the beach, should keep an eye peeled up and down the shoreline for this phenomenon.

Landlubbers think all waves are the same. Oceanographers, however, have classified them in more descriptive ways—generally as ocean waves, tidal waves, wind waves, sea swells, surf, and so on.

Destructive waves are *tsunamis* or seismic sea waves, which are caused by underwater earthquakes. These travel great distances, as much as two thousand to four thousand miles and at speeds up to five hundred knots. When they reach the continental shelf or shelving coastline they build up into waves of disastrous proportion, with several crests or oscillations spaced from ten to forty minutes apart. On the open sea a person in a boat would not even be aware of the passage of a *tsunamis*, but along a coastline they are fatal.

Storm waves are caused by winds and a sharp change in barometric pressure, and are also affected by tides. These are common in coastal regions.

Seiche is a stationary vertical wave which is caused by unusual tidal action, storm waves at sea, seismic sea waves, barometric pressure, and other factors. It is found in enclosed estuaries and bays and also superimposed on tidal currents. The *seiche* is a severe disturbance of the ocean surface, causing surges and horizontal oscillations, sometimes of violent proportions. Sometimes these are so severe that it is difficult to keep a ship tied up to a wharf.

Ocean waves can be anything from ripples and cat's-paws to huge buildups that have been measured at 150 feet in height, such as the one experienced by the heavy cruiser U.S.S. *Pittsburgh* in a 1945 typhoon. Usually, however, the maximum height does not exceed thirty to forty feet.

There are two types of "tidal waves"—the *tsunamis* and the hurricane induced storm tides common to the Caribbean.

Wind waves are those generated by the wind and moving across the open surface of a lake or ocean (and sometimes a river—I have seen six-foot waves on the Columbia above Bonneville Dam). Chop or whitecaps appear first in this condition, these becoming progressively higher and longer, developing into seas. The direction and velocity are dependent upon the wind, but they do not change direction immediately with a wind shift.

When wave trains, or a series of waves, moving across open water reaches the shallow water of coastal shelves, it begins to change form, its trough shortening and its height increasing. When the water depth reaches about 10 percent of the original swell length, the waves crest and break over into surf.

There are two types of wave forms—*trochoidal* and *cycloidal*. The former are shaped more like swells that have been flattened out by the wind. In deep water they are harmless, but when they reach shallow

Wave forms on North Pacific coastline, as the long swells come up on shallow water.

water and break they can be thundering monstrosities. The cycloids are short, choppy wind waves which are also dangerous to small craft.

Breaking waves come in two major sizes and shapes: *plungers* and *spillers*. The terms are self-explanatory, but the plungers are formed by long ground swells which, when reaching shallow water, build up and plunge over in heavy falls of water, trapping air and creating noisy surf. The spillers are gentler breakers which start with a small crest of spray spreading evenly down the wave. These breakers are caused by short sea swells that are not changed much in reaching shallow water.

The breakers found in inlets and on bars at the entrance to bays and estuaries are usually of the spilling type. The plungers are found on wide stretches of open beach and against exposed cliffs.

There are some basic techniques for dealing with all these sea conditions, and particularly with navigating through the kind of breaking waves found at the small bays, coves, and dog holes along the northern California, Oregon, and Washington coasts. This, however, is beyond the scope of this discussion except to call attention to the subject.

A few tips on boating safety might be mentioned in passing for the same reason. Along the North Pacific coast the standard system of small craft, gale, storm, and hurricane warnings are used by the Coast Guard. These can be seen posted on masts at many strategic centers along the coasts, and aural versions of these are broadcast at the usual intervals on marine radio frequencies and weather stations.

The Coast Guard publishes a number of pamphlets on water safety, among which are the *Bar Guides*, for each of the major inlets and bars frequented by fishing craft and small boats. They advise not to attempt to cross a rough bar on the ebb or shortly before. A swift ebb current meeting heavy seas rolling in at shallow entrances creates a

A sport fisherman returning to harbor in a sheltered "dog hole"

Hundreds of miles of almost deserted beaches offer solitude, peace, and surf fishing potential to the young of all ages along the North Pacific.

most dangerous condition, even on otherwise calm days. Boatmen should be tide
conscious, crossing from harbors to the
ocean on the slack or flood stages only.

On the Pacific Northwest coasts there are
usually two tides daily, caused by the grav-
itational pull of the moon and the sun. The
flood and ebbing of these tides varies at different points along the coast in time as well
as in intensity. In the waters of the Inland
Passage and among the islands off the British Columbia coast, these tidal currents of-

The sea crashing against the buttress of the North American continent draws spectators during storms just to watch
and marvel at the power of the Pacific.

ten reach velocities of ten miles an hour and
more—exceeding in many cases, the maximum speed of some small craft. Moreover,
most of the Northwest coast being heavily
timbered, with extensive logging operations, the tidewaters, bays, and even waters
far out to sea are subject to floating debris
ranging from pieces of bark to mammoth
logs and trees three feet in diameter. I have
seen large logs floating, half submerged,
twenty-five miles off the coast. These submerged or partly submerged logs, known locally as "deadheads," are extremely dangerous to navigation in broad daylight as well
as at night. A constant lookout must be
maintained by the man at the wheel or the
one responsible for the conn of the ship.

Along the Washington, Oregon, and
northern California coasts, the tides are usually relatively mild, with certain periods of
extreme minus tides during which clamming is considered best. In Alaska and British Columbia, however, the tide range may
reach thirty feet.

A salty old seafarin' friend of mine the
other day had a few choice comments on the
subject in general:

"I'm sure you know more about the fishing off the Oregon coast than I do, but what
I've seen there has made me a little sick of
the 'sportsmen' who continue to catch fish
after they have their salmon limit, hoping
to catch a larger one than those they have.
If they do, they dump the smaller dead fish
back into the sea.

"I've also seen them virtually plugging
the Columbia River bar, working two-year
fish that barely made their legal limit.

"I shouldn't worry too much about that,
either, for I feel certain that no run of salmon has been seriously impaired by any
type of legal fishing in the sea. Nets, of

course, are another matter, and the taking of spawners near the spawning grounds can be serious.

"But the real damage, particularly to the once consistently big run in the Sacramento River system, has been done by pollution, irrigation diversions, and the destruction of spawning beds.

"Incidentally, the Pacific north of San Francisco is not much used by cruising yachtsmen. It is too damn rough and too damn cold.

"Many owners of 50- to 65-foot yachts try it once, and then spend summers thereafter in the party area of the Sacramento delta, telling sea stories about their ocean cruising and boasting that 'if tomorrow, I made up my mind, I could stand out of here for Astoria, or down to Acapulco, just like that.' But they don't cast off that shoreside electric line that keeps the ice cubes coming for their martinis.

"I don't blame them a hell of a lot. If I had the money I too might get a big twin screw diesel yacht, complete with skipper, throw saltwater on the gold braid of my 50-fathom cap until I looked as salty as I needed to."

3.

Bait, Tackle and Gear

A sign of the inexperienced or amateur fisherman, says one Old Local Expert, is the detailed preoccupation with the selection of lures and bait, and even of tackle and gear.

I hereby offer *Holm's Rule* part I:

A fish—any fish—when feeding will take any lure that even remotely resembles or suggests something to eat, presented in a familiar way.

Part II of *Holm's Rule* goes like this:

A feeding fish can be hooked and landed on anything that will allow the angler to play and land it in a reasonable length of time.

The North Pacific is no different in this respect than any other part of the world. As a matter of fact, the "new" or "local" plugs, spinners, and other artificial lures are based on classic patterns in use in other parts of the world for centuries.

One of the most amusing examples of Madison Avenue hucksterism in recent years has been the capitalization of the marketing departments of the tackle and sporting goods manufacturers following the amazing coho salmon bonanza in Lake Michigan where no one had seen a fish bigger than a herring for fifty years.

Suddenly, the national sport magazines and other media blossomed out with "new"

tackle and gear "designed especially for Great Lakes coho salmon fishing." There were "Coho Killers," "Coho Wobblers," "Coho Plugs," "Coho This" and "Coho That." There were even "Coho Boats," "Coho Coats," "Coho Raincoats," "Coho Landing Nets," and no doubt "Coho Pipes" for the well-dressed Coho Fisherman.

Needless to say, this left thousands of old coho fishermen on the West Coast standing there with an amazed look on their faces. All these one hundred years or so they'd been catching coho salmon, and had not known about all these "Coho Killers."

A closer look at these "new" products, however, reveals merely the same old classic spoons, spinners, wobblers, and plugs, with different names, designed to catch more fisherman than fish.

The Indians along the Northwest coast, of course, fished with hook and line long before the white man arrived—and even used "modern" methods and gear such as offshore trolling for salmon, and jigging for halibut—the latter, incidentally, being much preferred by the Indians, as it was to the later Scandihoovian fishermen who made their living from the sea.

Up along the Washington coast, for example, the Makahs regularly went to sea in their cedar canoes to the offshore halibut banks around Cape Flattery (they called it "Big Point") and off the mouth of the Hoh. Almost identical gear and methods were used by other tribes, such as the Rogue River Indians far to the south. They went out not only for halibut, but for cod, bright salmon, and occasionally for whale.

Typically, the hooks of the Indians were made of wood steamed to a curved shape and sharply pointed, and attached to line made of woven fibers of cedar, or animal sinews, and even kelp. For bottom fishing, sinkers were made of stones attached to the line. Sometimes buoys made of bladders were used to mark a set line. Often two Indians in a canoe would have out 10 or 15 such set lines with flags on the buoys. Most of the fishing was done close to shore in 10 fathoms or so, but off Flattery the Indians were known to go 15 to 20 miles to sea in their canoes.

Captain William Clark recorded in the *Journals* of watching Snake Indians catching fish with what must have been a forerunner of the present "spinning" or "threadline" gear that was developed in Europe and brought to the United States after World War II.

A baited piece of bone, tied in the center to the line, was cast from an open frame or from a coil wound around the hand loosely. When a fish grabbed the bait, the bone got stuck crosswise in his gullet and the Indian reeled in quickly before it could be disgorged.

This is exactly the principle used in modern spinning gear, except for the hook.

Jim Heddon invented his famous plug about seventy-five years ago when he tossed a chunk of wood he had been whittling on, while waiting for the arrival of a friend, into a nearby pond. To his surprise a big bass charged and grabbed the piece of wood.

He could hardly wait to get home and whittle more plugs to the approximate size and shape of the one the bass took, and attached hooks to them. Thus was born a "new" industry.

Today hundreds of manufacturers turn out thousands of plugs, spinners, jigs, wobblers, and other deceitful booby traps with the ingenuity exceeded only by the missile engineers and the pinball machine designers.

Along with the coming of modern plugs and lures, there arrived a whole new folklore. There is scarcely an experienced fisherman who does not have his personal repertoire of anecdotes of his favorite plug or lure. Most of these are artful variations of old wives' tales that go back to the Neanderthal man, or at least to the Folsom man.

A favorite is the so-called "Killer Plug," of Puget Sound. Until about 1950 everyone who knew what he was talking about would assure anyone willing to listen that the *only* way you could catch a big salmon on trolled wooden plugs was with something like the "Lucky Louie." They assured you solemnly that for every, say one hundred plugs made, you would find one with just the right variations in manufacture that gave it just the right action, tint, shape, and allure that was irresistible to a chinook salmon. These plugs were identified only in the tackle boxes of the lucky owners by numerous teeth marks where chinook salmon had allegedly chewed on them.

Hundreds, perhaps thousands, of these plugs were sold to fishermen, each of whom hoped they were buying the rare Killer. It was like buying Cracker Jack, hoping to find a hundred-dollar bill as a prize instead of a cricket.

Until along came a fisherman who never heard of one of these lucky Killers, and began catching record salmon with mooched or trolled herring, the Killer Plug racket made a killing indeed. Many an enterprising entrepreneur sold these special Killers from under the counter, complete with "teeth marks" and aging.

When I first arrived in Oregon, I was surprised to learn that anyone who fished for salmon and didn't use a Bear Valley spinner, a McMahon wobbler, or a wooden plug trolled, might as well stay home. I did not understand this, since I had only had previous experience in Puget Sound, British Columbia, and Alaska waters where salmon were caught by "strip fishing" with bait, trolled and mooched herring, and even on streamer flies. Never one to go against local custom, I too equipped myself with the local brands—and caught nothing. Then some of the fellows from Puget Sound, who didn't know about local customs, showed up at Astoria during the big salmon derbies when prizes of thousands of dollars were offered, bringing with them some fresh herring and mooching gear.

They walked off with all the prizes, and ever since then mooching with fresh or frozen herring, or herring strips, has been the "deadliest" way of catching salmon.

Today, no matter where in the North Pacific you fish, you will find readily available at all fishing ports and sport centers, complete stocks of bait, lures, and terminal tackle that are used locally by local fishermen, and which can generally be relied upon as the most effective. Today you do not even have to bother with tying your mooching harness. These can be purchased ready-made anywhere in the Northwest. Moreover, all licensed guides and charter boat operators have tackle and equipment available for clients, all rigged and ready to go.

For this reason, I for one can't get much

worked up over the technicalities of tackle and equipment.

Anything that works, for my money, is the gear to use.

Strangers to the Northwest are often puzzled by the sight of anglers with towels hanging from their belts. These are not necessarily super-sanitary fishermen. More likely they are "fresh egg fishermen."

The use of fresh (or preserved) salmon eggs is not only legal in most places, but has long been a productive and favored method of meat fishing. Since it is almost impossible to buy fresh eggs when you want them, it is up to the angler himself to prepare his own stock.

To do this, as the old recipe goes, first you catch a salmon (or steelhead), a female that is full of spawn.

Remove the eggs from the fish carefully, without damaging the membrane or the egg sac. Wrap the skeins of eggs in paper towels or newspapers and allow to remain overnight in a refrigerator to drain them properly.

Next, split the skein, leaving some membrane on each of the chunks as they are cut off for bait. These chunks should be about the size of a small walnut. Drop these chunks in a paper bag containing Borax powder. Shake the sack to assure each chunk acquires a complete coating of Borax (*not* Boraxo).

When thoroughly coated, place them in small freezer containers or jelly jars, adding more Borax powder to cover the top and put the lid on.

Next, to keep them indefinitely, put in deep freeze.

Some fresh-egg fishermen put each chunk in a piece of red Maline cloth or netting when they tie them on the hook, but most don't bother with this, simply tying the chunks on with red thread or using a single hook leader tie with a slip knot into which the chunk is inserted.

Incidentally, you can make your own single egg bait, which is legal for trout in some states, by separating the eggs and placing in a saline solution which will float an egg or medium potato. The saline, or salt and water, solution is then heated to a simmer, but not boiled, until the eggs are of the proper consistency. Test them by sticking with a pin.

4.

Marine Game Species of North Pacific

MACKEREL SHARKS
Thresher   *Alopias vulpinus*   Cape Flattery south

REQUIEM SHARKS
Blue   *Prionace glauca*   British Columbia south
Brown   *Triakis henlei*   Northern California south
Leopard   *T. semifasciata*   Oregon south

EAGLE RAYS
Bat stingray   *Myliobatis californica*   Oregon south

STURGEONS
white   *Acipenser transmontanus*   N. Calif. to Alaska
green   *A. medirostris*   S. Calif. to Alaska

HERRINGS
American shad   *Alosa sapidissima*   San Diego to Alaska

SALMONS
chinook   *Oncorhynchus tshawytscha*   Monterey to Alaska
coho   *O. kisutch*   S. Calif. to Alaska
pink   *O. gorbuscha*   N. Calif. to Alaska
chum   *O. keta*   N. Calif. to Alaska
sockeye   *O. nerka*   Oregon to Alaska

SEA-RUN TROUTS
cutthroat   *Salmo clarkii*   N. Calif. to Alaska
steelhead   *S. gairdnerii*   S. Calif. to Alaska
Dolly Varden   *Salvelinus malma*   N. Calif. to Alaska

SMELTS
surf   *Hypomesus pretiosus*   Calif. to Alaska

night	*Spirinchus starksi*	Puget Sound south
longfin	*S. thaleichthys*	San Francisco to British Col.
eulachon	*Thaleichthys pacificus*	Mad River to Bering Sea

CODS

Pacific tomcod	*Microgadus proximus*	Calif. to Alaska
Pacific cod	*Gadus macrocephalus*	N. Calif. to Alaska

BASSES AND GROUPERS

striped bass	*Morone (Roccus) Saxatilis*	Central Calif to Washington
giant sea bass	*Stereolepis gigas*	Calif. south

JACKS

jack mackerel	*Trachurus symmetricus*	B. C. to Mexico

CROAKERS

white sea bass	*Cynoscion nobilis*	Alaska to Mexico
white croaker (kingfish)	*Genyonemus lineatus*	Vancouver Island south

SURFPERCHES

barred	*Amphistichus argenteus*	Bodega Bay south
calico	*A. koelzi*	Trinidad Head south
redtail	*A. rhodoterus*	Flattery to Monterey
walleye	*Hyperprosopon argenteum*	Vancouver Island south
silver	*H. ellipticum*	Washington south
spotfin	*H. anale*	California
pink sea perch	*Zalembius rosaceus*	Drake's Bay south
shiner perch	*Cymatogaster aggregata*	Calif. to Alaska
striped sea perch	*Embiotoca lateralis*	Calif. to Alaska
black	*E. jacksoni*	Bodega south
rainbow sea perch	*Hypsurus caryi*	Cape Mendocino south
rubberlip	*Rhaccochilus toxotes*	Bodega south
pile perch	*Damalichthys vacca*	Calif. to Alaska
white sea perch	*Phanerodon furcatus*	Calif. to B. C.

MACKERELS, TUNAS

Pacific mackerel	*Scomber japonicus*	Mexico to Alaska
Pacific bonito	*Sarda chiliensis*	Mexico to Vancouver Island
skipjack	*Euthynnus pelamis*	Vancouver Island south
bluefin	*T. thynnus*	Columbia River south
albacore	*T. alalunga*	Mexico to Alaska

ROCKFISHES

flag	*Sebastodes rubrivinctus*	Calif. to Alaska

treefish	*S. serriceps*	San Francisco south
greenstriped	*S. elongatus*	Vancouver Island south
China	*S. nebulosus*	Alaska south
black and yellow	*S. chrysomelas*	Eureka south
gopher	*S. carnatus*	Eureka south
blue	*S. mystinus*	Eureka south
black	*S. melanops*	S. E. Alaska south
grass	*S. rastrelliger*	Crescent City south
brown	*S. auriculatus*	S. E. Alaska south
kelp	*S. atrovirens*	San Francisco south
yellowtail	*S. flavidus*	Vancouver south
olive	*S. serrandoides*	San Francisco south
widow	*S. entomelas*	S. E. Alaska south
speckled	*S. ovalis*	San Francisco south
vermilion	*S. miniatus*	Vancouver Island south
rasphead	*S. ruberrimus*	Alaska south
canary	*S. pinniger*	Dixon Entrance south
copper	*S. caurinus*	S. E. Alaska south
rosy	*S. rosaceus*	San Francisco south
whitebelly	*S. vexillaris*	Crescent City south
swordspine	*S. rhodochloris*	San Francisco south
starry rockfish	*S. constellatus*	San Francisco south
greenspotted	*S. chlorostictus*	Eureka south
bocaccio	*S. paucispinis*	Eureka south
chilipepper	*S. goodei*	Eureka south
stripetail	*S. saxicola*	Calif. to Alaska
cow	*S. levis*	Monterey south

SABLEFISH

sablefish	*Anoplopoma fimbria*	Calif. to Alaska

LINGCOD AND GREENLINGS

kelp greenling	*Hexagrammos decagrammus*	Kodiak to Calif.
whitespotted	*H. stelleri*	N. Calif. to Alaska
rock	*H. superciliosus*	Alaska south
lingcod	*Ophiodon elongatus*	Alaska south
atka mackerel	*Pleurogrammus monopterygius*	Bering south

SCULPINS

cabezon	*Scorpaenichthys marmoratus*	B. C. south

BUTTERFISH

Pacific pompano	*Palometa simillima*	B. C. south

SILVERSIDES

jacksmelt	*Atherinopsis californiensis*	Oregon south
topsmelt	*Atherinops affnis*	Oregon south
California grunion	*Leuresthes tenuis*	Monterey south

LEFTEYE FLOUNDER

fantail sole	*Xystreurys liolepis*	Alaska south
bigmouth sole	*Hippoglossina stomata*	California
California halibut	*Paralichthys californicus*	California
longfin sanddab	*Citharichthys xanthostigma*	California
speckled sanddab	*C. stigmaeus*	S. E. Alaska south
Pacific sanddab	*C. sordidus*	Alaska south

RIGHTEYE FLOUNDER

curlfin sole	*Pleuronichthys decurrens*	Alaska south
Pacific halibut	*Hippoglossus stenolepis*	Bering south
rock sole	*Lepidopsetta bilineata*	Bering south
sandsole	*Psettichthys melanostictus*	S. E. Alaska south
diamond turbot	*Hypsopsetta guttulata*	N. California
English sole	*Parophrys vetulus*	Alaska south
buttersole	*Isopsetta isolepis*	Alaska south
starry flounder	*Platichthys stellatus*	Arctic south
rex sole	*Glyptocephalus zachirus*	Bering south
arrowtooth flounder	*Atheresthes stomias*	Bering south
slender sole	*Lyopsetta exilis*	S. E. Alaska south
petrale sole	*Eopsetta jordani*	Alaska south
dover sole	*Microstomus pacificus*	Alaska south

TONGUEFISHES

California tonguefish	*Symphurus atricauda*	Eureka south

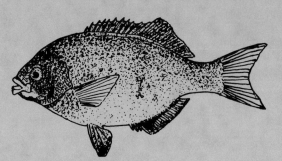
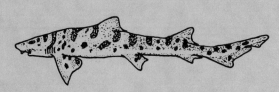